The Core Language Engine

ACL-MIT Press Series in Natural Language Processing

Aravind K. Joshi, Karen Sparck Jones, and Mark Y. Liberman, editors

The Core Language Engine

edited by Hiyan Alshawi

A Bradford Book
The MIT Press
Cambridge, Massachusetts
London, England

This book was printed and bound in the United States of America.

Library of Congress Cataloging-in-Publication Data

The Core language engine / edited by Hiyan Alshawi.
  p.   cm.—(ACL-MIT Press series in natural language processing)
Includes bibliographical references and index.
ISBN 0-262-01126-3
1. Computational linguistics. 2. English language—Machine translating.
3. English language—Translating into Swedish.
I. Alshawi, Hiyan. II. Series: ACL-MIT Press series in natural language processing.
P99.C583 1992
428'.02397'028563—dc20   91-27482
                                                                  CIP

Contributors

Hiyan Alshawi
SRI Cambridge Computer Science Research Centre

David Carter
SRI Cambridge Computer Science Research Centre

Jan van Eijck
Centre for Mathematics and Computer Science (CWI), Amsterdam, and
Department of Language and Literature, University of Utrecht

Björn Gambäck
Swedish Institute of Computer Science

Robert C. Moore
Artificial Intelligence Center, SRI International

Douglas B. Moran
Artificial Intelligence Center, SRI International

Fernando C. N. Pereira
AT&T Bell Laboratories

Stephen G. Pulman
SRI Cambridge Computer Science Research Centre, and
Computer Laboratory, University of Cambridge

Manny Rayner
SRI Cambridge Computer Science Research Centre

Arnold G. Smith
SRI Cambridge Computer Science Research Centre

All contributors were members of SRI International working at its
Cambridge Computer Science Research Centre when they carried out
the research reported in this book except for Björn Gambäck and Manny
Rayner who were at the Swedish Institute of Computer Science.

Contents

14   Swedish-English QLF Translation   277

Hiyan Alshawi, David Carter, Björn Gambäck, and Manny Rayner

Preface

In the mid-1980s, researchers at the SRI International Artificial Intelligence Centre and Cambridge University Computer Laboratory were looking at ways of setting up a collaborative research program that could take advantage of the theoretical advances and convergence of techniques then taking place in natural language processing. This research program was to take shape as a three-year project at SRI's newly established Cambridge Computer Science Research Centre. The project had the dual aims of furthering research in the field and producing a well-engineered natural language processing system embodying the research results in a form that could be used as the basis for experimentation and development at the laboratories of the industrial organizations sponsoring the work. Funding by these organizations (British Aerospace, British Telecom, Hewlett Packard, ICL, Olivetti, Philips, Shell Research, and SRI) was matched by a grant from the Department of Trade and Industry as part of the U.K. government information technology initiative.

This book describes the Core Language Engine (CLE), the natural language processor resulting from the project. It falls within the natural language processing paradigm that is largely concerned with translating between symbolic representations where the translation process starts and/or ends with natural language. The point of the exercise is that the artificial representations involved should be less vague, ambiguous, and syntactically varied than natural language, making them more suitable for a variety of purposes: for querying or adding information to a database, for reasoning about the truth or consequences of a statement, or for the mappings required by machine translation.

We believe that the CLE reflects the emphasis of the project on depth as well as breadth of coverage: we describe a wide-coverage unification grammar for English syntax and semantics; intermediate and contextually disambiguated logical form representations; efficient algorithms for parsing and generation; and mechanisms for quantifier scoping, reference resolution, and lexical acquisition. We hope that the mixture of scientific and engineering goals adopted in this work has repaid the fields motivating the research, both in developing models of natural language that are relevant to more than a few well-studied constructions and in making a concrete contribution to the emerging field of linguistic engineering.

Since the completion of the project in May 1989, we have been using the CLE as the basis for further work in natural language processing.

One such project, called CLARE, aims at combining linguistic and reasoning capabilities, and some developments of the CLE linguistic processing capabilities carried out within that project are covered in a separate chapter. Other projects include interfacing the CLE to a speech recognition system and building an interactive dialogue translation system by connecting the English CLE to a Swedish version.

We would like to thank the project funders listed, British Petroleum and the Royal Signals and Radar Establishment who joined British Aerospace, British Telecom and the DTI in funding CLARE, and the Swedish Institute of Computer Science for funding the translation project. SRI provided an ideal environment in which to carry out the style of research reported here. We are indebted to members of Cambridge University Computer Laboratory who contributed to the project by formal and informal consultation and support, particularly Karen Sparck Jones, without whom the work may not have been carried out, Richard Crouch, Julia Galliers, Roger Needham, and Barney Pell. Ted Briscoe made dozens of valuable comments on a draft of the text. We are also grateful to the Association for Computational Linguistics for giving us the opportunity to report, in papers cited in the book, on several aspects of this work through its journal and conferences. Finally, we thank Harry and Betty Stanton, Teri Mendelsohn, and Kathleen Caruso at the MIT Press and Bradford Books for all their help and encouragement.

Hiyan Alshawi, October 1991.

The Core Language Engine

1 Introduction to the CLE

Hiyan Alshawi and Robert C. Moore

1.1 Language Analysis and Interpretation

The Core Language Engine (CLE) is a general purpose device for mapping between natural language sentences and logical form representations of their meaning. For historical reasons, we tend to describe the translation processes from the perspective of deriving representations of natural language inputs, though lately we have been devoting considerable efforts to performing these processes in the reverse direction. The mappings are not purely formal syntactic transformations, but require the application of one or more sources of knowledge. In particular, we will refer to processes that translate natural language into syntactic or semantic representations using only linguistic knowledge as *analysis*, while processes that apply contextual knowledge will be referred to as *interpretation*.

A primary goal of the Core Language Engine (CLE) design was to achieve substantial syntactic and semantic coverage of English that is linguistically well motivated and as independent as possible of particular domains of discourse. These properties are intended to ensure that the CLE is extensible and suitable for a range of language processing applications. Given the requirements of some potential applications, it was also considered important that the meaning representations produced by the CLE should be capable of supporting reasoning. The starting point for the work was therefore strongly influenced by previous research on logical form representations of natural language in which the semantic analysis of a phrase is derived as a combination of the analyses of its constituent phrases.

We adopted a modular staged design for the CLE in which explicit intermediate levels of linguistic representation are used as an interface between successive phases of analysis. The final result is a set of fully specified *logical forms* (LFs) that represent possible literal meanings of the input sentence. As well as the usual scientific and engineering benefits of modularity, this approach means that the CLE can also be used in applications for which an intermediate level of linguistic representation is more suitable.

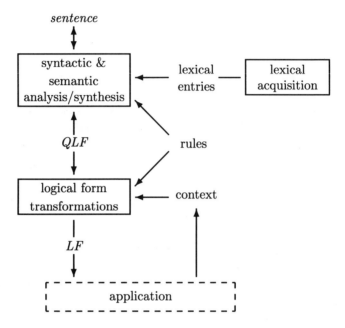

Figure 1.1
Broad overview of the CLE architecture

Two such levels are the parse trees produced by the syntactic analysis phase and *quasi logical forms* (QLFs) produced by the initial semantic analysis phase. QLFs, for example, are currently being used in an experimental interactive machine translation application. The CLE architecture evolved in such a way that the QLF representation, which may be thought of informally as a "contextually sensitive" logical form, became central to the overall design as shown schematically in Figure 1.1.

The QLF representation results from purely linguistic processing by the application of lexical entries and syntactic and semantic grammar rules independently of the influence of context. QLFs differ from fully specified logical forms in that they may contain quantifiers and operators whose scope has not yet been determined, and also "anaphoric expressions" that stand for entities and relations to be determined by reference resolution.

This approach allows the problems of compositional semantics to be tackled separately from those of scoping, reference resolution, and plausibility judgment. Our experience so far with the CLE has shown that the separation can effectively reduce the complexity of the system as a whole, and avoids multiplying out interpretation possibilities at an early stage, considerations which are important to achieving wide coverage in a natural language processing system. The separation also bears on theoretical considerations about the role of grammar versus that of other aspects of language understanding in the overall context of a cognitive system, but we will not be addressing such considerations in this book.

A central theme of the CLE design is the use of unification as the basic mechanism for passing information during linguistic analysis and generation, and, to a lesser extent, during interpretation processes. Unification is an operation that supports the incremental solution of systems of constraints as new constraints are added. The grammatical categories used in the system to classify the syntactic and semantic content of English phrases are defined by equational constraints on the various features of a phrase; grammar rules relate the constraints on a phrase to constraints on its constituent phrases. During the analysis of a sentence, unification is used to ensure that the constraints associated with its constituent phrases are compatible as specified by the rules of grammar.

The semantic analysis rules are also expressed in a unification-based formalism in which unification is used to build QLF representations of the meanings of sentences in a compositional way. In most cases, this is done without resort to more traditional formal devices for meaning representation and composition, such as lambda abstraction and lambda reduction (Montague 1974). This direct encoding of semantic composition is achieved by giving phrases parametric semantic representations. The composition of such parametric representations takes place by unifying the parameters, specified by certain features, with actual values that are the semantic representations of the phrases that syntactic and semantic rules identify as the fillers of the parameters. Since the unification-based rules and lexical entries are declarative and bidirectional, they are applied in the CLE for sentence generation as well as analysis. In particular, the unification approach to semantics allows practical generation from semantic representations because structures can be matched directly against rules without having to perform abstractions to reverse lambda reductions.

Selectional restrictions constraining the sorts of entities that can participate in a semantic relation are also compiled in such a way that the constraints they impose are combined incrementally by unification and incompatible sortal constraints lead to unification failure.

Quantifier scoping, reference resolution, and other contextually sensitive aspects of interpretation are usually implemented in natural language processing systems by purely procedural components, in contrast with the use of declarative rules in the better understood processes of morphology, syntax, and compositional semantics. We have addressed this issue in the CLE design to the extent that much of the knowledge about scoping and reference possibilities and preferences is also expressed by declarative rules. For example, applicable reference resolution rules are matched by unification and the results of resolution are combined with QLFs by unification, bringing us closer to declarative and reversible rules in interpretation as well as analysis.

In more recent research, Alshawi and Crouch (1991) have taken a further step in this direction by extending the QLF representation in a way that allows reference resolution and scoping to be carried out monotonically by instantiation rather than destructive manipulations.

1.2   Overview of CLE Components

The coverage of English syntax (Chapter 4), semantics (Chapter 5), referring expressions (Chapter 10), and ellipsis in the CLE includes the following constructions:

Major clause types: declaratives, imperatives, wh- and yes-no questions, relatives, passives, clefts, there-clauses.

Verb phrases: complement subcategorization, control verbs, verb particles, auxiliaries, tense operators, some adverbials.

Noun phrases: prenominal and postnominal modifiers, lexical and phrasal quantifiers/specifiers.

Coordination: conjunctions and disjunctions of a wide class of noun phrases, verb phrases, and clauses; adjectival, nominal, and adverbial comparatives.

Anaphoric expressions: definite descriptions, reflexive and nonreflexive pronouns, bound variable anaphora, implicit relations.

Ellipsis: 'one'-anaphora, intrasentential and intersentential verb phrase ellipsis, follow-on questions.

Morphology: inflectional morphology, simple productive cases of derivational morphology, special form tokens.

Such a list of constructions can, of course, only give a rough view of coverage, but there are as yet no widely accepted criteria for assessing the linguistic coverage of NLP systems. However, it might be helpful to give the result of an informal experiment conducted with naturally occurring text. A sample of 1000 sentences, restricted to being up to 10 words long and to contain only alphanumeric characters, was taken at random from the Lancaster Oslo Bergen corpus of printed British English. The sentences were processed by the CLE analysis subsystem with its lexicon augmented by a large word list containing only coarse part of speech information. QLF analyses were produced for 634 sentences i.e. 63 percent of the test set. It was also estimated, by sampling and manual inspection, that in 67 percent of these cases the QLF ranked first by the CLE would be valid in some context. (Exhaustive manual inspection of all QLFs produced was not attempted.) In a particular application, the ranking of QLFs is improved significantly by the use of selectional restrictions and domain specific preferences. Manual inspection of the sentences which failed analysis suggests that the point of diminishing returns has not yet been reached, so we expect that these figures will be improved by further grammar development. Larger scale experiments with a fully fledged lexicon would be necessary for a more systematic assessment of syntactic and semantic coverage.

Linguistic analysis is performed in the CLE by four processing phases: lexical analysis (segmentation), morphology, syntactic analysis, and semantic analysis. Further disambiguation and contextual interpretation is carried out by phases for sortal filtering, quantifier scoping, reference (and ellipsis) resolution, and plausibility checking. The inputs to the analysis and interpretation phases are summarized in Figure 1.2. There is also an interactive lexical acquisition component (Chapter 11) that allows application developers to extend the lexicon without knowledge of linguistics or the grammatical theory we have implemented. This facility was used to construct a core lexicon of around 1600 common English words, and to define sortal restrictions applicable to 2300 senses of these words.

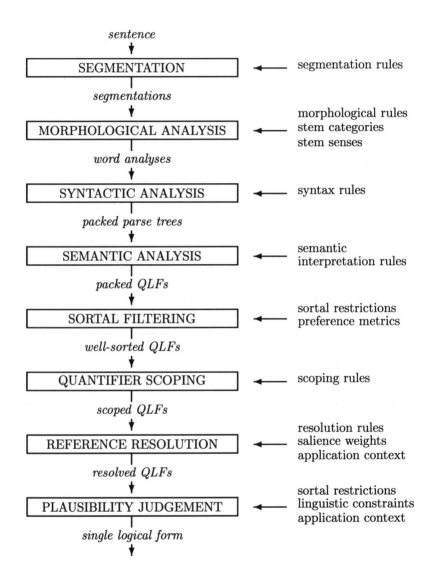

Figure 1.2
Inputs to CLE processing phases in analysis direction

The lexical analysis phase (Chapter 6) performs segmentation of words into stems and affixes, and other token-related tasks such as spelling correction and the recognition of open-ended tokens like dates and numbers.

Syntactic analyses are produced by bottom-up parsing with top-down constraints, using a "left-corner" parsing algorithm (Chapter 7). That is, the parser builds syntactic analyses bottom-up but checks every proposed constituent to make sure that it is compatible with the analysis of the preceding part of the sentence before basing any further analyses on it. The representation we use for local ambiguities, called "packing" after Tomita 1985, is a way of sharing structure between similar analyses of a constituent. During the project, we generalized the technique so that it could be applied to arbitrary category structures and to semantic representations as well as syntactic ones. The basic idea is that when a particular substring can be analyzed in multiple ways, but those subanalyses all enter into larger analyses of the sentence in the same way, the local ambiguities need not be "multiplied out" in building higher level structures. One important consequence of the use of packing is that we have been able to adopt the serial or staged approach to sentence processing even though this implies that analyses produced by one stage of processing are not constrained by information available at later stages. With packing we can efficiently compute and represent all syntactic analyses allowed by a realistically comprehensive grammar.

The semantic analysis phase (also covered in Chapter 7) operates directly on the packed syntactic structures producing packed semantic analyses. Semantic processing needs to be carried out only for constituents that form part of a complete syntactic analysis of a sentence. Word senses for morphologically complex words are derived in a similar way using semantic rules that apply at the sublexical level. Sortal restrictions (Chapter 9) are applied to any QLFs extracted from the packed structure to rule out semantically spurious interpretations that arise from legitimate syntactic analyses of a sentence. The sortal restriction mechanism we have implemented associates sorts with objects, properties, and relations, according to a declaratively specified sort hierarchy so that the only interpretations produced are those that combine properties and relations with objects of the sorts that are appropriate to them.

Quantifier scoping (Chapter 8) determines the scopes of quantifiers and operators, generating scoped logical forms in a preference order. The ordering is determined by a set of declarative rules expressing linguistic preferences such as the preference of particular quantifiers to outscope others. The scoper avoids producing multiple readings for some simple cases of logical equivalence. We have implemented several versions of the quantifier scoping component. The version described here extends earlier versions to support the more complex QLFs produced for comparatives, anaphora, definite reference and conjoined noun phrases. Much of the additional information needed by the scoper to deal with those phrase types is given by declarative specifications of the properties of logical form operators.

Reference resolution (Chapter 10) replaces QLF anaphoric expressions corresponding to pronouns, definite descriptions, and implicit relations with entity or relation constants or with bound variables. This process takes place according to an ordered set of reference resolution rules, each of which specifies a method for resolving expressions that match the rule. The CLE maintains salience weights associated with contextually accessible entities for the purpose of intersentential reference. Other ambiguities that are implicit in QLFs, including cases of the collective/distributive distinction and the "resolution" of determiners to quantifiers, are also made explicit during this phase.

Resolved QLF "interpretations", which are versions of QLF representations showing proposed scoping and resolution choices, are passed to the plausibility checking phase. This phase applies linguistic constraints on resolution and domain-based constraints in the form of sortal restrictions. The design of the reference and plausibility phases includes a carefully defined interface to allow the context provided by an application to influence the derivation of a single LF from the set of linguistically possible QLFs for an English utterance.

Sets of alternative QLFs and resolved interpretations produced by the processing components are ordered according to numerical preference measures. This reduces the burden on users during interactive disambiguation and increases the chances of the correct interpretation being selected without user intervention. The preference measures are arrived at by combining the effects of a variety of scoring functions, but these are largely heuristic in nature so we will be ignoring them for the most part when describing system components.

Chapter 12 outlines two test applications that we implemented to demonstrate the functionality and possible uses of the CLE. These were a database query system, implemented as a logical form to Prolog translator, and an interface to a simulated purchase order processing system. Chapter 13 describes some recent developments of the CLE linguistic processing capabilities, particularly the processing of ellipsis and comparatives and a component for the generation of English sentences using the grammar developed for analysis. Finally, Chapter 14 discusses a translation application based on interfacing the English CLE to a Swedish version to allow typed communication between monolingual users.

In general, there is consistency of analyses, and the notation in which they are expressed, across different chapters of the book. However, as noted at various points in the text, we have not always adhered to this strictly in order to allow some later developments of these analyses to be included by authors of particular chapters.

Since the logical forms generated by the CLE are the main goal of the processing that it performs, and its main interface to application systems, we discuss these first in Chapter 2 before moving on to descriptions of the grammatical formalism, syntactic and semantic rules for English, and the components for sentence processing and lexical acquisition.

2 Logical Forms

Jan van Eijck and Hiyan Alshawi

2.1 Levels of Logical Form in the CLE

While processing a sentence, the CLE generates representations corresponding to successive phases of linguistic analysis. These are orthographic analyses, morphological analyses, syntactic analyses, unscoped quasi logical forms, scoped quasi logical forms, resolved quasi logical forms and logical forms. In this chapter we will describe (unscoped) quasi logical forms (QLFs) and logical forms (LFs), giving a substantively revised and extended version of the material presented in Alshawi and van Eijck 1989.

Quasi logical form is the target language of the syntax-driven semantic analysis rules. Transforming QLF expressions into LF expressions requires:

(i) fixing the scopes of quantifiers and operators, giving scoped logical forms;

(ii) resolving pronouns, definite descriptions, ellipsis, underspecified relations and vague quantifiers, giving resolved quasi logical forms (RQLFs); and

(iii) extracting the truth conditional part of resolved quasi logical forms to give logical forms.

This last step is a purely formal operation. The RQLF representation is discussed in Chapter 10; it suffices to say here that it includes the information from both QLF and LF representations.

A particular QLF expression may correspond to several, possibly infinitely many, LF expressions. However, the LF language is in fact a sublanguage of the QLF language; there are additional "quasi logical" constructs for unscoped quantifiers, unscoped descriptions, unresolved references, and unresolved relations. LFs are therefore described first, with the additional QLF constructs being introduced at the end of the chapter.

2.2   Resolved Logical Form

LF Formalism Requirements

Logical forms are intended to satisfy the following requirements:

- LFs should be expressions in a disambiguated language; i.e., alternative readings of natural language expressions should give rise to different logical forms.

- LFs should be suitable for representing the literal "meanings" of natural language expressions; i.e., they should specify the truth conditions of (appropriate readings of) the original natural language expressions.

- LFs should provide a suitable medium for the representation of knowledge as expressed in natural language, and they should be a suitable vehicle for reasoning.

The formalism used in the CLE is a higher-order logic, in which extensions to first-order logic have been motivated by trying to satisfy the above requirements with respect to the range of natural language expressions covered. We will first present the predicate logic part, then cover the extensions. As descriptions of formal logics go, our presentation of the LF and QLF languages will be relatively informal. The term "translation" of a natural language sentence will be used for either QLF analyses or LFs corresponding to the sentence.

2.2.1   The Predicate Logic Part

The basis of the LF formalism is first-order predicate logic, with some peculiarities of notation motivated by computational convenience. The following BNF-like rules show the notational details.

$\langle formula \rangle \rightarrow$ [$\langle predicate \rangle$, $\langle argument_1 \rangle$, . . . , $\langle argument_n \rangle$]

$\langle predicate \rangle \rightarrow$ love1 | donkey1 | mule1 | tall2 | geq . . .

$\langle argument \rangle \rightarrow \langle term \rangle$

$\langle term \rangle \rightarrow \langle variable \rangle$ | $\langle constant \rangle$

$\langle variable \rangle \rightarrow$ X | Y . . .

$\langle constant \rangle \rightarrow$ dobbin1 | mary1 | titanic1 . . .

⟨*formula*⟩ → [not,⟨*formula*⟩]

⟨*formula*⟩ → [and,⟨*formula*⟩,⟨*formula*⟩]

⟨*formula*⟩ → [or,⟨*formula*⟩,⟨*formula*⟩]

⟨*formula*⟩ → [impl,⟨*formula*⟩,⟨*formula*⟩]

⟨*formula*⟩ → quant(⟨*quantifier*⟩,⟨*variable*⟩,⟨*formula*⟩,⟨*formula*⟩)

⟨*quantifier*⟩ → forall | exists

As can be seen from the rules, the Prolog list notation is used for the application of a predicate or logical operator to its arguments. This is convenient for later extensions, since it allows the possibility of having complex expressions in the functor position. We also follow the Prolog convention of starting variables with an uppercase letter and constants with a lowercase letter. In this notation, the logical form

    [or, [donkey1,dobbin1], [mule1,dobbin1]]

expresses the proposition that Dobbin is a donkey or a mule. Here donkey1 and mule1 are one place predicates,[1] dobbin1 is a constant, and or is the usual disjunction operator. As the rules above show, the logical connectives and, or, impl, and not are treated in LF syntax as any other operators; and, or, and impl are prefix operators with two arguments, not is an operator with one argument.

The notation for quantification caters for restricted first order quantifiers. For a simple sentence like *Every doctor visited Mary*, a logical form translation produced by the CLE will typically involve quantified variables (tense is ignored here):

    quant(forall,D,[doctor1,D],
            quant(exists,E,[event,E],
                    [visit,E,D,mary1])).

Here D and E are variables bound by the familiar first order logic quantifiers. It is well known that restricted first order quantifiers give the same expressive power as unrestricted ones. However, this is no longer the case for nonstandard quantifiers like *most* (Barwise and Cooper 1981). The notation for quantifiers with restrictions was chosen to ease the shift to a

---

[1]Predicates corresponding to different senses of a word are often distinguished by sense numbers or other suffixes, but these are sometimes omitted when giving example logical forms.

generalized quantifier perspective, the details of which will be explained
below. The use of event variables will also be explained shortly, but for
the moment this logical form can be paraphrased as "For every doctor
D, there is an event, E, of D visiting Mary".

2.2.2   Higher Order Extensions

The syntax of the extensions to the first order part of the logical form
language can be specified with the following additional BNF-like rules:

$\langle lf\_form \rangle \rightarrow$ [$\langle mood\_op \rangle$, $\langle formula \rangle$]

$\langle mood\_op \rangle \rightarrow$ dcl | whq | ynq | imp

$\langle argument \rangle \rightarrow \langle formula \rangle$

$\langle argument \rangle \rightarrow \langle abstract \rangle$

$\langle predicate \rangle \rightarrow$ believe1 | want1 | past | fut ...

$\langle quantifier \rangle \rightarrow$ most | several | wh | count ...

$\langle quantifier \rangle \rightarrow \langle variable \rangle \hat{} \langle variable \rangle \hat{} \langle formula \rangle$

$\langle quantifier \rangle \rightarrow$ set($\langle quantifier \rangle$)

$\langle quantifier \rangle \rightarrow$ amount($\langle variable \rangle \hat{} \langle variable \rangle \hat{} \langle formula \rangle$, $\langle functor \rangle$)

$\langle abstract \rangle \rightarrow \langle variable \rangle \hat{} \langle lambda\_body \rangle$

$\langle lambda\_body \rangle \rightarrow \langle formula \rangle$

$\langle lambda\_body \rangle \rightarrow \langle abstract \rangle$

$\langle term \rangle \rightarrow$ kind($\langle variable \rangle$, $\langle formula \rangle$)

$\langle constant \rangle \rightarrow$ 'U'([$\langle constant_1 \rangle$,..., $\langle constant_n \rangle$])

$\langle constant \rangle \rightarrow$ 'SF'($\langle functor \rangle$($\langle constant_1 \rangle$,..., $\langle constant_n \rangle$)).

The four kinds of $\langle lf\_form \rangle$ distinguished at top level are declaratives,
yes/no questions, wh-questions, and imperatives, as marked by the mood
operators dcl, ynq, whq, and imp respectively. However, we will often
omit these operators when displaying logical forms.

Constant terms of the form

'U'([$\langle constant_1 \rangle$,...,$\langle constant_n \rangle$])

are called *union terms*; they are used to refer to collections. Constant
terms of the form

'SF' (⟨functor⟩(⟨constant₁⟩,..., ⟨constant_n⟩))

are called *special form terms*; they are used for representing the meaning
of dates (e.g., 'SF'(date(2,12,1957))) and other terms with special
format lexical realizations. They can usually be thought of simply as
function applications (e.g., the result of applying the function date to
three numerical arguments).

The LF language extends the language of first order predicate logic
in three main ways. First, use is made of lambda abstraction for the
formation of higher order expressions. Second, the language is extended
with generalized quantifiers. Finally, tense operators, intensional operators, and other higher order operators are included. These extensions
are discussed below.

Abstraction and Application

Lambda abstraction is used to construct functions of arbitrary complexity (properties of objects, relations between objects, and so on). In
the LF notation, X^[heavy,X] corresponds to the more usual notation
$\lambda x.heavy(x)$. The BNF rules show that terms, formulae, and abstracts
can all act as arguments to a functor expression. For every functor expression the types of the arguments that it takes are fixed, although the
rules do not show that. The rules do convey that all functor expressions
except for "^" form expressions of type *formula*, that is, that functors
have result-type *proposition*. In other words, the only way of forming
higher order expressions is by means of the abstraction functor "^". The
logical counterpart of the abstraction functor "^" is the functor apply for
lambda application. This functor expresses the result of applying an abstract to an appropriate argument. Thus [apply,X^[woman,X],mary1]
reduces to [woman,mary1].

A simple example of the use of abstracts is the treatment of so-called
arbitrary control infinitives, such as the infinitive phrase in "It is nice *to
live in Paris*", in which the subject of *live* is unspecified. The translation
of the infinitive phrase abstracts over the subject variable:

```
A^quant(exists,E,[event,E],
        [and,[live,E,A],[in_location,E,paris1]]).
```

This can be paraphrased as "the property of being the subject of an event
of living which is located in Paris" (Section 2.2.7). Lambda abstraction

is also used in the LF translation of comparatives and superlatives (Section 2.2.12).

In the LF representations produced by the CLE, the only uses of `apply` reduce properties to formulae by applying them to terms. This special case can be expressed as follows in a specific BNF rule:

$\langle formula \rangle \rightarrow$ [apply,$\langle variable \rangle^{\wedge}\langle formula \rangle$,$\langle term \rangle$].

The functor `apply` is a logical functor in the sense that its interpretation is meant to be application-independent. Other such logical functors are the logical operators `not`, `and`, and `or`. See Pereira and Shieber 1987 for the general background on the representation of standard logical operators in computational semantics for natural language.

2.2.3 Generalized Quantifiers

Logical form quantifiers are not restricted to existentials and universals; these are simply special cases of generalized quantifiers. A generalized quantifier is a relation Q between two sets A and B (where A is called the *restriction set* and B the *body set*) that satisfies some specific requirements. Useful background information about generalized quantifiers in natural language is provided by van Benthem (1986) and van Eijck (1988). For present purposes it is enough to note that the requirements can be summarized as the condition that Q be insensitive to anything but the cardinalities of the sets A (the *restriction set*) and the set $A \cap B$ (henceforth: the *intersection set*). Thus a generalized quantifier with restriction set A and body set B is fully characterized by a predicate $\lambda n \lambda m . \mathbf{Q}(n, m)$ on n and m, where $n = |A|$ and $m = |A \cap B|$ (Figure 2.1). Here are some examples:

- *All representatives voted* is true if and only if the restriction set (the set of representatives) equals the intersection set (the intersection of the set of representatives and the set of voters).

- *At least three representatives voted* is true if and only if the intersection set contains at least three individuals.

- *Not all representatives voted* is true if and only if the the restriction set does not equal the intersection set.

- *Most representatives voted* is true (in neutral contexts) if and only if the size of the intersection set is greater than half the size of the restriction set.

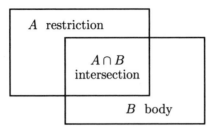

Q is a predicate on n and m, where $n = |A|$ and $m = |A \cap B|$

Figure 2.1
Generalized quantifier sets

- *At least four and at most ten representatives voted* is true if and only if the intersection set contains at least four and at most ten individuals.

As explained later in Sections 2.2.9 and 2.2.10, the LF quantifier notation is further extended to deal with collectives and mass terms. In particular, our treatment of collective readings assumes a more complex interpretation of logical form variables in which they range over sets of entities.

In the LF language the quantifier relations are expressed by means of predicates on two numbers, where the first variable abstracted over denotes the cardinality of the restriction set and the second one the cardinality of the intersection set. In simple cases, these predicates are abbreviated by means of mnemonic names, such as **exists**, **notexists**, or **forall**. In general, the quantifier predicate is built up from numerical relations such as ">", "$\geq$", "=" (in CLE notation: **gt**, **geq**, **eq**), and **ratio**, where [**ratio,M,N,K,L**] states that "the ratio between M and N is at least K/L".

Here are the translations for the quantifiers in the above examples ($\rightsquigarrow$ is used to abbreviate 'translates into'):

- *every* $\rightsquigarrow$ N^M^[eq,N,M]
  i.e., $\lambda n \lambda m (n = m)$.
  (This quantifier is abbreviated as **forall**.)

- *at least three* `N^M^[geq,M,3]`
  i.e., $\rightsquigarrow \lambda m(m \geq 3)$.
- *not every* $\rightsquigarrow$ `N^M^[not,[eq,N,M]]`
  i.e., $\lambda n \lambda m(n \neq m)$.
- *most* $\rightsquigarrow$ `M^N^[ratio,N,M,1,2]`
  i.e., $\lambda n \lambda m(n \geq m/2)$.
  (The ratio for *most* is, in reality, context sensitive.)
- *at least four and at most ten*
  $\rightsquigarrow$ `N^M^[and,[geq,M,4],[leq,M,10]]`
  i.e., $\lambda m(4 \leq m \leq 10)$.

Simplified logical forms (ignoring "event variables") for *Every representative voted*, *Not every representative voted*, and *At least four and at most ten representatives voted* now look like this:

```
quant(forall,X,[representative1,X],[past,[vote1,X]])
```

```
quant(N^M^[not,[eq,N,M]],
          X,[representative1,X],[past,[vote1,X]])
```

```
quant(N^M^[and,[geq,M,4],[leq,M,10]],
          X,[representative1,X],[past,[vote1,X]]).
```

Note that in the cases of quantifiers that depend only on the cardinality of their intersection set, the abstraction over the cardinality of their restriction set will be vacuous. These are called *absolute* quantifiers (example: *at least three*); quantifiers that depend on the cardinalities of both restriction and intersection set are *relative* (example: *not all*). The absolute quantifiers turn out to be the quantifiers that are "symmetrical": *At least three representatives were men* is true just in case *At least three men were representatives* is true. Formally, the property of symmetry can be expressed thus:

```
quant(Q,Var,A,B)   <=>   quant(Q,Var,B,A).
```

The quantifiers with this property constitute a linguistically well-defined class: they are the quantifiers that can occur in the NP position in "There are NP". See Barwise and Cooper 1981 and van Eijck 1988 for further discussion.

Table 2.1
LF tense and aspect operators

tense/aspect	example	translation
simple present	*Birds fly*	[pres, *LF*]
simple past	*John left*	[past, *LF*]
present perfect	*John has left*	[pres, [perf, *LF*]]
past perfect	*John had left*	[past, [perf, *LF*]]
present progressive	*John is talking*	[pres, [prog, *LF*]]
past progressive	*John was talking*	[past, [prog, *LF*]]
present perfect prog.	*John has been talking*	[pres, [perf, [prog, *LF*]]]
past perfect progressive	*John had been talking*	[past, [perf, [prog, *LF*]]]

2.2.4 Tense, Aspect, and Modality

Logical operators such as not, and, and or are extensional: the truth values of propositions of which they are the main functors depend on the extensions (the truth values) of their propositional arguments. Tenses of verbs and modal auxiliaries give rise to logical operators that are not extensional: the truth values of propositions of which they are the main functors do not depend only on the truth values of their arguments, but rather on functions from indices (possible worlds, contexts) to truth values.

As the above examples show, the past tense is translated into a one place operator past. Generally, we express aspect, tense, and modality in logical forms by operators on formulae in which the event or state variables have been bound. Table 2.1 illustrates how the English tense and aspect system is treated.

In English, reference to the future is expressed by means of the auxiliaries *will* and *shall*, which translate into a future operator fut in logical form. Similarly, modal auxiliaries translate into the operators shown in Table 2.2. Formulae within the scope of a tense or modal operator will always contain a bound event (or state) variable. The modal operators in the table can be transformed into first order quantifications over events and time intervals; in fact, such explicit quantification is useful in applications. The modal operator representation at LF level was chosen partly for conciseness of representation. We will not dwell on the formal semantics of these operators, especially since our more recent efforts are based on a different representation of tense and aspect information in

Table 2.2
LF modal operators

auxiliary	example	translation
shall	*I shall work*	[fut, *LF*]
will	*John will talk*	[fut, *LF*]
may	*John may talk*	[may1, *LF*]
can	*John can talk*	[can1, *LF*]
should	*John should talk*	[should1, *LF*]
must	*John must talk*	[must1, *LF*]
might	*John might talk*	[might1, *LF*]

LF and QLF (see Section 10.5.4).

As an example,

> *John may have been working.*   (1)

is assigned a logical form translation with operators for both modality
and aspect:

```
[may1,
    [perf,
        [prog,quant(exists,A,[event,A],
                    [work,A,john1])]]].
```

2.2.5   Statements, Questions, and Commands

The logical forms that the CLE assigns to questions and commands (imperative sentences) are similar to those for declarative statements. Logical forms for yes/no questions are distinguished from those for declarative statements by the top-level (mood) operator **ynq**. Logical forms for
imperative statements are distinguished from logical forms for declaratives by the top level **imp** operator. For example, the logical form for
(3) is the same as that for (2) except that the operator **dcl** is replaced
by **ynq**.

> *John designed a house.*   (2)
> *Did John design a house?*   (3)

Imperatives, such as *Stop* and *Send it to John*, are translated in the
same way as the corresponding present tense declaratives with a second

person pronoun as subject. Thus, except for the top level operator
imp *Send it to John* receives the same translation, after resolution of
the pronoun, as *You send it to John*. These translations are initially
expressions in the quasi logical form language since they will contain
"anaphoric terms" corresponding to pronouns (Section 2.3.3 below).

One possible way to think of the semantics of the ynq operator is as a
relation between states of the world: the [ynq,LF] representation for a
yes/no question denotes the reflexive relation on the set of states of the
world (or the current database), consisting of precisely those pairs $\langle s, s \rangle$
for which LF evaluates to true in s. Similarly, the [imp,LF] representation for a sentence in imperative mood can be thought of as denoting
a transition relation on the set of states of the world, with $\langle s, s' \rangle$ in the
relation just in case LF evaluates to true in s'. Nothing hinges, however,
on these particular interpretations.

Logical forms for wh-questions are like those for declaratives except
for top-level operator whq and the fact that they contain at least one wh-
quantifier (a quant expressions in which the quantifier position is filled
by the symbol wh1 or count). For example, (simplified) LF translations
of the following sentences:

> *Which house did John design?* (4)
>
> *Who did John laugh at?* (5)

are, respectively:

```
[whq,quant(wh1,A,[house_building,A],
          [past,[design1,john1,A]])]

[whq,quant(wh1,A,[person,A],
          [past,[laugh_at1,john1,A]])].
```

Typically, in an application, these forms are interpreted as requesting
the set of all bindings of the wh-variable that satisfy both the restriction
and the body. In the first example, this corresponds to the set of houses
that John designed in the past. In cases involving embedded clauses, for
example,

> *Which doctor did Mary want John to visit?* (6)

the CLE's treatment of long-distance dependencies (Chapters 4 and 5)
ensures that the wh-variable appears inside the interpretation of the

embedded clause, giving the following logical form (shown in full with
event variables):

```
[whq,quant(wh1,A,[doctor1,A],
        [past,
            quant(exists,B,[event,B],
                [want,B,
                    mary1,
                    quant(exists,C,[event,C],
                            [visit,C,john1,A])])])]).
```

2.2.6   Events and States

Event Variables

The event variables employed in the CLE's treatment of verb phrases
will now be discussed in more detail. Verbs are not treated simply as
relations between a subject and a number of VP complements. Following
Davidson 1967, the event being described is introduced as an additional
argument. Thus, the full logical form for *Every representative voted* is
as follows:

```
quant(forall,A,[representative1,A],
    [past,quant(exists,B,[event,B],[vote1,B,A])]).
```

Informally, this says that for every representative, at some past time,
there existed an event of that representative voting.

The presence of an event variable allows optional verb phrase modifiers
to be treated as predications on events, in first-order fashion, which
in turn permits a uniform interpretation to be given to prepositional
phrases, whether they modify verb phrases or nouns. The reading of

John designed a college in Cambridge.   (7)

in which *in Cambridge* is taken to modify the verb phrase gives rise to
the following logical form:

```
quant(exists,A,
    [college_place,A],
    [past,
    quant(exists,B,[event,B],
            [and,[design1,B,john1,A],
                [in_location,B,cambridge1]])]).
```

The same interpretation of the prepositional phrase takes part in the reading involving noun phrase modification (Section 2.2.8); on one reading it expresses a property of the college, and on the other a property of the event of designing the college.

Event variables are also employed in the treatment of wh-moved PPs, as in the following example:

> *Where did John eat?*   (8)

for which the LF translation is:

```
quant(wh1,A,[place,A],
    [past,
     quant(exists,B,[event,B],
         [and,[eat,B,john1],[in_location,B,A]])]).
```

State Variables

Adjectives in predicative position give rise to state variables in their translation. States are like events, but unlike events they cannot be instantaneous. For example:

> *John is nice.*   (9)

is translated as:

```
quant(exists,A,[state,A],[nice1,A,john1]).
```

One should think of this translation as a rather coarse-grained account of the meaning of (9). In an appropriate application context, contextual lexical resolution of **nice1** will result in a more fine-grained translation. Such further lexical resolution is necessary to bring out out the equivalence in meaning between (9) and (10).

> *John is a nice person.*   (10)

Like event variables, state variables are employed in the account of PP modification, as in the translation of *John is happy in Cambridge*:

```
quant(exists,A,[state,A],
    [and,[happy1,A,john1],
         [in_location,A,cambridge1]]).
```

To interpret this we assume that states can be located, or in other words, that properties can be relativized to locations.

2.2.7   Infinitives

The analysis of "free control" infinitive verb phrases (i.e., those for which
the sentence does not provide a subject) makes use of lambda abstraction. The translation of the example given earlier, *It is nice to live in
Paris*, is a statement about the property of living in Paris:

```
[pres,
 quant(exists,A,[state,A],
     [be,A,
      [nice1_property,
       B^quant(exists,C,[event,C],
               [and,[live1,C,B],
                    [in_location,C,paris1]])]])].
```

An unreduced application of a lambda abstraction appears in the
translation of *John expected Mary to go*:

```
[past,quant(exists,E,[event,E],
    [expect1,E,john1,
     [apply,A^quant(exists,E1,[event,E1],[go,E1,A]),
            mary1]])].
```

This logical form is equivalent to the following reduced version:

```
[past,quant(exists,E,[event,E],
    [expect1,E,john1,
     quant(exists,E1,[event,E1],[go,E1,mary])])].
```

The analysis using the unreduced application has three motivations.
First, it gives a treatment that is uniform with arbitrary control infinitives, in the sense that infinitives have the same translation in different
syntactic positions. Second, it allows reference resolution rules to establish the right intrasentential anaphoric links for examples like *John
expected himself to go* (Section 10.4.3). Finally, it affords simpler verb
subcategorization, so that, for example, expect1 takes the same number
of arguments in the translation of *John expected that Mary would arrive*
as in the above example.

2.2.8   Nominal Modifiers

The logical forms resulting from prenominal and postnominal modification are in many cases translated simply as additional conjuncts con-

straining the variable introduced by a noun phrase. This is true for relative clauses, prepositional phrases modifying NPs, and (intersective) adjectives. Compound nominals and possessives also result in conjuncts constraining the NP variable, but these are treated as implicit relations and are considered in Section 2.3.4.

The event-modification reading of *John designed a college in Cambridge* was given earlier. The reading in which *in Cambridge* is a postnominal modifier is assigned the logical form:

```
quant(exists,A,
    [and,[college_place,A],[in_location,A,cambridge1]],
    [past
        quant(exists,B,[event,B],[design1,B,john1,A])]).
```

Example (11) involves nominal modification by both an intersective adjective and a relative clause.

John reads every interesting book that Mary buys.   (11)

This results in a logical form with nested conjunctions in the restriction of the universal quantifier:

```
quant(forall,B,
    [and,
        [and,[book1,B],[interesting1,B]],
        [pres,quant(exists,E,[event,E],
                    [buy,E,mary1,B])]],
    [pres,quant(exists,D,[event,D],[read,D,john1,B])]).
```

2.2.9   Distributive and Collective Readings

Sentences involving plurals often have different readings corresponding to collective/distributive distinctions (Fauconnier 1975), i.e., whether sets of objects take part in relations collectively or as individuals. Conjunctions of proper names can be read either distributively or collectively.

John and Mary left.   (12)

The reading of (12) expressing that there was an event of John leaving and an event of Mary leaving—that is, the distributive reading—is expressed as follows:

```
[and,
 [past,quant(exists,A,[event,A],[leave,A,john1])],
 [past,quant(exists,B,[event,B],[leave,B,mary1])]].
```

The reading expressing that there is one leaving event is represented by means of a 'union term' denoting a collection:

```
[past,quant(exists,A,[event,A],
            [leave1,A,U([john1,mary1])])].
```

For this example, the collective reading does imply the distributive reading, but in general this need not be the case. The collective reading of *John and Mary bought a house* does not imply the distributive one, or vice versa.

This treatment of collectives leads to the interpretation of variables as always ranging over sets, with "normal" individuals corresponding to singleton sets (cf. Scha 1981). Thus properties like X^[dog,X] can be true of singletons (e.g., the referent of *Fido*), as well as of larger sets (e.g., the referent of *the three dogs we saw yesterday*). Quantified variables bound by quant are restricted to ranging over individuals (singletons), unless a set(...) or amount(...) operator indicates otherwise (amount quantifiers are discussed in the next section).

Let us look at the collective/distributive distinction for quantifiers.

> *Two companies ordered five computers.*   -   (13)

Example (13) has readings involving differing numbers of computers, depending on whether each of the quantifiers is taken as distributive or collective. The reading in which both quantifiers are distributive involves ten computers and ten ordering events. This reading is assigned by the CLE using the generalized quantifier notation introduced in Section 2.2.3:

```
quant(N^M^[eq,M,2],A,[company,A],
      quant(K^L^[eq,L,5],B,[computer,B],
            [past,quant(exists,E,[event,E],
                        [order,E,A,B])])).
```

What this says is that for each of two companies there were five computers such that the company ordered the computer, in other words, the two companies both placed five orders for one computer; hence the total of ten ordering events.

Collective readings for such examples are also generated by the CLE; these require a different mode of quantification involving a 'set' quantifier. The variable for set quantifiers ranges over sets (of computers in the following reading):

```
quant(N^M^[eq,M,2],A,[company,A],
    quant(set(K^L^[eq,L,5]),B,[computer,B],
        [past,quant(exists,E,[event,E],
                         [order,E,A,B])])).
```

This is the reading where each of two companies takes part in an ordering event involving a (possibly different) set of five computers. Another reading, with the quantifiers set(N^M^[eq,M,2]) and set(K^L^[eq,L,5]) would say that two companies (acting together) took part in purchasing a collection of five computers. Clearly, further readings can be represented by reversing the scopes of the quantifiers.

More generally, in quantifiers of the form set(Q), Q is a predicate of two numbers. A quantification (i.e. quant expression) with set(Q) holds if Q holds of the cardinality of the union of sets satisfying the restriction and the cardinality of the maximal subset of this union satisfying the body.

Distributive readings for plural definite descriptions are expressed with the subset predicate in conjunction with a normal (distributive) quantifier.

The two representatives voted.   (14)

In (14), if the context contains a suitable set to serve as antecedent for the definite description, say the set consisting of John and Mary, then the description gets resolved to this set (represented as the term U([john1,mary1])). The distributive reading for the resolved logical form is expressed as follows:

```
quant(forall,A,
    [subset,A,U([john1,mary1])],
        [past,quant(exists,E,[event,E],[vote1,E,A])]).
```

In cases where no suitable antecedent for a definite description is found the description is turned into a quantifier that may be distributive or collective. A fuller discussion of the interaction between quantifiers, distributivity, and reference is given in Chapter 10.

2.2.10   Measure and Kind Terms

Measure Terms

A further extension of the quantifier notation, which can be seen as a generalization of the 'set' quantifiers just described, gives a treatment of (collective) measure terms. The objects in the domain of quantification can be measured quantities as well as sets of entities. In case the quantifier translates a measured expression such as *two pounds of butter* the items in the restriction set and the intersection set are amounts of butter measured in pounds. Units of measurement thus correspond to functions from amounts of stuff to the real numbers. They form an open class category including, for example, `pound`, `inch`, `meter`, and `foot`.

Where 'set' quantifiers involve counting to determine the cardinality of sets, 'amount' generalized quantifiers involve measuring by application of the measurement unit function. Our approach, which is related to proposals that can be found in Pelletier 1979, leads to the following translation for *John bought at least five pounds of apples*:

    quant(amount(R^I^[geq,I,5],pound),A,
        [apple,A],
        [past,quant(exists,E,[event,E],[buy,E,john1,A])]).

In this representation the variable A is bound to an amount of apples which is such that pound(A) is at least five. Representing the 'set' quantifier for the collective reading of *John bought five apples* in a parallel fashion would involve the quantifier

    amount(R^I^[geq,I,5],cardinality).

With this view of amount quantification, it does not matter whether the head of the noun phrase is a count noun, like *apple*, or a mass noun, like *butter*; the only requirement is that a particular amount of the stuff can be assigned a number by the chosen measure. The representation used is the same in both cases.

Kind Terms

Terms in logical forms may also refer to natural kinds (Carlson 1977), which are individuals of a specific nature. The term

```
kind(V,[pred,V])
```

can be loosely interpreted as the typical individual satisfying **pred**. All properties, including composite ones, have a corresponding kind term in our formalism. Kind terms can be used in the translations of examples like (15) and (16).

> *Birds fly.*   (15)

> *Angry bears are dangerous.*   (16)

The logical form for (16) is as follows:

```
[pres,quant(exists,A,[state,A],
        [dangerous1,A,
            kind(B,[and,[bear_animal,B],[angry1,B]])])].
```

Kind terms also appear in the logical forms for compound nominals, so the LF for *computer message* uses `kind(C,[computer1,C])` (see Section 2.3.4).

In reasoning about kinds, the simplest approach possible would be to have a rule of inference stating that if a "kind individual" has a certain property, then all "real world" individuals of that kind have that property as well: if the "typical bear" is an animal, then all real world bears are animals. Of course, the converse rule does not hold: the "typical bear" cannot have all the properties that any real bear has, because then it would have to be both white all over and brown all over, and so on.

In English, bare plurals like *birds* can either refer to kinds or serve to indicate existential quantification. The distinction between the two interpretations is rather subtle and is influenced by tense and aspect. The statement

> *Birds were flying.*   (17)

is not about the kind *bird* but about some individual birds. A different treatment of bare plurals, which may allow contextual factors to be taken into account, is presented in Chapter 10.

2.2.11   Predicate Nominals

In order to have a uniform treatment of the predicate nominals in all the following examples,

> *Fido is a dog.*   (18)

John is my best friend.   (19)

Most bishops are men.   (20)

Dogs are animals.   (21)

the translation of *be* plus predicate nominal employs a predicate **be** that is used to link a state to a proposition; the proposition will have **eq**, the equality predicate, as its main predicate. Thus, the general format of the translation of a predicate nominal construction is:

```
[Tense,
    quant(exists,S,[state,S],[be,S,Proposition])].
```

Here **Tense** is the tense operator and **Proposition** is a proposition involving equality. For example, (18) can be paraphrased as "Fido is in the state of being equal to some dog":

```
[pres,quant(exists,A,[state,A],
    [be,A,quant(exists,B,[dog1,B],[eq,fido1,B])])].
```

Bare plurals can be assigned an existential interpretation when they occur as objects of *be*, so (20) produces the following logical form:

```
quant(R^I^[ratio,I,R,1,2],C,[bishop1,C],
    [pres,
        quant(exists,D,[state,D],
            [be,D,
                quant(exists,E,
                    [man_male_human,E],[eq,C,E])])]).
```

The predicate **be** is also used in the representation of *'there'* existential sentences such as (22), which receives the following translation:

How many bishops are there in London?   (22)

```
[pres,
    quant(count,
        A,
        [bishop1,A],
        quant(exists,B,[state,B],
            [be,B,[in_location,A,london1]]))].
```

2.2.12   Comparatives and Superlatives

In this section we discuss the LF representation of simple adjectival comparatives and superlatives. A more general treatment of comparatives is discussed in Section 13.2. Here we assume that "gradable" adjectives (such as *tall*) have a corresponding degree relation between individuals and integers, so, for example, the following might hold:

    [tall1_degree,john1,176].

Intuitively, the meaning of a comparative, as in (23), is that one of the two items being compared possesses a property to a higher degree than the other one. The meaning of a measured comparative, as in (24), is that the degree to which one item possesses a property exceeds the degree to which the other item possesses it by some specified measure.

> *Mary is taller than John.*   (23)
>
> *Mary is two inches taller than John.*   (24)

Taking the second form as basic, comparatives are treated in terms of graded predicates, generalized amount quantifiers and a four-place higher order predicate more:

    [more,P,Item1,Item2,Degree]

This is true just in case the degree to which Item1 satisfies graded predicate P exceeds the degree to which Item2 satisfies P by Degree. The LF for (24) using more is:

    [pres,
      quant(exists,A,[state,A],
        [be,A,
          quant(amount(B^C^[eq,C,2],inch),D,
                [degree,D],
                [more,E^F^[tall1_degree,E,F],
                      mary1,john1,D])])],

and that for (23), using existential quantification over amounts, is:

    [pres,
      quant(exists,A,[state,A],
        [be,A,

```
quant(amount(B^C^[gt,C,0],units),D,
    [degree,D],
    [more,E^F^[tall1_degree,E,F],
     mary1,john1,D])])].
```

Examples like the following get similar translations:

Mary is less happy than John.   (25)

Mary is as tall as Bill.   (26)

The first of these uses the operator less that parallels more; the LF for
the second is expressed in terms of more, with 'degree' argument 0:

```
[pres,
 quant(exists,A,[state,A],
   [be,A,
    [more,B^C^[tall1_degree,B,C],mary1,bill1,0]])].
```

The meaning of a superlative, as in (27), is taken to be the possession
of a property to the highest degree among all the items in a certain set.

Mary is the nicest woman I know.   (27)

In the example the property is that of being nice and the set is all the
women known to the speaker. This treatment makes the assumption
(unrealistic in some contexts) that any gradable adjective imposes a
linear order on the set of objects to which it applies.

Superlatives can be related to comparatives in the following way: A
is the Adj-est N just in case there is exactly one pair of (not necessarily different) Ns such that A is the second member of that pair, and
the first member of such pairs is at least as Adj as the second member. Thus a reduction of superlative to comparative can be performed
by expressing the superlative in terms of the predicate more. However,
for a more readable representation of superlatives, a predicate order is
used corresponding to a higher-order relation between properties, degree predicates and integers. The relation holds of X just in case X is
the thing occupying the position indicated by the integer in the ordering induced by the degree predicate on the set of things satisfying the
property. For example, the following predicate would be satisfied by the
heaviest wrestler:

X^[order,X,Y^[wrestler,Y],K^L^[heavy_degree,K,L],1].

The representation of superlatives in terms of **order** can be thought of as an abbreviation for the reduction to comparatives mentioned above. This treatment engenders an elegant treatment of ordinal-superlative combinations. Thus in the representation of *the third oldest building*, the ordinal contributes the appropriate numeral to the **order** predicate:

X^[order,X,Y^[building,Y],K^L^[old_degree,K,L],3].

Definite determiners followed by ordinals without superlatives can then be treated in cases where the appropriate degree predicate is to be inferred from the context. *The third college in Cambridge* might mean the third oldest, the third as you go down the main street, and so on. The CLE notation that is used to indicate that the appropriate piece of information (a degree predicate in this case) is still lacking is covered in the next section.

2.3   Quasi Logical Form

As stated earlier, the quasi logical form (QLF) language is a superset of the LF language; it contains additional constructs for unscoped quantifiers, and unresolved terms and relations. The linguistic constraints and algorithms for quantifier scoping are discussed in detail in Chapter 8, while the reference resolution mechanism is covered in Chapter 10. Here, we simply present the additional constructs in sufficient detail to allow an understanding of the results of the semantic analysis phase.

A process akin to reference resolution can also be invoked for contextual resolution of lexical ambiguities. However, the CLE makes the usual approximation of treating most content words as having a fixed set of distinct senses that give rise to distinct QLFs when they are not ruled out by selectional restrictions.

2.3.1   Syntax of the QLF Language

The basic constructs by which the QLF language extends the LF language are the following:

1. Terms for unscoped quantified expressions (**qterms**). These are used to get ambiguous translations for quantifiers at the prescoping

level: *no woman, every man*; and for definite descriptions: *the bishop, these five farmers.*

2. Terms for unresolved references (a_terms). These are used to translate pronouns, reflexives and indexicals (anaphoric terms that do not have scope): *he, it, myself, today*, etc.

3. Formulae for implicit relations (a_forms). These are used to translate genitives (*John's book*), relational 'of' (*the bishop of Ely*), compound nominals (*a computer message*); and for unresolved ellipsis: *Did Mary?, an expensive one, more horses than John.*

The BNF rules for the additional QLF term constructs are:

⟨*term*⟩ → qterm(⟨*category*⟩,⟨*variable*⟩,⟨*formula*⟩)

⟨*term*⟩ → a_term(⟨*category*⟩,⟨*variable*⟩,⟨*formula*⟩)

⟨*term*⟩ → a_index(⟨*variable*⟩)

⟨*term*⟩ → term_coord(⟨*category*⟩,⟨*variable*⟩,⟨*term*⟩,⟨*term*⟩)

and those for the additional QLF formula constructs are:

⟨*formula*⟩ → a_form(⟨*category*⟩,⟨*variable*⟩,⟨*formula*⟩)

⟨*functor*⟩ → ⟨*variable*⟩

⟨*formula*⟩ → [island,⟨*formula*⟩].

The ⟨*category*⟩ arguments are categories in the sense of collections of linguistic attributes. They are used to pass linguistic information, including syntactic information, to the scoping and reference resolution phases. This can include information on number, reflexivity, the surface form of quantifiers, and so on. The notation used for these "QLF categories" will be a sequence of feature-value pairs enclosed in angle brackets:

<*Feature1* = *Value1* , . . . , *FeatureN* = *ValueN*>.

The features used will be t specifying the *type* of anaphoric expression (e.g., ref for noun phrase reference); p for the *phrase* type (e.g., pro for pronoun, def for definite description); l for *lexical* information; n for *number*; and a for specifying intrasentential *antecedents*. A fuller discussion of the information passed by QLF categories is given in Chapter 10.

2.3.2 Quantified Terms and Descriptions

In quantified qterms, the category gives the lexical form of the determiner and marks the singular/plural distinction. The QLF analysis of *Some bishops gathered* (ignoring tense) is:

```
[gather,
  qterm(<t=quant,n=sing,l=ex>,E,[event,E]),
  qterm(<t=quant,p=det,n=plur,l=some>,A,[bishop1,A])].
```

The qterm for an event variable has a pseudo-lexical value ex. Information in qterm categories is used by scoping and reference resolution to decide the scope of a determiner, the quantifier it corresponds to, and whether a collective interpretation is possible. In the current example, the resulting preferred LF would be:

```
quant(set(exists),
      A,
      [bishop1,A],
      quant(exists,B,[event,B],[gather1,B,A])).
```

The term_coord term construct is used for unscoped distributive coordination. One QLF translation of *John and Mary arrived* uses such a term:

```
[past,
   [arrive,
      qterm(<t=quant,n=sing,l=ex>,E,[event,E]),
      term_coord(<op=and1>,C,john1,mary1)]].
```

The term_coord notation forces parallel scoping of the elements of the term. In the case at hand, the term is distributed over the proposition after scoping:

```
[and,
  [past,quant(exists,F,[event,F],[arrive,F,john1])],
  [past,quant(exists,G,[event,G],[arrive,G,mary1])]].
```

The coordinated terms may themselves be qterms as in

Most doctors and some engineers read every article.   (28)

for which one QLF analysis is:

```
[pres,
  [read,
    qterm(<t=quant,n=sing,l=ex>,E,[event,E]),
    term_coord(<op=and1>,C,
                qterm(<t=quant,p=det,n=plur,l=most>,
                      A,[doctor1,A]),
                qterm(<t=quant,p=det,n=plur,l=some>,
                      B,[engineer1,B])),
    qterm(<t=quant,p=det,n=sing,l=every>,
          D,[article1,D])]].
```

The `island` operator shown in the BNF rules serves to prevent un-scoped quantifiers in its range from having wider scope than the operator. In particular, it is used to block the raising of `qterms` out of relative clauses during the scoping procedure (Section 8.3.2).

Definite descriptions are also represented as quantified terms in QLF. For example the noun phrase in *The Irish bishop arrived* is translated as the `qterm`:

```
qterm(<t=ref,p=def,l=the,n=sing>, B,
      [and,[bishop1,B],[irish1,B]]).
```

Definite description `qterms` are scoped in the same way as quantified noun phrases during the scoping phase. After that, reference resolution determines whether to replace the description with a referent (giving a referential reading), for example

```
quant(exists,E,[event,E],
      [arrive1,E,john1]),
```

or whether to convert it into a quantification (giving an attributive reading):

```
quant(exists,B,
      [and,[bishop1,B],[irish1,B]],
      quant(exists,E,[event,E],
            [arrive1,E,B]).
```

Plural definite descriptions such as *the three bishops* include a further `qterm` for quantifying over the subsets of a collection:

```
qterm(<t=quant,n=plur,l=all>,
    S,
    [subset,S,
        qterm(<t=ref,p=def,l=the,n=number(3)>,
            X,[bishop1,X])]).
```

2.3.3   Anaphoric Terms

Pronouns are represented in QLF as a_terms in which the restriction places constraints on a variable corresponding to the referent, and the category contains linguistic information that guides the search for possible referents. For example, in the QLF for *Mary thinks that John likes her*, the a_term for *her* is:

```
a_term(<t=ref,p=pro,l=her,n=sing,a=[john1,mary1]>, X,
    [and,[female,X],[personal,X]]),
```

while the representation of *himself* in *Every bishop admires himself* is:

```
a_term(<t=ref,p=refl,l=him,n=sing,a=[-X]>, Y,
    [and,[male,Y],[personal,Y]]).
```

where X is the variable bound to *every bishop*. The value of the antecedents feature 'a' in the a_term category is a list of possible antecedents within the same sentence. It contains indices to the translations of noun phrases that precede or dominate the given pronoun in the sentence, allowing, for example, reference to bound variables.

Demonstrative pronouns like *this* and indexicals like *there* are also represented as a_terms in QLF:

```
a_term(<t=ref,p=dem,l=there,n=sing>, X, [place,X]),
```

while the QLFs for adverbial senses of indexical expressions like *here* and *today* consist of a predication involving an a_term:

```
[in_location,Event,a_term(<t=ref,...>,V,[place1,V])]

[in_time,Event,a_term(<t=ref,...>),V,[day1,V])].
```

In some later versions of the CLE, proper names are also represented in QLF as a_terms, but we will only show them as constants in this book.

Terms of the form a_index(Var) are used to link terms binding variables to other argument positions in the same QLF where such linking is governed by the grammar. Examples are the treatment of control verbs and verb phrase coordination, as in:

I want to go.   (29)

Every child jumped and shouted.   (30)

In (29) *to go* has the same subject as *want*, namely, the speaker:

```
[want1,
  qterm(<t=quant,n=sing,l=ex>,E1,[event,E1]),
  a_term(<t=ref,p=pro,l=i,a=[]>,X,[personal,X]),
  [apply,
    Y^[go1,
        qterm(<t=quant,n=sing,l=ex>,E2,[event,E2]),
        a_index(X)]]].
```

In (30), the two verb phrases have the same subject:

```
[and,
  [jump1,
  qterm(<t=quant,n=sing,l=ex>,E1,[event,E1]),
  qterm(<t=quant,p=det,n=sing,l=every>,X,[child1,X])],
  [shout1,
  qterm(<t=quant,n=sing,l=ex>,E2,[event,E2]),
  a_index(X)]].
```

2.3.4 Anaphoric Relations and Formulae

The format for unresolved relations is given by the following BNF rule:

⟨*formula*⟩ → a_form(⟨*category*⟩, ⟨*variable*⟩, ⟨*formula*⟩)

where the ⟨*formula*⟩ in the righthand side of the rule contains an occurrence of ⟨*variable*⟩ in functor position. Such relation variables only occur in positions where they are "bound" by an a_form.

Compound nominals, which are very common in English, provide the classic case of a construction with unresolved relations. Rather than positing a fixed set of possible underlying relations, we assume that there may be arbitrarily many, the correct one being chosen by the reference resolution mechanism on the basis of context (McDonald 1982, Alshawi 1987). At the QLF level, the unresolved relation implicit in *a computer message* is indicated as follows:

```
qterm(<t=quant,p=det,n=sing,l=a>,X,
  a_form(<t=pred,p=nn>,R,
         [and,[message,X],
          [R,kind(Y,[computer_thing,Y]),X]])).
```

The phrase to be translated does not identify the envisaged relation: a computer message might be a message about computers, to a computer, from a computer, or relayed by computer, among other things. The category simply indicates that the unresolved relation was one underlying a compound nominal. In order to avoid a link to a particular computer, the unspecified relation is a relation between the message and a kind term for computers. Unresolved relations are also used in the translations of possessive constructions, such as *John's house*:

```
qterm(<t=ref,p=def,...>,X,
  a_form(<t=pred,p=poss>,R,
         [and,[house,X],[R,john1,X]])).
```

The CLE representation of one-anaphora (Webber 1979) is in terms of a_forms, but here the functor variable ranges over one place predicates. For example, the QLF for *Mary bought a yellow one* contains an unresolved predicate P:

```
[buy1,
  qterm(<t=quant,n=sing,l=ex>,E,[event,E]),
  mary1,
  qterm(<t=quant,p=det,l=a,n=sing>,X,
        [and,a_form(<t=pred,p=one>,P,[P,X]),
         [yellow1,X]])].
```

Finally, we note that a_forms have also been used in the QLF representation of unresolved temporal relations and ellipsis as discussed in later chapters.

For some of the QLF constructs discussed above, it is fairly straightforward to formulate a semantics. For instance, a_form constructs can be interpreted as denoting second order quantifications over relations. Similarly, a_terms are naturally interpreted as functions from contexts to individuals. It is more difficult, however, to formulate a semantics for unscoped qterms that is not indirect in the sense that it relies on the set of possible scopings of an unscoped QLF.

3 Categories and Rules

Hiyan Alshawi

3.1 Constraints, Components, and Rules

At an abstract level, most current formalisms in computational linguistics can be viewed as representing (implicitly or explicitly) linguistic information in terms of a set of constraints on various aspects of linguistic objects. The objects under consideration can be of widely differing sizes: sentence constituents, phonemes, discourse segments, etc. A particular set of constraints corresponds to a linguistic object type—for example, a type of sentence constituent—to which there will correspond a (possibly empty) set of tokens realizing that type in actual language use. The constraints can be expressed in a variety of ways, perhaps even as statements in some logic, but that is not relevant to this abstract characterization. One of the most common ways of expressing the constraints is as feature-values equations, which we can interpret as stating the values assigned to linguistic objects by particular functions.

The constraints are usually divided into subclasses of constraints that are identified with different "levels" of linguistic description, phonemic, orthographic, syntactic, semantic, and so on. In terms of theories of language processing, this classification is relevant to defining the functional properties of the components of a language processing architecture. For example, the constraints might be classified for a particular architecture into four subsets (orthographic form, constituent attributes, logical structure, referents) corresponding to the positions in the following tuple:

$$(\langle Orth \rangle, \ \langle Cat \rangle, \ \langle Log \rangle, \ \langle Ref \rangle).$$

The sentence analysis component might then take a such a linguistic description in which only constraints on the orthographic form for a sentence are present and return a linguistic description including constraints on the constituent attributes (syntactic and semantic features) and logical structure (the predicate-argument structure, say). A reference resolution component might take a tuple with constraints on the constituent structure and logical structure (together with contextual information) and return constraints on the referents. A paraphrase compo-

nent could produce constraints on the constituent structure and orthographic form starting with constraints on logical structure and referents.
In other words, there is a correspondence between the processing components of the architecture and the classification of information about
linguistic objects into constraints on different levels of representation.

Linguistic objects are typically thought of as being composed of, or
standing in a "dominance" relation to, other linguistic objects, which can
also be represented as sets of constraints. The specification of a linguistic
object therefore often includes constraints on these subsidiary linguistic
objects. This can be expressed as a pair consisting of a tuple of the kind
described above for the main linguistic object (the mother), together
with a sequence of tuples corresponding to the subsidiary objects (the
daughters):

$$(\langle mother\ tuple\rangle, \quad [\dots\langle sequence\ of\ daughter\ tuples\rangle\ \dots]).$$

Pairs of this form that show the relationship between constraints on
well-formed linguistic objects and their daughters correspond to grammar rules specifying well-formed expressions of a particular language.
Such rules, embodying much of the linguistic knowledge of the language
processing system, form additional inputs to the system components.

A sequence (as opposed to a set) of daughter tuples is required to
allow multiple daughters of the same type and to allow unique reference
to such daughters. In many grammatical formalisms, the order in which
daughters appear in such a rule also corresponds to the precedence relation on their surface realization. Although such rules can in principle
contain constraints in all tuple positions, in practice the rules applied
by some components tend to be more restricted in scope. For example,
syntax rules could be rules that are only (or primarily) concerned with
constraints on syntactic attributes of mothers and daughters. Lexical
entries (for stems, i.e., ignoring morphology) correspond to rules of this
kind that have no daughters. Again a syntactic lexical entry, for instance, is one that is primarily concerned with constraints on syntactic
information.

The framework for linguistic constraints, components, and rules described in this section is particularized in the CLE to a specific language
processing system in which there are different ways of representing the
constraints for the different aspects of linguistic information. Processing
components often also take input and rules, and produce output, that

correspond to only some of the fields of a linguistic description tuple of the kind just discussed; this is possible because of the modular design of these components. Other parts of the CLE are a more direct implementation of this framework, examples of this being word sense entries, semantic analysis records, and the RQLF representation (Chapter 10).

3.2   Categories for Linguistic Analysis

In the CLE, information about the syntactic and semantic properties of linguistic constituents is represented by assigning to each constituent a complex category. Categories, which appear in syntax rules, semantic rules, and lexical entries, are specified by a principal category symbol augmented by a set of constraints on the values of syntactic and semantic features. Matching and merging of the information encoded by categories is carried out by unification.

The categories allowed in our formalism are similar to those of Generalized Phrase Structure Grammar (GPSG) (Gazdar et al. 1985), but we do not impose the restrictions on category-valued features that limit GPSG grammars to a finite set of categories. The way semantic features are used in the CLE grammar bears some resemblance to the way f-structures are used for building "semantic forms" in LFG (Kaplan and Bresnan 1982), although we do not make a principled distinction between categorial and functional information, nor do we postulate a universal set of grammatical functions, as LFG does. We omit such restrictions because we do not want the category formalism itself to embody substantive linguistic constraints.

In this respect the CLE formalism for categories is similar to PATR-II (Shieber 1986). (The CLE also includes rules and representations for components that were not intended to be covered by PATR-II.) In fact, for the most part, the CLE category formalism and PATR-II are notational variants; the main notational difference is that constraints expressed in PATR-II by path unifications in feature structures are expressed in our formalism by shared logical variables. Our category formalism does, however, extend the possible ways of specifying feature values, as compared to PATR-II. For example, CLE feature values can be boolean expressions, subject to constraints (Section 3.5) that allow such features to be matched efficiently.

The notation used externally by a grammar writer for specifying feature values, including boolean expression values, is converted into a fixed internal format for more efficient processing. Specifically, the internal format allows category unification to be implemented as Prolog term unification. Most of the examples show the external format, which is more easily readable.

3.3   CLE Categories

A category consists of a category symbol and a set of feature-value pairs (or feature specifications) represented as a list:

$\langle category\text{-}symbol \rangle : [\langle pair_1 \rangle , \ldots , \langle pair_n \rangle]$.

The category symbol is a constant (i.e., a Prolog atom), and the list of feature specifications may be empty (i.e., "[]"). It is not necessary to give an explicit pair for each feature associated with a category symbol; those that do not appear on the list take a default value (Section 3.6). The category symbol can be regarded as the value of a distinguished feature giving a coarse classification of constituents. Its special treatment is motivated by implementation and efficiency considerations. (To simulate the GPSG method of encoding major category distinctions without the use of category symbols, we could give all categories the dummy symbol cat, and use features n, v, bar, etc., with values as in GPSG.)

The feature-value specifications in a category may appear in any order. Each specification consists of an atomic feature name and a value, which can be an arbitrary Prolog term:

$\langle feature\text{-}name \rangle = \langle value \rangle$.

In particular, feature values may contain variables or categories. For example, in the category represented below, the value of the gapsin feature is a Prolog term consisting of a list structure containing a category with symbol np:

s: [type=Type,form=tnsd,gapsin=[np: [num=N]]] .

Variables appearing in feature values (e.g., Type and N above) are used to express unification constraints on feature values between categories and within the same category, or to stop a feature value from being set to the default specified for that feature. The variables are in fact ordinary Prolog variables, so they start with a capital letter or the underscore character ("_"), and their scope is the largest term in which they occur (for example, a syntax rule).

There can be multiple specifications for a feature in a single category, in which case the constraints from all the specifications are taken to hold together. This is useful, for example, if it is necessary to give a substantive constraint on the value of a feature (e.g., that it is not equal to **singular**), and also to name that value with a variable so that it can be equated with some other feature, perhaps in a different category.

3.4 Category Unification and Subsumption

Category unification in the CLE is Prolog term unification of the internal representations of the categories. This means that, for two categories to unify, they must have the same category symbol and that, for each feature associated with the symbol, the corresponding values must unify as Prolog terms, with consistent variable bindings across all the features. The feature values involved take into account any feature default declarations, which are applied when the category is first internalized, and also the encoding of feature values that are boolean expressions into a form suitable for unification (Section 3.5). Categories appearing as feature values must also unify by applying this definition recursively.

For example, in the absence of default declarations the two categories

```
s:[form=tnsd,gapsin=[np:[num=plur]]]
s:[gapsin=[np:[]],form=F,type=ynquestion]
```

will unify resulting in a category equivalent to:

```
s:[form=tnsd,gapsin=[np:[num=plur]],type=ynquestion].
```

If, on the other hand, the feature **type** had been declared to have a default value **declarative**, then the unification would fail.

For one category to subsume another they must be able to unify, and each feature value of the subsumed category must be an instance of the value of the subsuming category, taking into account any feature default declarations. In the above example neither category subsumes the other. Subsumption is a frequent operation in our generalization of local ambiguity packing (Section 7.4) to constituents with complex categories.

Category subsumption and unification correspond to operations on sets of linguistic objects described by the categories: If we think of a category having variables as standing for the set of fully instantiated instances of it, then category unification and subsumption correspond simply to set intersection and inclusion respectively, and unification failure corresponds to an empty intersection.

3.5   Boolean Expression Feature Values

If we wish to express that the uninflected verb *live* can agree with a singular subject that is in the first or second person, or any plural subject, then these cases might be covered by the three categories:

```
v:[number=sing,person=1,...]
v:[number=sing,person=2,...]
v:[number=plur,person=_,...].
```

Boolean expression values allow us to express this more compactly in a single category having the agreement feature "not third person singular" (\, \/, and /\ are used here for negation, disjunction, and conjunction, respectively):

```
v:[...agreement=\(sing/\3),...].
```

Rules can also be made more general by using boolean expression values; for example, a single syntax rule might allow a class of postnominal modifiers except for superlatives. Further evidence of the need for negation and disjunction of feature values is given by Karttunen (1984) for the case of noun phrase coordination.

The boolean expressions can be regarded as specifying subsets of a cross product, this being

$$\{1, 2, 3\} \times \{sing, plur\}$$

for the agreement example above. In order for the value of the agreement feature to be treated this way rather than as a literal term, there is a declaration for the cross product:

```
syn_feature_space(agreement,[[1,2,3],[sing,plur]])
```

The sets of atomic values from which the boolean combinations are constructed are restricted to finite sets in the CLE. This is enforced by having these sets explicitly listed in the value space declarations, as in the above example. The reason for this restriction is that we want to be able to encode these feature values in such a way that the constraints they impose can be checked by unification.

For such an encoding to work, it must be the case that the terms encoding two boolean expressions unify if, and only if, the constraints they impose are consistent. Furthermore, the result of successfully unifying these terms should be the same as the term encoding of the conjunction of the two expressions, so that the incremental description semantics of category unification is preserved. We use an encoding that satisfies these properties (see Mellish 1988), which is due to A. Colmerauer.

This encoding, which is carried out by the system when categories are compiled, is as follows. A boolean expression value is represented as a term with a fixed number of argument positions, the arguments being "0", "1", or a variable. Each adjacent pair of argument positions corresponds to a point in the cross product. We therefore need seven argument positions for the six agreement alternatives (i.e., points in the cross product: first person singular, first person plural, etc.) in our example. For each of these alternatives that does not satisfy the boolean expression, the pair of arguments corresponding to that alternative are unified together. To complete the encoding, the first and last argument positions of the term are unified with "0" and "1" respectively. For example, we get the following encoding for the value `plur`:

```
plur       --> bv(0,0,Y,Y,Z,Z,1),
```

because the expression `plur` is not satisfied at the points (1,`sing`), (2,`sing`), and (3,`sing`) in the cross product, for which the following unifications of adjacent positions are made in the encoded value:

```
bv(X,X,_,_,_,_,_),bv(_,_,Y,Y,_,_,_),bv(_,_,_,_,Z,Z,_).
```

Similarly, we obtain these encodings for 'singular' and 'not third person singular':

```
sing        --> bv(0,A,A,B,B,1,1)
\(sing/\3) --> bv(0,_,_,_,C,C,1).
```

To see why this encoding has the desired properties, observe that a pair of adjacent argument positions which are not unified together corresponds to a point in the cross product that satisfies the boolean expression. If there are no such pairs remaining, there is no way of satisfying the expression, and there will be an attempt to unify "0" with "1" since all argument positions will now be unified.

3.6   Feature Sets, Defaults, and Macros

Each category symbol has associated with it a set of syntactic features and a set of semantic features. These classes of features are distinguished as follows:

1. Any feature that appears in a category in a syntactic rule (or morphological rule) is included in the set of syntactic features for the category symbol of that category.

2. A feature, other than a syntactic feature, that appears in a category in a semantic analysis rule (or sense derivation rule) is included in the set of semantic features for the category symbol of that category.

These feature sets are therefore determined when the corresponding rules are loaded; there are no explicit declarations for associating features with category symbols. The distinction between syntactic and semantic features is motivated partly by the fact that this leads to a more concise grammar. Another consideration is that sentence analysis, using the techniques we have developed, is more efficient if an initial analysis phase, the syntactic parser, does not distinguish between categories on the basis of semantic feature values.

The value for a feature on a category appearing in a rule or lexical entry is determined by one of the following, in the order listed:

1. values stated explicitly in feature-value pairs,

2. the value given in a feature-default declaration, and

3. a unique uninstantiated variable.

(If there is more than one specification for the feature, then the values from these specifications are unified to give the feature value.) In particular, the ordering implies that if the value of a feature is given explicitly as a variable (including "_"), then the value remains uninstantiated regardless of the presence of a default declaration for the feature in question. Feature values are also determined in this way for categories that themselves appear in feature values. The syntactic feature `lexform` is treated as a special case when reading the lexicon: the value of this feature (if it needs to be present for a particular category) is set to be the word stem for the lexical entry.

There are two types of feature defaults: those that are applied when filling out the categories in syntax rules, morphology rules, and syntactic lexical entries, and those that are applied when filling out semantic interpretation rules, sense derivation rules, and word sense entries. The defaults applied to syntax rules and entries have the form

> `feature_default(⟨feature⟩,⟨value⟩)`

whereas those applied to semantic rules and sense entries have the form

> `semantic_feature_default(⟨feature⟩,⟨value⟩)`.

Defaults are global in the sense that they are not dependent on category symbols but are simply associated with feature names.

The CLE category formalism also allows grammar writers to define "macros" which expand into frequently used sets of feature specifications. These macros can take parameters, increasing their usefulness in stating feature constraints in rules and regularities in the lexicon. Even so, macros are just notational "sugar" that can be expanded at category compilation time and their use is primarily relevant to grammar maintenance and development. We will not be using macros in examples but instead simplify categories in the presentation by omitting many of the feature specifications.

3.7   Internal Category Representation

When a category is compiled into its internal representation, macros are first expanded, then the value of each syntactic and semantic feature for the category is determined by applying defaults as appropriate in the way described in the previous section. The completed list of features is then placed in a canonical order, and boolean expression feature values are encoded (Section 3.5). A term representing the category can now be constructed having the category symbol as its functor and subterms with the values of syntactic and semantic features in fixed argument positions:

⟨*category_symbol*⟩(syn(⟨*syn-val*⟩,...),sem(⟨*sem-val*⟩,...)).

For example, the category

```
vp:[form=fin,eventvar=E,pred=sleep1,
   gapsin=[np:[agreement=plur]]]
```

might be translated into:

```
vp(syn(fin,[np(syn(bv(0,0,A,A,B,B,1),...),
                sem(notprednom,...))],...),
   sem(E,sleep1,...).
```

Here the semantic feature value `notprednom` for the embedded `np` category has been filled in as a default. Given the fixed argument positions for feature values, and the encoding of boolean expression values, compiling categories with the above procedure means that category unification and subsumption operations can be carried out efficiently as Prolog term unification and subsumption.

3.8   Grammar Rules

In the remaining sections of this chapter we present the rule types making use of the category notation described above. These rules embody the grammatical knowledge used for morpho-syntactic and semantic analysis. They are applied after segmentation (i.e., orthographic analysis) of a sentence, resulting in a set of QLF analyses. Details of the CLE English grammar using these rule types are presented in Chapters 4 and 5. The example rules presented in this chapter, however, are for expository purposes only; they do not form part of the CLE grammar for English.

3.9 Syntax and Morphology Rules

The basic form of CLE syntax rules is that of phrase structure rules that specify a local syntax tree in terms of the category $\langle mother \rangle$ of a constituent dominating daughter constituents with categories $\langle dau_1 \rangle, \ldots, \langle dau_n \rangle$. This is written as:

$$\text{syn}(\langle \textit{rule-identifier} \rangle, \ \langle \textit{rule-group} \rangle, \ \langle \textit{mother} \rangle \ \text{-->}$$
$$[\langle dau_1 \rangle, \ldots, \langle dau_n \rangle]).$$

The order in which daughter categories appear in the rule corresponds to the surface order of the daughter constituents. Thus linear precedence cannot be expressed separately from the dominance relation as it is in the IDLP format of GPSG (Gazdar et al. 1985), nor is there a special construct for indicating that a particular set of daughters is unordered; unrestricted word order needs to be expressed by multiple rules in our formalism. The easiest way to allow the CLE to economically capture free-order properties exhibited by some languages (this did not appear necessary for English and Swedish) would be to include annotations expanding rules into several fixed-order rules. This would enable the rest of grammar compilation and the parsing algorithm to remain unchanged.

Allowing arbitrary structures with variables as the feature values in categories means that the rule formalism is not limited to describing context free grammars. In practical terms, however, the more powerful formalism is used mainly in order to produce a more compact and perspicuous grammar.

The example rule below specifies a sentence (s) composed of a noun phrase (np) and a verb phrase (vp). The identifier chosen for the rule is the mnemonic s_np_vp_Normal:

```
syn(s_np_vp_Normal, core,
    s:[type=T, subjcase=S, vpform=V,
       gapsSoughtIn=Gi, gapsSoughtOut=Go, ... ]
    -->
    [np:[agr=Ag,  type=T, form=S, nform=Sfm, ... ],
     vp:[agr=Ag, subcat=[], tnsd=Tns, form=V,
         gapsSoughtIn=Gi, gapsSoughtOut=Go, ... ]]).
```

Prolog notational conventions for terms are used in the rules, so variables start with capital letters and square brackets delimit lists. As in

DCG grammars (Pereira and Warren 1980), shared variables are used to express constraints between rule daughters (e.g., the variable Ag enforces number agreement between the noun phrase and verb phrase daughters in this rule) and to pass information up and down a syntactic structure (e.g., by unifying the values of the gapsSoughtIn features that appear on the s and the vp in this rule).

Syntax rules are partitioned into rule groups, the group for a particular rule being indicated by a rule group identifier (core in the above example, though we will often omit these identifiers when displaying rules). Different subsets of the grammar can be activated by specifying which rule groups are to be included when the grammar is preprocessed into the form used for parsing. This allows some provision for excluding sets of linguistically valid rules that are nevertheless judged to be inappropriate in the context of a particular application. Just as important, this facility for selecting subsets of the rules is helpful during the grammar development testing cycle, especially since derivation of the reachability table (Section 7.1.2) from a full set of rules takes a considerable time for a wide coverage grammar.

Morphological Rules

The morphosyntactic rules for word structure have a similar format to syntax rules, except that these rules are not classified into groups:

morph($\langle rule\_identifier \rangle$, $\langle mother \rangle$ --> $\langle dau_1 \rangle$,...,$\langle dau_n \rangle$]).

The daughters are categories for stems or affixes, though the latter tend to be literal affixes in the English morphology rules. A typical example is the past tense inflection rule for verbs:

```
morph(vp_vp_ed_Past,
    v:[agr=A, form=fin, lexical=y, subcat=S, ...] -->
    [v:[agr=A, form=inf, lexical=y, subcat=S, ...],
    ed]).
```

These rules operate on strings and affixes produced in accordance with segmentation rules for affixes or affix combinations. Segmentation is discussed in Chapter 6 together with other aspects of surface lexical analysis.

Special Cases of Syntax Rules

The parser accepts an input string of words if, and only if, the complete string can be analyzed according to a derivation starting from the distinguished category sigma. There thus needs to be at least one rule in which the mother is sigma, though in practice there are several covering both complete and elliptical sentence types.

Although the ⟨mother⟩ in a syntax rule is always a category, other items in the rule can be literal words (or affixes, as in the suffix ed in the morphology rule given above). This is just a convenience for the grammar writer; when the grammar is read in by the system, special lexical entries are given to literal words. For example, if the literal how occurs as one of the daughters in a rule, then a lexical entry for this word with category symbol how will be generated, and this entry will be incorporated into the system when the lexicon is recompiled.

When writing rules to cover the grammatical description of empty categories and complement subcategorization, we can take advantage of the fact that the daughter categories in a grammar rule form a list structure. For categories that rewrite as the empty string (i.e., "gap" categories) there is simply an empty list of daughter categories:

```
syn(empty_np, gaps,
    np:[agr=A,gapsIn=[np:[agr=A]|Rest],gapsOut=Rest]
    --> []).
```

Complement subcategorization is covered by allowing daughter categories, or lists of categories, to be represented as variables in the rule which get instantiated from category-valued features in the lexicon during parsing. In the CLE English grammar, this is used for rules covering verbal, adjectival, and nominal complements so that the variety of possible complements can be specified in the lexicon rather than by the proliferation of grammar rules. For example, in the following possible verb complement subcategorization rule the first category on a feature specifying the complement list for a verb phrase is unified with the daughter that follows it in the rule:

```
syn(vp_vp_comp, core,
    vp:[subcat=OtherComps, ... ] -->
    [vp:[subcat=[Comp|OtherComps], ... ],Comp]).
```

Alternatively, a flatter structure can be achieved by using a variable ranging over a list of categories:

```
syn(vp_v_comps, core,
    vp:[ ... ] -->
    [v:[subcat=Complements, ... ] | Complements]).
```

Here the list `Complements` for a particular verb is unified with the tail of the list of daughter categories (| is the Prolog list constructor). We have followed a pragmatically motivated restriction on the use of variables ranging over categories. This restriction, which results from the CLE parsing strategy, is that the leftmost daughter of the rule cannot be a variable; it must have at least the category symbol instantiated.

In an earlier version of the CLE grammar formalism, "tests" as well as daughter categories were allowed to follow the mother category in a syntax rule. These took the form of Prolog procedure calls, meant to be declarative in the sense of having no side effects, which had to succeed for the syntax rule to apply. These tests were thus a restricted form of the arbitrary calls to Prolog allowed in DCGs. However, in the grammars developed so far, we have been able to avoid the use of such mechanisms in favour of rules which only make use of unification.

3.10   Semantic Rules

Semantic Rules

There are one or more semantic rules associated with each syntax rule. Such rules are often called *semantic interpretation rules* in the literature, but we tend to use the term *semantic analysis rules* reserving *interpretation* for later processes. Instead of a rule group, which a semantic rule inherits from the syntax rule, there is a semantic rule identifier distinguishing it from other cases for the semantics of the same syntax rule:

> sem($\langle$*syntax-rule-id*$\rangle$,$\langle$*semantic-rule-id*$\rangle$,
>   ($\langle$*logical-form*$\rangle$,$\langle$*mother-category*$\rangle$) -->
>   [$\langle$*daughter-pair$_1$*$\rangle$,...,$\langle$*daughter-pair$_n$*$\rangle$]).

The logical form paired with the mother category is a QLF expression, not normally fully instantiated, corresponding to the semantic analysis of the constituent analyzed by the syntax rule whose identifier is ⟨*syntax-rule-id*⟩. The mother logical form typically contains variables that are unified with the semantic analyses of the daughter constituents. Such variables appear as the left-hand elements of the daughter pairs:

   (⟨*daughter-qlf-variable*⟩, ⟨*daughter-category*⟩)

In the semantic rule below, the variables Det and Nbar stand for the semantic analysis of the first and second daughters, and these variables appear in the logical form template associated with the mother:

```
sem(np_det_nbar, quantified,
    (qterm(<l=Det,n=N>,X,Nbar),
       np:[quantform=y,handle=X,number=N,
           gapValsIn=Gin,gapValsOut=Gout]) -->
    [(Det,det:[quantform=y,num=N]),
     (Nbar,nbar:[arg=X,
                 gapValsIn=Gin,gapValsOut=Gout])]).
```

Logical variables of the logical form language itself are represented as Prolog variables. The noun phrase meaning variable X in the example rule is such a variable.

Categories appearing in semantic rules may include specifications for the values of syntactic features (i.e., features that have appeared in some syntax rule) as well as semantic features. Semantic features are often used to hold logical form fragments passed between mother and daughter constituents (gapValIn in the rule above). In a parallel fashion to the corresponding syntactic rules, there are cases where the set of daughter items in a semantic rule is empty, or where a daughter position may be unified with part of the feature structure of another daughter.

In a sense, our syntax rules can be viewed as underinstantiated semantic rules in which the QLF expressions are completely unspecified, and where the features in the categories allow an initial skeletal analysis to be derived efficiently during the parsing phase. In principle, the information in a syntax rule could be unified into the corresponding semantic rules before application; this is done, in fact, when the rules are being used for generation (Section 13.3).

Sense Derivation Rules

Sense derivation rules have a similar format to semantic analysis rules, except that the daughter positions in the rules are often placeholders for literal affixes. A typical example is the following rule for deriving the logical form and semantic category for the past tense of a verb from its infinitive form:

```
deriv(v_v_ed_Past, only,
  ([past,V],
   v:[arglist=Compmeanings,eventvar=E,subjval=A]) -->
   [(V,v:[arglist=Compmeanings,eventvar=E,subjval=A]),
   (_,ed)]).
```

Sense derivation rules operate on the results of morphology rules during the semantic analysis phase (Section 7.3).

Ordering and Preference

The order in which syntactic and semantic rules appear in the rule files does not affect the set of analyses that the CLE associates with a particular sentence. Rule ordering can be used as a way of indicating a (local) preference for the analyses generated by one rule over those produced by another. However, this does not allow the effects of different preference criteria to be combined in a sensible way. Our current approach to preference is to employ measures computed for semantic analyses by summing over scoring functions corresponding to different preference criteria. Because much of the phrasal structure of a sentence is implicit in its QLF analyses, the preference criteria covered are not limitied to semantics but can also include essentially syntactic preferences such as minimal attachment. Hobbs and Bear 1990 discuss the effectiveness of a number of such preferences.

3.11   Lexical Entries

The CLE lexicon is divided into two parts, one of which contains information about the syntactic behavior of words and the other about word senses. As well as these syntactic and semantic components of the lexicon, the sortal restrictions on word senses can be regarded as supplying pragmatic information for lexical items; selectional restrictions will be discussed separately in Chapter 9.

Lexical entries in the CLE are created in one of two ways. They can be entered directly in the form shown below, or they can result from user interaction with the lexical acquisition component (VEX; see Chapter 11). Direct entry is the only option for function words and also for the entries of "paradigm" words that exhibit behavior that is typical of a class of nouns, verbs, or adjectives. These paradigm entries are used as templates by VEX to construct entries for new words whose behavior is covered by the paradigms.

Lexical Syntax Entries

A syntactic lexical entry associates a word with a syntactic category:

lex($\langle word \rangle$, $\langle category \rangle$) .

For example the entry for *whom* shown below has two such entries distinguishing its use in wh-questions from relative pronouns.

```
lex(whom,np: [pron=y,wh=y,rel=n,type=q,
              agr=3,form=nonsubj,...])
lex(whom,np: [pron=y,wh=y,rel=y,type=r,
              agr=3,form=nonsubj,...]).
```

A verb taking different lists of complements (as specified by the subcat feature) would also have multiple entries, though the use of features with boolean expression values can conflate entries with minor differences:

```
lex(want,v: [agr=(\(sing/\3)),vform=(inf\/fin),
             subcat=[vp: [vform=to,...]]])
lex(want,v: [agr=(\(sing/\3)),vform=(inf\/fin),
             subcat=[np: [...],vp: [vform=to,...]]]).
```

In general, the CLE English lexicon contains word stems and words formed by derivational morphology processes. Words formed from the stems by regular inflectional morphology are covered by the morphology rules, so they do not require lexical entries. Irregular forms are covered by entries indicating their analysis in terms of morphological rule identifiers. This mechanism for irregular morphology is explained in Chapter 6 where it is also shown how open-ended lexical forms—for example, numbers, dates and library catalogue numbers—can be declared

in terms of regular expressions. A lexical entry associated with the pseudoword identifying such a regular expression specifies the category given
to tokens that it matches.

Sense Entries

Entries in the sense lexicon associate a word (or sequence of words) with
a QLF expression representing a possible meaning of the word provided
that the category for the word unifies with the category specified in
the sense entry. There may be more than one entry for a particular
word–category combination, each entry taking the form:

  sense($\langle string \rangle$, $\langle category \rangle$, $\langle quasi\text{-}logical\text{-}form \rangle$),

where $\langle string \rangle$ is a word or a nonempty list of words, and $\langle category \rangle$
may include specifications for the values of semantic features as well as
syntactic ones.

  Typically $\langle quasi\text{-}logical\text{-}form \rangle$ will be a QLF containing an entity or
predicate constant that we often loosely refer to as a 'word sense'. This
may be the name of an individual, a one-place predicate for a common
noun, or a three-place predicate for a transitive verb, and so on. For
example, the following sense entries contain the word senses `darwin2`,
`woman1`, and `design1`:

```
sense(darwin,np:[...], darwin2).
sense(woman,nbar:[arg=A,...], [woman1,A]).
sense(design,
      v:[arglist=[(B,np:[...])],eventvar=E,subjval=A],
      [design1,qterm(<t=quant,l=ex>,E,[event,E]),A,B]).
```

Sense entries can also be specified for sequences of words, in order
to give lexicalized meanings to phrases, i.e., meanings that are not constructed from the meanings of subphrases. For such an entry to apply,
the sequence must be a well-formed syntactic constituent whose category matches the one in the entry. An example of a phrasal sense entry
is:

```
sense([the,red,lion], np:[...], red_lion_inn).
```

The presence of such an entry for a phrase does not rule out the derivation of other, compositional, meanings. Since a phrase with a lexicalized

meaning is not treated specially with respect to syntax, there is no need for syntactic category entries corresponding to the semantic ones.

4 Unification-Based Syntactic Analysis

Stephen G. Pulman

This chapter gives a brief guide to the approach taken to the description of English syntax in the CLE. Rather than exhaustively discuss every single construction covered, we concentrate instead on several central areas in which the use of a unification-based formalism seems to lead to a reasonably elegant and simple analysis. However, the coverage of the grammar *is* fairly wide, by current standards: all basic verb, noun, and adjectival complement types are covered; passives; wh-questions (NP, PP, AdjP and AdvP) and yes/no questions (both direct and indirect); finite and nonfinite relative clauses; the phenomena often referred to as 'raising', 'subject-extraposition', 'tough-movement', and so on; pre- and postmodification of nominal and verbal constructs; topicalization; existentials; clefts; adjectival comparatives; complex determiners and nominals of various types; conjunction; and of course all of the above in combination. This gives a reasonable coverage of the types of sentences that are likely to be used in interactive dialogues with information systems of various kinds—certainly enough that one can usually express what is required— although of course there is still a large residue even of this variety of English that the system fails to analyze properly.

4.1 Theoretical Background

The approach to the description of English syntax taken here is most directly influenced by Generalized Phrase Structure Grammar (Gazdar et al. 1985). However, our formalism is less complex than theirs, and the use of unification with logical variables and boolean features allows for a more succinct treatment of many grammatical phenomena. In some cases, these are phenomena that are taken within the GPSG tradition as motivating extensions to the formalism, or the introduction of new metagrammatical principles (e.g., in the treatment of unbounded dependencies, or various types of default feature principles). In the CLE formalism, there are no metagrammatical principles. Simple default values for features are allowed, but these are global compile-time defaults only. This, in our experience, has meant that complex linguistic descriptions are in practice much easier to develop. This is because it is possible, by looking at rules or lexical entries, to see what the effects of unification will be at run time. In a system where complex conditional defaults can have an effect during processing, it is often very difficult to predict just by inspection of a rule exactly what its consequences for the overall grammar might be.

4.2 Subcategorization

Verbs, adjectives, and some nouns "subcategorize" for particular complements. That is, they expect particular syntactic constituents, or "complements", to be associated with them in some way and will not make up a well-formed constituent if those complements are not present.

The first version of the CLE grammar, developed during the first year of the project, followed the GPSG treatment of subcategorization (Gazdar et al. 1985) and had one verb phrase rule[1] for each different syntactic type of verb:

```
VP --> [v:[subcat=intransitive]]
VP --> [v:[subcat=transitive], NP]
VP --> [v:[subcat=ditransitive], NP, NP]
etc.
```

In this version of the grammar, most of these rules had to be duplicated for adjectives, which take almost the same range of complements as verbs. This approach is feasible, but clumsy, and generates 30 to 60 rules for verb phrases, depending on how refined a system of subcategorization is chosen. There is also a practical disadvantage in the context of an NLP system designed for use by non-linguists, in that such a system makes it impossible to add new types of verb-complement combinations to the lexicon (which could conceivably be done on the basis of analogy with existing examples: cf. Chapter 11) without also making appropriate additions to the grammar. Adding rules to a grammar is a much riskier process for the nonlinguist.

During the second year of the project we used a different method of associating verbs and adjectives with their complements, which was essentially that described in Shieber 1986.

---

[1]Here and throughout, categories are given in CLE notation, where lowercase items are constants and uppercase ones are variables, when the internal structure of the category is being referred to. Categories with no features indicated, like 'VP', 'AdvP', etc. and beginning with upper case, are to be taken as abbreviations for vp:[f1=v1,f2=v2,...] etc.

A first minor modification is to follow a tradition prevalent in categorial grammar and identify verbs (V) with verb phrases (VP), and analogously for adjectives. (The feature lexical is available to distinguish them where necessary.) The second major change made use of the ability in our grammar formalism to have variables over whole syntactic categories (provided these are not mothers or leftmost daughters; while declaratively correct, the latter use of variables would not lead to efficient parsing with the algorithm we employed). With this convention, we could write something that is formally a rule schema, although it can be treated as an ordinary rule within our notation. This allows for a somewhat more readable analysis than that available in PATR-style formalisms, in which a theory of lists usually has to be encoded within the feature system.

```
vp:[subcat=Tail,...] -->
    [vp:[subcat=[Category|Tail],...], Category].
```

The lexical entries for verbs and adjectives specify as the value of the subcat feature a list of the complement categories expected. The rule combining a VP with a subject NP to form a sentence requires the value of subcat to be the empty list. (Alternatively, one could require the final item on the subcat list to be a specification of the subject NP.) Repeated applications of the VP rule schema then combine a verb or adjective with its complements one at a time, each time resulting in a category that is looking for the remainder of the items on the subcat list. An abstract example will illustrate this:

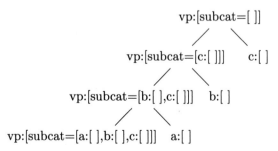

This method has several advantages: it keeps the size of the grammar down, although lexical entries have to be correspondingly more complex, and it allows the semantics for verbs to be located almost completely in their lexical entries, since there is a description of the arguments they will combine with explicitly listed as the value of the subcat feature. Furthermore, adding new complement types is now just a matter of adding a new lexical entry: the syntactic rules do not need to be added to or changed in any way.

While an improvement in many respects on the GPSG treatment, we are left with potentially deep recursion inside VP, which is there simply as an artifact of the use of the rule schema. Since syntactic structures are not an end in themselves, but merely a prerequisite for semantic analysis, this is by no means a fatal objection. There are some practical drawbacks of a not-too-serious kind: with our parsing algorithm this recursion leads to a certain amount of inefficiency in parsing. (This type of analysis can also lead to problems in generation, as commented on in Shieber et al. 1990.)

In later versions of the grammar we have kept a more general form of this subcategorization mechanism, using a feature of our formalism that we had not explicitly designed but that turned out to be highly desirable. Verbs and adjectives are once again distinct from VP and AdjP. The lexical entries for V and Adj are otherwise as they were as far as subcategorization information is concerned, but the schema that combines them with their complements cannot now operate one at a time, since the input to the rule is now V rather than VP and we have no recursion inside VP. Instead it must combine the verb with all its complements at once. Hence the form of the rule:

```
syn(vp_v_comp,
    vp:[agr=A, vform=V, ...] -->
    [v:[agr=A, vform=V, subcat=X, ...] | X]).
```

Notice that the vertical bar signifies that the X variable is the tail of the list of categories constituting the right-hand side of the rule. Thus a verb like put, which will be subcategorized [NP,PP], will result in a verb phrase with the structure

```
[VP [V put] [NP ...] [PP ...]].
```

The list containing the NP and the PP will unify with the subcat feature, and this will instantiate the tail of the list of daughters to these categories, giving the same effects as if we had had a rule

```
VP --> [V, NP, PP]
```

for V of the type of **put**. Now the subcat feature need not appear on VPs at all. Thus we achieve a non-nested VP structure while still preserving the generality of the analysis of subcategorization.

Neither the original GPSG based analysis, nor this one, allow for the possibility of optional modifiers like PP or AdvP to appear between elements on a subcat list. While usually such modifiers are VP initial or VP final, it is possible to get some adverbials in other positions:

John said quietly that he was leaving
He put a flower with great delicacy into the vase.

In the recursive VP analysis, this was handled by having rules allowing modifiers before or after a VP,

```
vp:[subcat=S] --> [vp:[subcat=S], PP]
vp:[subcat=S] --> [vp:[subcat=S], AdvP]
vp:[subcat=S] --> [AdvP, vp:[subcat=S]].
```

In order to allow for this within the final treatment adopted we have to have a version of the subcategorization schema that *splits* the list of complements and allows a modifying structure to intervene.

Auxiliary verbs are treated just like any other verb with respect to subcategorization. They are also marked with a binary feature (the equivalent of GPSG **inv**) that allows them to occur in sentence-initial position in yes/no questions. However, this feature is not quite coextensive with the feature used to distinguish auxiliaries from main verbs (**mainv**): for example, the passive auxiliary *be* can appear initially in yes/no questions, but it is in most other respects like a main verb. For example, like main verbs but unlike true auxiliaries, it can be the complement of progressive or perfective auxiliaries.

The connection between auxiliaries and their complements is treated by the same subcategorization mechanism as for main verbs and their complements. Thus the fact that the auxiliary *have* requires a following verb phrase to have its verb in the *-ed* form is captured in the same way as the requirement of a transitive verb to have an NP object, with agreement between features of the auxiliary and the complement verb phrase, by giving *have* a subcategorization feature:

```
subcat=[vp:[vform=ed,...]].
```

(Notice that the `vform` feature is passed down from VP to V by the complement-combining rule given above.) Representative subcategorization entries for auxiliaries and main verbs that act as auxiliaries in at least some respects are:

be leaving:
```
lex(be,v:[inv=y,mainv=n,vform=inf,
          subcat=[vp:[inv=_,mainv=y,vform=ing,...]]])
```
be left, being left:
```
lex(be,v:[inv=y,mainv=y,vform=inf,
          subcat=[vp:[mainv=y,vform=passive,...]]])
```
be a doctor:
```
lex(be,v:[inv=y,mainv=y,vform=inf,
          subcat=[np:[...]]])
```
have left:
```
lex(have,v:[inv=y,mainv=n,vform=inf,
            subcat=[vp:[inv=_,mainv=_,vform=en,...]]])
```
have a cold:
```
lex(have,v:[inv=y,mainv=y,vform=inf,
            subcat=[np:[...]]])
```
may leave:
```
lex(may,v:[inv=y,mainv=n,vform=fin,
           subcat=[vp:[inv=_,mainv=_,vform=inf,...]]])
```
doesn't leave:
```
lex(doesn't,v:[inv=y,mainv=n,vform=fin,
               subcat=[vp:[inv=_,mainv=_,vform=inf,...]]])
```
(Note that there are only 'inv=y' entries for finite
forms of auxiliary *do*.)

The values of `vform` are

inf	(infinitival)
fin	(simple present or past)
en	(perfective)
passive	(passive)
ing	(progressive)
to	(singles out *to* and VPs headed by *to*).

It is a boolean feature, and so any combination of these values is possible: for example, for many verbs, as far as morphology is concerned, the suffix *-ed* can equally well signal a passive or a perfective (*en*). Thus such a verb form might be labeled `vform=(en\/passive)`.

Subcategorization, logical variables, and boolean features mean that the complex set of feature defaults used in theories like GPSG to get the syntax of auxiliaries right is unnecessary. The "start category" (see below) for simple sentences, or subcategorization for embedded sentences, ensures that the main VP is finite, unless specified otherwise. This entails that modals or auxiliary *do*, if present, occur only as the first of any auxiliaries, because they are `vform=fin`. The subcategorization on perfective *have* and progressive *be* ensure that the following verbs have the appropriate endings.

Most of the "transformational" relations beloved of early generative grammar ('Dative', 'Raising', 'Subject Extraposition', etc.) are treated in the CLE as lexically based. For example, *give* will have two entries:

```
lex(give,v:[subcat=[np:[...],pp:[pform=to,...]],...])
lex(give,v:[subcat=[np:[...],np:[...]],...]),
```

and other verbs like *seem*, *worry*, etc., will also receive multiple entries characterizing their occurrences in different contexts.

'Control' or 'Equi' verbs are not given any special treatment. A verb like *try* or *want* is simply given a subcategorization like:

```
lex(try,v:[subcat=[vp:[vform=to,...]],...])
lex(want,v:[subcat=[vp:[vform=to,...]],...])
lex(want,v:[subcat=[np:[],vp:[vform=to,...]],...]),
```

ensuring that it has an infinitival complement. The semantic rules and entries will ensure that, in this case, the subject of *try* and of the first entry for *want* is also the subject of the infinitive complement, and that in the second entry for *want* the NP on the subcat list is the subject of the infinitival VP following it.

By general convention, a feature `lexform` appears on all lexical items and has as value the stem form of that item. This enables reference to be made to selected lexical items within the feature system. Thus one can capture phenomena like 'phrasal verbs' and other quasi-idiomatic phenomena very easily:

```
lex(put,v:[subcat=[p:[lexform=up],
                   p:[lexform=with],np:[]],...]).
```

The appropriate semantic entry (which is, approximately, 'tolerate') can then be associated with this in such a way as to ignore the regular meanings of *put*, *up*, and *with*, as is required to capture what *put up with* means.

4.3   Start Categories

The "start symbols" for the grammar are given as a series of "sigma" rules. The start symbol **sigma** is known to the parser and rules expanding **sigma** in effect tell the parser what type of category to look for as a complete analysis. Sigma rules in the CLE characterize the major types of sentences, but in later work (Chapter 13) this has been extended to cover a wider range of phrases and incomplete sentences in coverage of elliptical phenomena. The start categories in the original CLE grammar are those corresponding to sentences of the following types:

- Wh-questions like *What did he do?* or *What killed him?*
- Topicalized sentences like *That woman, I would never vote for*
- Declaratives like *The cat sat on the mat*
- Yes/no questions like *Did the cat sit on the mat?*
- Imperatives like *Be quiet!* or *Don't do it!*

The sigma rules also serve to set features constraining possible parses: for example, the requirement that in a main clause nonimperative sentence the verb must be tensed is imposed top-down by the sigma rule, rather than by anything in the rules that parse the sentence structure itself (the relevant feature is **vform=fin**).

Here is an example sigma rule:

```
syn(sigma_YNQorDECL,
    sigma --> [s:[inv=_,type=norm,whm=n,hascomp=n,
                  subjcase=subj,vform=fin]]).
```

This particular one characterizes both yes/no and declarative sentence types, since the feature that distinguishes them (**inv**) can have either a **y** or an **n** value.

Table 4.1
Features for sentence types

	type	whm	inv	vform	
declarative	norm	n	n	fin	*Wren lives*
yes/no question	norm	n	y	fin	*does Wren live*
subject wh-question	q	n	n	fin	*who designed Trinity*
main non-subj wh-ques.	q	y	n	fin	*what does Wren do*
topicalized	norm	y	n	fin	*Trinity, Wren designed*
finite subject relative	r	n	n	fin	*... who designed Trinity*
finite non-subj relative	r	y	n	fin	*... Wren designed _*
non-finite *to* VP	norm	n	n	to	*... to deal with _*
non-finite *for* NP *to* VP	norm	n	n	to	*... for you to deal with _*

4.4 Sentence Types

The main rule for building ordinary sentence structures of a variety of
types is:

```
s: [agr=Ag,type=T,subjcase=S,vform=V,sai=A,gaps=G,...]
-->
[np: [agr=Ag,type=T,case=S,nform=Sfm,...],
 vp: [agr=Ag,vform=V,sai=A,gaps=G,subjform=Sfm,...]].
```

The type of the sentence is defined by that of the subject, via **type**. The
possible values of **type** are q (question), r (relative), and norm (normal).
The feature **type** defaults to norm; **whm** (wh-moved) and **inv**, not explicitly appearing on the rule, default to n and these three features, together
with **vform**, jointly classify sentence types as shown in Table 4.1.

4.5 Subject-Auxiliary Inversion

Inversion of auxiliaries in yes/no questions and other constructions is
treated as a local "movement". The relevant rules in schematic form
are:

```
syn(s_v_s_YNQ,
 s: [type=ynq,inv=y] -->
 [v: [mainv=n,inv=y,subcat=X,...],
  s: [sai=v: [mainv=n,subcat=X,...]]])
```

```
syn(empty_V,
    v:[mainv=n,subcat=X,sai=v:[mainv=n,subcat=X]] --> []).
```

The value of the feature sai is passed down into the daughter S, then
into its VP, and finally down to be unified with the appropriate feature
on the empty_V rule. This ensures that whatever follows the empty V is
an appropriate complement for the fronted V, via the usual mechanism
for subcategorization. The final structure is like this:

```
[s can [s [np john] [vp [v []] [vp [v swim]]]]].
```

4.6   Unbounded Dependencies

Unbounded dependencies are treated entirely within the feature system,
using a technique originating with Pereira (1981), and referred to as "gap
threading" by Karttunen (1986). The idea is that in a sentence like *Who
did you give the book to _?*, the filler *who* is connected to the gap position
marked by '_'. Recognizing this connection gives us the information
we need to determine which argument of the verb is being questioned,
which is necessary to interpret the sentence correctly. The connection is
established by making the rules that introduce fillers pass down features
to the rest of the sentence that cause a corresponding gap to be found.
In the following rule for wh-movement, an interrogative NP is introduced
as a filler, and in its sister S an NP is placed on the gapsSoughtIn list.
Requiring the gapsSoughtOut list to be empty ensures that a gap must
be found if the sentence is to be grammatical. Furthermore, we have
also a pair of features, gapsFoundIn and gapsFoundOut, with lists of
markers (g) for gaps that have had fillers associated with them. We
require the 'in' list to contain n markers when going into the relevant
constituent, and the 'out' list to contain exactly $n+1$. We will see below
why four features, rather than just two, are needed.

```
syn(s_np_s_WhMvt,
    s:[gapsSoughtIn=G, gapsSoughtOut=G,
       gapsFoundIn=Fr, gapsFoundOut=Fr,...] -->
    [np:[wh=y,agr=A,...],
     s:[gapsSoughtIn=[npgap:[agr=A,...]],
        gapsSoughtOut=[],
        gapsFoundIn=[], gapsFoundOut=[g],...]]).
```

Note that in practice, these four features are treated as a single feature called **gaps**, whose value is a 4-tuple: gaps=(Gi,Go,Fi,Fo).

Each rule and lexical entry "threads" the incoming gaps through all the constituents that can contain the missing constituent. Thus the rule that provides the analysis of the verb phrase

[*vp* [*vp* *saw a book*] [*pp* *in the library*]]

threads the gap features through both the VP and the PP, since either the VP or the PP might contain the gap.

```
syn(vp_vp_pp_OptMod,
      vp:[gapsSoughtIn=Gi, gapsSoughtOut=Go,
          gapsFoundIn=Fi, gapsFoundOut=Fo,...]   -->
      [vp:[gapsSoughtIn=Gi, gapsSoughtOut=Gnext,
           gapsFoundIn=Fi, gapsFoundOut=Fnext,...],
       pp:[gapsSoughtIn=Gnext, gapsSoughtOut=Go,
           gapsFoundIn=Fnext, gapsFoundOut=Fo,...]]).
```

Likewise, the lexical entry for a verb like *give* will thread the gaps through the relevant items on the subcat list:

```
lex(give,
      v:[gapsSoughtIn=Gi, gapsSoughtOut=Go,
         gapsFoundIn=Fi, gapsFoundOut=Fo,
         subcat=
         [np:[gapsSoughtIn=Gi, gapsSoughtOut=Gnext,
              gapsFoundIn=Fi, gapsFoundOut=Fnext],
          pp:[lexform=to,
              gapsSoughtIn=Gnext, gapsSoughtOut=Go,
              gapsFoundIn=Fnext, gapsFoundOut=Fo]]]).
```

Of course, we assume that the vp_v_comp rule above passes the value of the gap features from the VP to the V in order for the "thread" not to be broken.

The general pattern for threading a feature through several constituents is:

```
[in=In,out=Out] -->
    [[in=In,out=A],[in=A,out=B],...,[in=Z,out=Out]].
```

If a constituent is an "island" or does not happen to contain a gap in this instance, then its 'in' and 'out' values are unified:

```
[...in=G,out=G...]
```

which does not break the thread but does not allow a gap to be found at this point. So, for example, all lexical NPs would have the gap features co-instantiated in this way: a lexical item does not contain a gap, but may occur on the route from a filler to a gap and so must not break the thread.

Gaps are "found" by rules like:

```
syn(np_Gap,
    np:[agr=A,
        gapsSoughtIn=[npgap:[agr=A,...]|Sought],
        gapsSoughtOut=Sought,
        gapsFoundIn=Found, gapsFoundOut=[g|Found],...]
    --> []).
```

The gapsSoughtIn feature is regarded as a stack: if we are looking for an empty NP, we can find it at any point in the input, pop that request off the stack, and continue looking for one fewer empty NPs.

What this means is that the structures below will all involve the same verb phrase rules as the ungapped versions:

the man to whom I gave the book _
the man (who) I gave the book to _
the man (who) I gave _ to the soldiers
the man (who) I gave the name of _ to the police.

The gap threading analysis is a considerable practical improvement on the metarule treatment of Gazdar et al. 1985, which would involve a separate rule not only for each different subcategorization, but for each gap position for each version.

In the vast majority of cases, only one gap is ever being looked for within one constituent so using a stack is not strictly necessary. Having the relevant category as the value of a gap feature would be sufficient. However, there are some cases where two gaps can be involved:

Which babies were the toys easiest to take _ from _?

The sentence is interpreted as a variant of *It was easiest to take the toys from which babies?* The simple, two-feature 'in/out' gap threading breaks down on such structures. Consider what happens at the point where the *easiest* ... clause is entered. One NP is on the `gapsSoughtIn` list and (ultimately) the `gapsSoughtOut` list is required to be null. We add another NP on top of the `gapsSoughtIn` list and identify the topmost `gapsSoughtOut` value with the one associated with the embedded sentence. Both gaps must be found. In this case both are found, and in the correct order, because the `gapsSoughtIn` feature is a stack. Fillers and gaps are nested (in English) $F_1, \ldots, F_n, G_n, \ldots, G_1$, so that the most recently encountered filler will be associated with the the next gap found: exactly the behavior guaranteed by using a last-in-first-out stack.

However, this simple regime will not always guarantee that the gap sought within the lower sentence will be found within that sentence. Consider what would happen with a sentence like:

Which babies [did he claim that [the toys were easiest to take _ from _] in his report to the committee?]

Since the only constraint on the `gapsSoughtOut` feature is that it should be empty on the upper node (the outermost brackets), this feature will be threaded through material coming after the sentence contained in the innermost brackets (*in his report* ...). So, as far as the upper node is concerned, a gap found there would do just as well. This means that the grammar would accept as well-formed the sequence

Which babies did he claim that [the toys were easiest to take food from the children] in _ to _?

where the fillers *which babies* and *the toys* have erroneously been linked to two gaps, at least one of which is in the wrong place. Notice that we cannot simply require the `gapsSoughtOut` feature of the embedded sentence to be empty, as that would rule out the following sentence, which seems to be perfectly acceptable:

To which committee [did he claim that [the children were difficult to deal with _] _?]

In other words, although the two-feature gap-threading mechanism allows us to say that a gap must be found *somewhere* in the whole sentence, it does not allow us to say that it must be found in some particular constituent, which is what is needed. To solve this problem we use the `gapsFoundIn` and `gapsFoundOut` features (following a suggestion by Mark Johnson and Stuart Shieber) which keep track of where gaps have been found. Each time a gap is found, a marker is added to the list threaded by the `gapsFoundIn` and `gapsFoundOut` features, and each time a constituent that must contain a gap is exited, a marker is removed from the list. If any constituent contains fewer gaps than it is supposed to, there will be no markers on the list to remove and the parse will fail.

In the following sections, to aid readability, we will represent the gap features using the notation `gaps=(In,Out)`, etc., to indicate the thread.

4.7   Passives

The original starting point for the analysis of passives in the CLE was that presented by Gazdar et al. (1985). In the GPSG framework, passive VP rules are derived by a metarule from active VPs:

VP → NP, W ⇒ VPpas → W, (PPby).

The interpretation of this metarule is as follows: for every rule expanding VP that introduces an NP daughter, there is also to be a rule that has the VP marked as passive, does not contain that NP daughter, and may contain a PP headed *by*. Feature principles ensure that the verb heading the VP will have passive morphology in this latter case.

There are several problems with this account (see Pulman 1987 where an earlier version of the analysis used here is described). First, the metarule treatment will fail to get the right results in those instances where the passivized NP is not a daughter of VP. There are several different cases here including so-called double passives like:

Kim was taken advantage of
Advantage was taken of Kim.

If *take advantage of* is treated as a complex V only one passive will be derived, for *advantage* will not be a daughter of NP. There are also "prepositional passives" like:

Kim can't be relied on
That meal wasn't paid for

where the "object" NP is actually inside a PP. That it is a PP is demonstrated by the fact that the constituent can be fronted, as in:

On Kim, you can rely absolutely
For that meal, the company will pay.

Passives for which there are no active equivalents will fail to be derived
(by the metarule, at least):

Sandy was said to be a CND activist
*They said Sandy to be a CND activist.

Second, there is a problem about agent PPs. The metarule treatment
allows for an optional agent phrase as a constituent of the passive VP.
The ID/LP format presupposed in GPSG allows for some freedom of
ordering between PPs that are introduced by a VP: thus the output of
the metarule for an input like:

VP → V[...], NP, PP

will allow possibilities like:

A book was given by Kim to Sandy
A book was given to Sandy by Kim.

But optional PP modifiers of VP are (correctly) introduced by a rule:

VP → VP, PP.

There is thus no way of accounting for cases where a non-subcategorized-
for PP intervenes between verb and agent PP:

John was [[[[arrested] in the park] on Friday] by the Special Branch]

even though such cases are freely possible.

Passives are often regarded as prime candidates for a "lexical" treatment. For example, Bresnan (1982) presents an analysis of passives
within the LFG framework in which lexical entries for passive forms of
verbs are derived from those for the active form via a lexical rule that
makes the appropriate morphological and semantic changes. Then passive VPs are parsed using the same context free phrase structure rules
as for actives, with principles of functional coherence and completeness
making sure that subcategorization requirements are met, and the appropriate interpretations arrived at.

However, there are several descriptive problems with Bresnan's proposed lexical treatment of passives, at least one of which could be regarded as fatal.

Bresnan's lexical rules operate within the lexicon and not during a derivation. They "express patterns of redundancy that obtain among large but finite classes of lexical entries" (Kaplan and Bresnan 1982, 180). This has the consequence that the lexical analysis can only be sustained if there is a finite number of passivizable verbs in English. However, derivational processes of various types mean that this is not in fact the case. Several derivational phenomena demonstrate this. For example, there is no upper limit to the number of proper names in English: we can always make up new ones, and we can always concatenate existing names to form new ones: *Slater-Walker, Hewlett-Packard,* etc. But we can form verbs using *-ise* from all of these: *Bresnanise, Hewlett-Packard-ise,* etc. And these verbs are all passivizable (*Thatcherised, Marks-and-Spencerised*); hence, there is a potentially infinite number of passive verbs. Without an infinitely large lexicon the lexical treatment will be unable to cope.

A unification-based formalism like that used in the CLE allows for a treatment of passives that is both more elegant and more adequate than those just discussed. As with the treatment of gap threading described earlier, the use of logical variables provides us with a flexible and succinct mechanism for capturing linguistic generalizations.

Essentially the idea is to capture literally the observation that, syntactically, a passive VP is just like an active VP except that the verb has passive morphology, and there is an NP missing. The missing NP is treated as a kind of "bounded dependency". In the same way that GPSG style analyses introduce unbounded dependencies at the top of a sentence for wh-constructions, we will introduce a bounded dependency at the top of a passive VP.

We will assume that regular passive verbs are derived by a productive morphological process attaching a passive affix, *en/ed*. This process will apply to any verb of the appropriate class, whether or not it is itself the product of prior morphological processes. The syntactic effect of this affixation is that passive verbs are marked **vform=passive**. We also introduce a feature distinguishing passive from active VPs and Vs: **passive= +/-**. This feature can also occur on NPs and PPs, for a reason that will be immediately apparent. The default value for **passive** is -.

In the CLE grammar, passive VPs are introduced in three environments: as complements to verbs like *be* or *get*; as postnominal modifiers, when not headfinal; and, when headfinal, as prenominal modifiers.

The appropriate lexical entry for a verb like *be* will be of the form:

```
lex(be, v:[gaps=(In,Out),
           subcat=[vp:[passive=+,vform=passive,
                       gaps=([np:[passive=+]|In],Out)]]]).
```

The entry puts an NP gap onto the gaps list of the subcategorized VP and requires it to be found within that VP. In the corresponding semantic entry, this NP is associated with the subject of the sentence.

A transitive verb that can be passivized will have an entry like:

```
v:[passive=P,gaps=G,subcat=[np:[passive=P,gaps=G]]].
```

In collaboration with the `vp_v_comp` rule, such an entry will normally generate ordinary transitive VPs. But when the structure built by that rule appears as a complement to *be*, it will require passive morphology on the verb and will contain an NP marked `passive=+`. A passive NP is an empty NP, found by the same rule as unbounded dependency gaps, but featurally distinct from wh-gaps. (This prevents the same NP from being both passivized and wh-moved in the same VP.) All other NPs default to `passive=-`.

Syntactically, then, a passive version of a transitive VP looks just like the active, except that the object is empty. Notice that the features guarantee that the passive NP is empty if and only if the verb is in the passive form. The attraction of this treatment is that it is generally the same rules and entries that generate both the active and the passive versions: no extra lexical or metarule machinery is required.

Some lexical entries for other verbs that passivize will illustrate the analysis further:

(i) Verb-particles:

```
lex(switch,
    v:[passive=P, gaps=G,
       subcat=[p:[lexform=off],
               np:[passive=P,gaps=G]],...])
```

allowing things like:

The light was switched off.

Notice that we can choose whether it is the moved (NP P) or the un-moved (P NP) version which is capable of passivising: but only one of them, for otherwise passives will get two parses.

(ii) Phrasal verbs:

```
lex(look,
    v:[passive=P, gaps=G,
        subcat=[p:[lexform=up],p:[lexform=to],
               np:[passive=P,gaps=G]],...])
```

giving:

John was looked up to by his children.

(iii) The raised version of "object raising" verbs:

```
lex(believe,
    v:[passive=P,gaps=(In,Out),
        subcat=[np:[passive=P,gaps=(In,Next)],
               vp:[vform=to,gaps=(Next,Out)]],...]).
```

(iv) Both types of dative:

```
lex(give,
    v:[passive=P,gaps=(In,Out),
        subcat=[np:[passive=P,gaps=(In,Next)],
               pp:[lexform=to,gaps=(Next,Out)]],...])
lex(give,
    v:[passive=P,gaps=(In,Out),
        subcat=[np:[passive=P,gaps=(In,Next)],
               np:[gaps=(Next,Out)]],...]).
```

We prevent passives from applying where they should not by sim-ply leaving out the **passive** feature on the relevant categories: it then defaults to value -.

For passives that have no active equivalent, we rely on the same mech-anism. There are two types of cases, those like *said, rumored* etc., and those like *surprised at, astonished at*. For the *say* type cases, the passive version will be listed directly in the lexicon with the relevant subcategorization. There will be no entry for the active version on that subcategorization. The absence of the active version guarantees that we will not generate things like:

They rumored him to be a spy

because the only lexical entry for *rumor* with the appropriate subcategorization is the passive form, and the features guarantee that this cannot co-occur with a full NP in this structure. The familiar *promise/persuade* alternation is precisely the inverse of this: we can simply arrange for the lexical entry for *promise* on this subcategorization to be marked as not undergoing affixation by the passive morpheme. Thus we will get the following pattern:

John promised/persuaded Bill to leave
*Bill was *promised/persuaded to leave.*

For the *surprised* cases, we assume that there are actually two different verbs, with different semantics. The ordinary transitive verb denotes an event and behaves regularly:

John surprised Bill
Bill was surprised by John.

The other denotes a state and does not have an active form; it subcategorizes for *at* and is listed directly as a passive, with the appropriate semantics:

The noise was surprising at Bill
Bill was surprised at the noise

```
lex(surprise,
    v:[passive=+,vform=passive,gaps=G,...,
       subcat=[p:[lexform=at],np:[passive=+,gaps=G]]]).
```

Now we turn to the *rely on* type of case. Here the problem is that the missing NP is not a daughter of the VP: a fatal problem for the metarule treatment. Our solution is to pass on the bounded NP dependency down through a PP:

```
lex(rely,
    v:[passive=P,gaps=G,
       subcat=[pp:[lexform=on,passive=P,gaps=G]],...])

pp:[passive=P,gaps=G,lexform=L] -->
   [p:[lexform=L], np:[passive=P,gaps=G]].
```

However, this is as far as the passive feature can go, unlike true unbounded dependencies:

> *On John, you can depend*
> *John, you can depend on*
> *John can be depended on*
> *John, you can depend on the promises of*
> **John can be depended on the promises of.*

As before, the default feature value for passive can be relied on to get the right result.

A notorious problem for many analyses of passive is the case of verbs like *sleep* and *walk* which appear to be subcategorized as intransitives, but occur in passives like the following:

> *This bed was slept in by the queen*
> *The new grass shouldn't be walked over.*

Apparently, an NP inside an optional modifier can be passivized. A simple account of this can be given by adding the following rule:

```
vp:[vform=passive, passive=+, gaps=G] -->
   [v:[subcat=[],vform=passive],
    pp:[passive=+,gaps=G]].
```

This claims that any intransitive verb can behave in this fashion, which seems approximately correct:

> *The plane was first flown in last year*
> *The film was snored through/sneered at by most of the audience.*

The semantic counterpart of this rule has to make the connection between the subject of the VP and the "empty" passive NP inside the PP.

Thus, the use of a local gap threading, a few special lexical entries, and a couple of extra features allows us to implement a virtually exhaustive analysis of the English passive that is descriptively superior to many other current candidates.

4.8 Conjunctions

In the CLE grammar, we treat two types of coordinated conjoined constituents: those with a binary structure, like *both X and X*, and those that can be indefinitely long, like *X, X, X, ... and X*. There are two rules for each different type of constituent, one for the binary, and one for the *n*-ary case, with most categories of the grammar instantiating X in the schematic representation given here.

```
X --> [CONJ:[infix=I], X,
            CONJ:[lexform=I,conjoins= X], X]
X:[simple=n,...] -->
            [ X:[simple=y],
              CONJ:[conjoins= X], X:[simple=_,...]]]
```

John and Mary
either John or Mary
likes trains and hates cars
both ate the food and drank the wine
in the water and under the trees
neither in the water nor under the trees

and similarly for other categories. In the nonbinary case, features impose a right branching analysis, using the `simple` feature. Binary conjunctions "agree" with each other (*either/or*, *both/and*, etc.). All conjunctions carry a boolean feature saying what type of constituent they can conjoin: for example, *and* can conjoin most things, whereas *but* can only conjoin Ss and VPs. Commas are treated as if they were conjunctions.

The only minor originality in the treatment of conjunctions is the way in which number agreement in NP is handled, a traditional problem for feature systems (Karttunen 1984). Conjunctions have, as well as the ordinary agreement feature, features to pick up the agreement from each conjunct and to set the agreement on the resulting new constituent. The

relevant rules pass around the values of these features in the appropriate
way.

```
np: [agr=A,...] -->
     [np: [agr=L],
      conj: [conjoins=np,agr=A,agrL=L,agrR=R],
      np: [agr=R]].
```

Given this mechanism, we then have two *ands*, one for NPs, which
yields a plural, whatever the number of its own constituents, and one
for non-NPs. We also have 3 *ors*, one for identical number in each NP,
yielding the same number for the conjoined NP, and one each for the
remaining two possibilities, yielding plurals in both cases:

```
lex(and, conj: [conjoins=np,ctype=infix,agr=plur])
lex(and, conj: [conjoins= \(np),ctype=infix,
                agr=A,agrR=A,agrL=A])

lex(or, conj: [conjoins=A,ctype=infix,
               agr=B,agrR=B,agrL=B])
lex(or, conj: [conjoins=np,ctype=infix,agr=plur,
               agrR=sing,agrL=plur])
lex(or, conj: [conjoins=np\/det,ctype=infix,agr=plur,
               agrR=plur,agrL=sing]).
```

This will predict, correctly, that only the following patterns are grammatical:

Either John or Bill is coming
Either the girls or John are coming
Either John or the girls are coming
Either the girls or the boys are coming.

This may not be the most elegant solution to this problem, but is a very
simple one.

The analysis of conjunction meshes cleanly with the gap-threading
analysis of wh-movement. In an "across the board" construction like:

What does John like _ or depend on _?

the gap thread is "copied" into both daughter VPs by the VP conjunction rule. This entails that the wh-phrase is interpreted as the object of
both verbs, as required.

5 Semantic Rules for English

Jan van Eijck and Robert C. Moore

The semantic analysis rules of the CLE generate quasi logical form (QLF) expressions, the format of which was described in Chapter 2. Although the output of these rules is an intermediate step in the CLE processing, the unscoped quasi logical form expressions constitute a key level of representation and are central to the CLE enterprise as a whole. The semantic analysis component applies three kinds of rules: (phrasal) semantic rules, morphological derivation rules, and sense entries for individual words. These are considered in general terms first, then the principles that underlie the CLE semantics are explained, and finally the semantics of specific English constructions are discussed.

5.1 Semantic Rules and Senses

5.1.1 Semantic Rules

Semantic rules indicate how the meaning of a complex expression is composed of the meanings of its constituents. Every syntactic rule has one or more corresponding semantic rules.

The general format of the semantic rules was given in Section 3.10. The rules describe how the logical forms of the daughter constituents plus their syntactic and semantic features constrain the logical form and the features of the mother. This is a simplified version of the rule that corresponds to the syntactic rule $S \to NP\ VP$, which is the only syntactic rule employed in the construction of:

John sneezed. (1)

The translation of (1) is:

```
[past,[sneeze1,
       qterm(<t=quant,n=sing,l=ex>,E,[event,E]),
       john1]].
```

Here `qterm(<t=quant,n=sing,l=ex>,E,[event,E])` indicates an existential quantification (in prescoped form) over the event denoted by the verb phrase. See Section 5.1.3 for the use of `qterms` to denote verb phrase events and states.

The semantic rule for $S \rightarrow NP\ VP$ indicates how the translations of subject and predicate combine. In this example, the translation of the subject is john1. The translation of the predicate is an expression with an open argument slot:

```
[past,[sneeze1,
     qterm(<t=quant,n=sing,l=ex>,E,[event,E]),_]]
```

The second argument slot in the translation of the predicate, the one that is left open, is the value of a feature subjval on the predicate, so all that the semantic rule has to do is specify that the translation of the mother is equal to the translation of the predicate daughter, with the subjval feature unified with the translation of the subject NP (other features have been omitted):

```
sem(s_np_vp_Normal,
    (Vp,s:[...]) -->
    [(Np,np:[...]),
    (Vp,vp:[subjval=Np,...])]).
```

In the case of this example rule, the real semantic complexity is not in the rule but in the sense entry for the verb phrase.

Semantic rules are reviewed in detail in the discussion of the semantics of specific constructions below.

5.1.2 Sense Entries

Sense entries are the semantic counterparts to the lexical entries in the syntactic component of the CLE. Their general format is described in Section 3.11.

Logical forms for sense entries can be constants or complex logical form expressions. Senses for proper names are examples of the first:

```
sense(dobbin,np:[...],dobbin1).
```

The sense entry for the auxiliary *can* introduces a complex logical form expression:

```
sense(can,
      vp:[arglist=[(A,vp:[subjval=B,...])],
          mainv=n,subjval=B,...],
      [can1,A]).
```

The entry shows that the auxiliary *can* takes an argument of category vp: [] (the main verb) to make a complete VP and applies the functor can1 to it. The resulting expression has the same subjval as its main verb argument. See Section 5.2.4 below for more information on the use of the feature arglist.

A sense entry for a full VP introduces a logical form with a qterm occupying the first argument slot and an uninstantiated second argument slot for the subject of the VP.

```
sense(vote,
   vp:[eventvar=E,subjval=A,...],
   [vote1,qterm(<t=quant,n=sing,l=ex>,E,[event,E]),A]).
```

The features subjval and eventvar are carried along until the logical form expression can be "closed off".

Adjectives that can be predicated of propositions, as in (2), and those that can be predicated of properties, as in (3), have separate sense entries to handle such cases.

> *It is likely that John lives in Cambridge.*   (2)
>
> *It is nice to live in Cambridge.*   (3)

The distinguishing feature here is subjType, which can take the values normalNP for the normal case of an adjective with a subject denoting an individual, property for adjectives with property-type subjects, and proposition for adjectives with proposition-denoting subjects.

5.1.3 Morphological Derivation

Morphological derivation rules provide senses for regularly formed combinations of words and one or more affixes (prefixes or suffixes). The general format of a morphological derivation rule is described in Section 3.10. The semantics of plural Nbar formation, verb phrase inflection, negative adjective prefixes, agentive nominalization, adverbial formation, and comparative and superlative inflection are all taken care of by derivation rules.

Plural Nbars Both singular and plural Nbars translate into predicates with open argument slots. In the case of a singular Nbar, the variable in the slot ranges over singleton sets, for plural Nbars over arbitrary sets. This treatment entails that the derivation rule for plural Nbars leaves the sense unaffected.

VP inflection   Derivation rules are used for constructing the meanings of the VP inflection forms from the present tense infinitive. For instance, the logical form for *sneeze* (present tense infinitive) is:

```
[sneeze1,qterm(<t=quant,n=sing,l=ex>,E,[event,E]),A].
```

Here A is a variable for the subject. The rule that derives the past tense from the sense of the infinitive is:

```
deriv(vp_vp_ed_Past,
      ([past,Vp],vp:[subjval=A,...]) -->
      [(Vp,vp:[subjval=A,...]),
       (_,ed)]).
```

Agentive nominalization   Morphological derivation also deals with simple cases of agentive *er*-nominalization. The meaning of *voter* is derived from the sense of the present tense infinitive *vote* by taking the part of the VP sense that consists of its predicate and arguments, but with the event qterm left out (this part is kept track of by the feature body), filling the argument slot for the event with suitable information, and linking the subjval variable of the VP daughter to the arg feature of the Nbar mother:

```
deriv(nbar_v_er_Agentive,
      (Vp,nbar:[arg=A,...]) -->
      [(Vp,v:[subjval=A,eventvar=kind(E,[event,E]),...]),
       (_,er)]).
```

The agentive derivation rule gives the following translation for *voter*:

```
[vote_intr,kind(E,[event,E]),A].
```

The variable A is bound to the feature arg. The sense entry expresses that a voter is an individual engaged in an event (or events) of the voting kind, in some timeless way. Although only roughly correct, this turns out to be a very useful approximation.

Negative prefixes Morphological derivation rules take care of the
semantics of adjective formation by means of the negative prefix 'un-':

```
deriv(adj_un_adj,
      ([not,Adj],adj:[subjval=A,...]) -->
      [(_,un),
       (Adj,adj:[subjval=A,...])]).
```

An adjective with a negative prefix like *unhappy* gets its sense entry
from this rule and the logical form entry for *happy*:

```
[happy1,A]
```

where **A** is the value of the **subjval** feature.

Adverbials Adverbials formed out of adjective + *-ly* are treated as
modifiers of the verb event.

John left quickly.   (4)

In the eventual logical form for this example, after scoping of the event
qterm, quickness is predicated of the leaving event:

```
[past,
  quant(exists,E,[event,E],
  [and,[leave1,E,john1],[quick_physev,E]])].
```

In other words, the prescoped logical form has to look like this:

```
[past,
  [and,[leave1,
        qterm(<t=quant,n=sing,l=ex>,E,[event,E]),
        john1],
   [quick_physev,E]]].
```

To achieve this result, the adverb sense has to conjoin the verb predicate with the sense of the adjective that the adverb derives from. The
following derivation rule for adverbs has the desired effect:

```
deriv(advp_adj_ly,
      ([and,VpSense,Adj]],
       advp:[arg=VpSense,eventvar=E,...]) -->
      [(Adj,adj:[arglist=[],subjval=E,...]),(_,ly)]).
```

When an adverb—category **advp:[]**—is combined with a verb phrase,
the value of **arg** is unified with the verb sense.

5.2   General Principles of the CLE Semantics

5.2.1   Building Translations by Unification

A basic technique that runs throughout the semantic rules in the current
version of the CLE is that semantic analyses are built up by unification
rather than by functional application. In the traditional treatments of
formal natural language semantics, the interpretation of a complex constituent is specified by applying the interpretation of one of the daughter
constituents to the interpretation of the others. In the rest of this chapter apply is used as the operator for lambda application (for arbitrary
types), to illustrate the traditional approach. If this approach were used
in the CLE, the semantic interpretation rule for the basic sentence pattern $S \rightarrow NP\ VP$ might look like this:

```
sem(s_np_vp,
    ([apply,Vp,Np],s:[]) -->
    [(Np,np:[]),
     (Vp,vp:[])]).
```

This rule says that the interpretation of the sentence is the interpretation
of the verb phrase applied to the interpretation of the subject noun
phrase.

The problem with this approach is that when the verb phrase itself is
semantically complex, as it usually is, a lambda expression has to be used
to express the verb phrase interpretation and then a lambda reduction
must be applied to express the sentence interpretation in its simplest
form (Dowty, Wall, and Peters 1981, 98–111). With the sentence *John
likes Mary*, the logical form for *John* could simply be john1 but the
logical form for *likes Mary* would have to be something like this (we use
X^ for λx, and for convenience we assume in this section that the event
quantifiers have been scoped already):

```
X^quant(exists,E,[event,E],
                 [like1,E,X,mary1]).
```

The logical form for the whole sentence would then be:

```
[apply,
    X^quant(exists,E,[event,E],
                     [like1,E,X,mary1]),
```

john1].

This must be reduced to yield the desired logical form:

```
quant(exists,E,[event,E],
      [like1,E,john1,mary1]).
```

Moreover, lambda expressions and the ensuing reductions would have to be introduced at each intermediate stage in building up interpretations of complex constituents such as verb phrases. To accommodate modal auxiliaries, as in *John might like Mary*, involves ensuring that *might like Mary* receives the same type of interpretation as *like(s) Mary* in order to combine properly with the interpretation of the subject. The only reasonable way to do this seems to be to give a complex interpretation to modals, so that *might* would have a logical form like P^Y^[might1,[apply,P,Y]]. When the semantic counterpart of a rule *VP → AUX VP* applies the interpretation of *might* to the interpretation of *like Mary* to produce the interpretation of *might like Mary*, the result is:

```
[apply,
    P^Y^[might1,[apply,P,Y]],
    X^quant(exists,E,[event,E],
            [like1,E,X,mary1])].
```

This needs to be reduced to:

```
Y^[might1,quant(exists,E,[event,E],
            [like1,E,Y,mary1])].
```

It is simpler and more efficient to use the feature system and unification to do explicitly what lambda expressions and lambda reduction do implicitly, that is, assign a value to a variable embedded in a logical form expression. In this approach, instead of the logical form of a verb phrase being a logical predicate, it is the same as the logical form of an entire sentence, but with a variable as the subject argument of the verb and a feature on the verb phrase bound to the same variable. The rule that produces the interpretation for *likes Mary* would need to give it the logical form:

```
quant(exists,E,[event,E],
        [like1,E,X,mary1]).
```

The subject variable is tracked by giving the VP the category:

```
vp:[subjval=X].
```

The sentence interpretation can then proceed by the rule that was given in Section 5.1.1. The application of this rule unifies john1 directly with the variable X to produce the desired result. Modal auxiliaries can be handled equally easily by a similar mechanism.

This technique does not permit the elimination of all lambda expressions and reductions from semantic interpretation. Lambda expressions must still be introduced where expressions that are normally used as predicates are used as arguments instead. These situations are tied to particular syntactic constructions, however, so the use of lambda expressions can be strictly limited. Also, special care must be taken if unification is used for the semantics of control phenomena and conjunction, where it might be necessary to distinguish semantically between occurrences of terms and occurrences of the variables bound by these terms (see Section 5.3.2). However, the unification style of semantic rules turns out to have practical advantages for generation (Section 13.3). For a theoretical perspective on unification-based semantic processing, see Moore 1989.

5.2.2   Unbounded Dependencies

There is a major difficulty in stating semantic rules. Constituents frequently appear syntactically in places that do not directly reflect their semantic roles. Semantically, the subject of a sentence is one of the arguments of the verb, so it would be much easier to produce logical forms of sentences if the subject were part of the verb phrase. The use of the subjval feature, in effect, provides a mechanism for taking the translation of the subject from the place where it occurs and inserting it into the verb phrase translation where it "logically" belongs.

The use of features on constituents for this purpose is particularly striking in the case of the unbounded dependencies in wh-questions. Take the example:

Who did Mary love?   (5)

As a translation of (5) we would like to generate the quasi logical form:

```
[past,[love,
       qterm(<t=quant,n=sing,l=ex>,E,[event,E]),
       mary1,
       qterm(<t=quant,l=wh>,B,[personal,B])]].
```

The problem is how to get the `qterm` that translates the wh-phrase in the appropriate argument slot of the VP predicate (the open slot of `love` that corresponds to the noun phrase gap at the end of the verb phrase).

Just as we handle long-distance dependencies by threading a list of syntactic gap fillers in the syntactic rules, in the semantic rules we thread a list of semantic gap fillers. These gap fillers are the senses of the NPs that are linked to the gaps. In some cases semantic feature information associated with the moved NPs is needed for a correct interpretation of the gaps. For this reason moved NPs are threaded as pairs consisting of a sense and a semantic category.

In Section 4.6 it was explained that for the syntactic gap threading to work correctly four lists are needed: a list of the gaps that are threaded in, a list of the gaps that are threaded out, a list of marks for gaps that have been consumed, and a list of marks for gaps that are still to be found. Since the semantic analysis can proceed on the assumption that all the gaps have been found in the right places, only two lists are needed: a list of semantic gaps threaded in, and a list of semantic gaps threaded out. Otherwise, the semantics of long-distance dependencies follows the syntax as closely as possible.

A semantic gap feature `semGaps` specifies the two lists that are used for semantic gap threading through a category. The format is as follows:

`semGaps=(⟨ Input_List⟩, ⟨ Output_List⟩).`

The items on the lists are sense-category pairs:

`[((⟨ sense₁⟩,⟨ category₁⟩)),...,((⟨ senseₙ⟩,⟨ categoryₙ⟩))].`

The following semantic rule shows how the semantic gap threading mechanism works:

```
sem(s_np_s_WhMvt,
    (S,s:[arg=Arg,semGaps=(G,G),...]) -->
    [(Np,np:[arg=Arg,handle=X,...]),
     (S,s:[semGaps=([(Np,npgap:[handle=X,...])],[])])]).
```

The **semGaps** input and output lists of the mother are unified, and the sense of the moved NP is placed on the gap threading input list of the daughter S, while the output list of this S is specified to be empty. Unifying the gap threading lists of the mother ensures that no filler from outside can consume a gap inside the sentence: sentences are islands with respect to wh-movement. The roles of the features **arg** and **handle** will be explained shortly.

The wh-NP *who* has the sense entry:

```
sense(who,
      np:[wh=y,rel=n,handle=V,...],
      qterm(<t=quant,l=wh>,V,[personal,V])).
```

The sense of *who* is an appropriate **qterm**; the **qterm** variable is linked to the feature **handle**.

The NP gap that has been put on the **semGaps** in-list by the semantic rule for moved wh-phrases is threaded through until it is consumed by a special gap rule. This rule takes the first gap sense from the **semGaps** in-list and binds it to the sense of the gap constituent:

```
sem(np_Gap,
    (Np,np:[handle=X, ... ,
            semGaps=([(Np,npgap:[handle=X...])|Rest],
                     Rest)])
    --> []).
```

This rule ensures that in (5) the gap would receive the translation:

```
qterm(<t=quant,l=wh>,X,[person,X]).
```

Also, the rule binds the **handle** feature of the gap NP to the **qterm** variable X. This feature is used in the treatment of control phenomena. In

Which man did John ask to leave?   (6)

the wh-term in the object slot of *ask* has to control the subject of *to leave*. This is done by having the **handle** feature of the wh-phrase bind the **subjval** of the VP *to leave*. See Section 5.3.2 for further examples.

The gap threading mechanism is also used in the semantics of relative clauses. The word *who* in the following example is not a wh-NP but a relative pronoun:

The woman who John loves is beautiful.   (7)

Here is the sense entry for the relative pronoun *who*:

`sense(who,np:[rel=y,handle=V,arg=V,...)],V).`

The relative pronoun *who* has a variable as its sense; this variable is linked to the features `arg` and `handle`. As can be seen in the rule `s_np_s_WhMvt`, the `arg` feature variable of the moved wh-phrase is passed up to the mother S. The rule that combines an Nbar and a relative clause to form a complex Nbar will link the free variable in the sense expression for *who John loves* to the free variable in the sense expression for *woman* and conjoin the two expressions to get an appropriate translation for *woman who John loves*.

5.2.3   Threading of Antecedents Lists

The threading technique is also used to maintain a list of possible intrasentential antecedents for pronouns and referential NPs. The antecedents list is maintained in the form of a stack. Every constituent through which it is passed gets its antecedents stack input as the value the feature **anaIn**, and passes an output stack as the value of its **anaOut** feature. Variable binding noun phrases contribute a variable to the antecedents stack; constant noun phrases contribute a constant (a copy of the NP sense) to the stack.

Copies of proper name senses are placed on the antecedents list by the proper name sense entries:

```
sense(john,
      np:[handle=john1,simpleTerm=simpleTerm,
          semGaps=(G,G),anaIn=Al,anaOut=[john1|Al]],
      john1).
```

Variables for quantifiers and other variable binders—all these have feature **simpleTerm** set to **notSimpleTerm**—are put on the antecedents list by the semantic rules. The rule that forms singular descriptive phrases provides an example:

```
sem(np_det_nbar,
  (qterm(<t=ref,p=Rt,l=Det,n=Dnr,a=Ain>,V,Nbar),
  np:[quantform=ref,handle=V,semGaps=Gaps,
      anaIn=Ain,anaOut=Aout]) -->
  [(Det,det:[quantform=ref,reftype=Rt,detnr=Dnr,
             agr=sing,anaIn=[-V|Ain],anaOut=Anext]),
   (Nbar,nbar:[arg=V,semGaps=Gaps,
               anaIn=Anext,anaOut=Aout])]).
```

The reader who finds this example rule with all its features rather opaque at first sight has our full sympathy. Bear with us, and the use of the features will gradually become clear.

The value of the **anaIn** feature of the mother figures in the quantifier category of the description that is being built, giving the list of possible intrasentential antecedents for the NP sense under construction. Next, the variable of the mother node's sense is put on the antecedent list of the first daughter, with a marker '-' to indicate that the antecedent is singular. If we look at the sense entry for singular **the** we can see what happens next:

```
sense(the,det:[quantform=ref,agr=sing,
               mass=n,reftype=def,
               detnr=sing,anaIn=A,anaOut=A],
      the).
```

The antecedents list is threaded through the determiner without modification and passed to the Nbar node.

Threading an antecedent list as indicated in the above rules results in lists containing handles of all *preceding or dominating* NPs. The following illustrates that dominating NPs can act as possible intrasentential antecedents.

[The man who said that he had designed it] left.   (8)

The fact that *he* can be anaphorically linked to *the man who said that he had designed it* is borne out by the antecedents list for *he*, which contains a copy of the variable used to translate this dominating NP.

5.2.4   Lexicalization of the Semantics

The English syntax rules deal with "movement transformations" like dative shift and passivization respectively by providing appropriate lexical entries for datives and by having an appropriate morphological rule to link passives to active infinitive forms of verbs. This treatment is carried through in the semantics as well. Likewise, the rule schema format for subcategorization (described in Section 4.2) is also employed in the semantics. Finally, the semantics of grades of comparison is dealt with by providing "graded" senses for gradable adjectives in the sense lexicon. The result of all this is that much of the complexity of the semantic analysis has been transferred from the semantic rules to the sense entries, and to a lesser extent to the sense derivation rules. This makes the semantics of the CLE lexicon-driven to a large extent.

The semantics of movement: passives The senses of passive VPs are derived from the active VP senses by morphological derivation rules such as:

```
deriv(v_v_ed,
  (V,v:[vform=passive,arglist=List,eventvar=E,
      agentAbove=agentAbove,agentval=Agent,
      subjval=Patient,tnsd=n,...]) -->
  [(V,v:[vform=inf,arglist=List,eventvar=E,
      subjval=Agent,subjType=Stype,objval=Patient]),
  (_,ed)]).
```

Note that the mother constituent has no binding for the subjval feature. The subjval feature of the daughter (i.e., the subjval feature of the active sense) becomes the agentval feature of the passive sense. The agentval feature on a passive VP is to be unified with the sense of an agent *by*-phrase, if there is one. This ensures that the agent *by*-phrase fills the argument slot in the passive VP that corresponds to what was the subject argument slot of the active VP.

The feature value agentAbove=agentAbove indicates that an agent has to be found above to fill the agentval slot. The rules that introduce VP daughter nodes (e.g., the rule $S \longrightarrow NP\ VP$) set the feature agentAbove to notAbove on the VP daughter; the rule that finds the agent flips this value to agentAbove. The agent can either be an agent *by*-phrase or an existential quantification over the agent position in case no suitable *by*-phrase is found. Here is the rule that finds an agent *by*-phrase:

```
sem(vp_vp_pp_OptMod,
  (Vp,vp: [semVpType=passive,agentAbove=notAbove,
          eventvar=E,subjval=A,handle=X,...])
  -->
  [(Vp,vp: [semVpType=passive,agentval=Agent,
           agentAbove=agentAbove,eventvar=E,
           subjval=A,handle=X,...]),
   (Agent,pp: [lexform=by,pptype=subcategorized])]).
```

The following rule introduces an agent by existential quantification:

```
sem(pred_vp_Passive,
  (Vp,pred: [semPredType=passive,agentAbove=notAbove,
            eventvar=E,subjval=A,handle=X,
            agentval=qterm(<t=quant,n=sing,l=ex>,
                           Agt,[entity,Agt])])
  -->
  [(Vp,vp: [eventvar=E,agentAbove=agentAbove,
           semGaps=([[(A,npgap:[handle=X])|Gin],Gout),
           agentval=Agt,vform=passive])]).
```

This rule also illustrates the use of the **semGaps** feature to indicate that the passive verb phrase has a noun phrase gap (see the discussion of the syntax of passive constructions in Section 4.7). The rule ensures that the NP gap that occurs in the position of the direct object of the verb phrase is interpreted as the subject of the passive VP. In the sense entry for the verb, the sense of the direct object NP that the VP is subcategorized-for is linked to the object slot in the VP predicate. This links the subject of the passive VP to the appropriate predicate slot.

The semantics of movement: dative shift   Another "movement" phenomenon that is lexicalized is dative shift. The traditional account of the relation between the examples (9) and (10) postulates a movement transformation.

John gave the flowers to Mary.   (9)

John gave Mary the flowers.   (10)

The CLE semantics treats these examples by having two entries for ditransitive verbs like *give*, one with subcategorization list *[NP, PP]*,

and the other one with subcategorization list *[NP, NP]*, where the first
NP on the list is linked to the indirect object slot of the predicate `give1`,
and the second one to the direct object slot.

Subcategorization   The rule schema format in the CLE syntax that is
described in Section 4.2 is also employed in the semantics. The semantic
counterpart to the syntactic feature `subcat` is the feature `arglist`. This
feature gives the list of semantic complements. The format is:

`arglist=[((` $sense_1$ `),(` cat_1 `)), ... ,((` $sense_n$ `),(` cat_n `))]`.

In the sense entries for verb phrases, the `arglist` feature plays an important role. The sense entry for a transitive verb like *design*, for example,
has an argument list with one element: a sense-category pair for the
direct object of the verb.

```
sense(design,
    v:[arglist=[(B,np:[semGaps=Gaps])],
        vform=inf,eventvar=E,subjval=A,semGaps=Gaps],
    [design1,
        qterm(<t=quant,n=sing,l=ex>,E,[event,E]),A,B]).
```

The sense of the NP complement is linked to the appropriate argument
slot of the `design1` predicate. Note that the `semGaps` feature of the VP
is set equal to the `semGaps` of the NP complement. What this says is that
any gap to be found in the whole VP is to be found in the complement.

In case the `arglist` contains several items, the list of semantic gaps
is threaded through all items that may contain gaps, as is shown in the
sense entry for *give*:

```
sense(give,
    v:[arglist=[(B,np:[semGaps=(Gin,Gnext)]),
                (C,pp:[pptype=subcategorized,
                        semGaps=(Gnext,Gout)])],
        eventvar=E,subjval=A,semGaps=(Gin,Gout)],
    [give1,
        qterm(<t=quant,n=sing,l=ex>,E,[event,E]),A,B,C]).
```

The feature `pptype` selects the right kind of PP sense: PPs that are
subcategorized-for are interpreted like NPs. As explained above, a second entry for *give* will have two NP arguments, with their senses linked
to the argument slots of `give1` in reversed order.

Because the work of linking the relevant features between functor and argument(s) has been carried out in the lexicon, the semantic rule that combines a verb with the items on its argument list can be very simple:

```
sem(vp_v_comp_Normal,
    (V,vp:[eventvar=E,subjval=A,handle=X,semGaps=Gaps,
            agentval=Agent,agentAbove=Ab,vform=P,...])
    -->
    [(V,v:[eventvar=E,subjval=A,handle=X,semGaps=Gaps,
            agentval=Agent,agentAbove=Ab,vform=P,
            arglist=Complements,...])
    | Complements]).
```

This rule says that the mother gets all the features of the V daughter, except for the `arglist` feature. The `arglist` feature of the V daughter is unified with the list of V complements—note that this entails all the unifications that are specified in the V sense entry—and the result is a semantically complete VP.

5.3 The Semantics of Specific Constructions

5.3.1 Complements of 'be'

Syntactically, complements of *be* are divided into constituents of category `comp:[]` and those of category `pred:[]`. NP complements of **be** have category `comp:[]`; complements of category `pred:[]` can be passive VPs, *-ing* VPs (progressives), adjectives, PPs, or cleft sentences. Semantically, the sense entries for both subcategorizations of **be** behave similarly; no distinction is made between the copula sense and the auxiliary sense of *be*.

Basically, all that the sense entries of **be** do is wrap the appropriate tense operators around the LFs for their complements. Here is an example sense entry (the sense entry for `subcat=[comp:[..]]` looks similar):

```
sense(was,
    v:[subcat=[pred:[...]],
        arglist=[(A,pred:[agentAbove=Ab,agentval=Agent,
                            eventvar=E,subjval=B,
                            handle=X,semGaps=Gaps,...])],
```

```
eventvar=E,subjval=B,handle=X,semGaps=Gaps,
   vform=fin,agentAbove=Ab,agentval=Agent,...],
[past,A]).
```

The rules that form predicates out of NPs, adjectives, or PPs introduce
an existential quantification over a state. The rule that forms predicates
out of adjectives provides an example:

```
sem(pred_adjp,
   ([be,qterm(<t=quant,n=sing,l=exs>,S,[state,S]),Adjp],
   pred:[semPredType=adjp,eventvar=S,subjval=A,
         handle=X,semGaps=Gaps,...]) -->
   [(Adjp,adjp:[subjval=A,handle=X,semGaps=Gaps,...])]).
```

The translation of *John was happy* is:

```
[past,
   [be,qterm(<t=quant,n=sing,l=exs>,S,[event,S]),
      [happy1,john1]]].
```

It might be thought that the following simpler translation would do just
as well:

```
[past,[happy1,john1]].
```

However, such a translation would make it difficult to treat cases where
the complement is modified by a PP:

> *John was happy in Cambridge.*   (11)

Under the state quantification treatment, (11) can be translated as:

```
[past,
   [and,
      [be,qterm(<t=quant,n=sing,l=exs>,S,[state,S]),
         [happy1,john1]]
      [in_location,S,cambridge1]]].
```

Predicates formed out of passive VPs and *-ing* VPs derive their existential quantification over an event from the lexical entries for VPs.
These predicates are distinguished from predicates that do not derive
from real VPs by the feature semPredType.

The logical forms assigned by the CLE to predicate nominals have been explained in Section 2.2.11. The rule that forms a complement out of a noun phrase introduces an existential quantification over a state variable and the basic equality predicate:

```
sem(comp_np,
    ([be,qterm(<t=quant,n=sing,l=exs>,S,[state,S]),
        [eq,A,Np]],
    comp:[subjval=A,eventvar=S,semGaps=Gaps,...])
    -->
    [(Np,np:[genType=nonGeneric,semGaps=Gaps,...])]).
```

The rule vp_v_comp_Normal that was discussed in Section 5.2.4 combines the be with its complement.

The way in which passive VP complements to be are handled semantically is described in Section 5.2.4. The handling of -ing VP complements is straightforward. PP complements are formed by the rule:

```
sem(pred_pp,
    ([be,qterm(<t=quant,n=sing,l=exs>,S,[state,S]),Pp],
        pred:[semPredType=pp,subjval=A,eventvar=State,
        semGaps=Gaps,...])
    -->
    [(Pp,pp:[arg1=A,semGaps=Gaps,...])]).
```

The treatment of *there* complements, such as those in the examples below, is rather special.

There is no bishop in Cambridge. (12)

There are many beautiful women in Cambridge. (13)

There are computers that are designed in Cambridge. (14)

Complements to *be* in *there are* ... constructions have to be quantified noun phrases. Actually, a more precise constraint is possible: the quantifier has to be symmetric, but the semantic rules do not impose this further constraint.

The three *there* complement rules set a feature scopedForm on the NP that they dominate; NPs with this feature translate into quant expressions rather than qterms. This is done to avoid spurious scopings: in the current scoping algorithm, a quant expression that is put in place explicitly by the semantic rule always gets narrowest possible scope.

The following sentences provide examples of cleft constructions:

It was John who designed a house.   (15)

It is in Cambridge that John wants to live.   (16)

The treatment of these examples employs the gap threading mechanism in a straightforward way. Example (15) gets the translation:

```
[past,
 quant(exists,A,
     [house_building,A],
     [past,[design1,
          qterm(<t=quant,n=sing,l=ex>,E,[event,E),
          john1,A]])].
```

5.3.2   Verb Phrases

VP control phenomena   The semantics of VP subcategorization was described in Section 5.2.4. This section explains the way in which the subcategorization mechanism is used to handle control phenomena, as in:

John wanted to leave.   (17)

Every man wanted to leave.   (18)

John wanted to try to leave.   (19)

John allowed Mary to leave.   (20)

The semantics of control is dealt with in the sense entries. The entry for *want (to VP)* is:

```
sense(want,
    v:[vform=inf,subcat=[vp:_],
       arglist=[(B,vp:[subjval=X,handle=X,
                       semGaps=(Gin,Gout),...])],
       eventvar=E,subjval=A,handle=X,
       semGaps=(Gin,Gout),...],
    [want1,
       qterm(<t=quant,n=sing,l=ex>,E,[event,E]),A,B]).
```

This entry shows that *want* has a VP on its complement list. The subjval feature of the complement VP is set equal to the handle feature of *want*. This ensures that the embedded VP gets an appropriate subject. If the subject of *want* is a proper name, its handle will be a copy of that name. If it is a quantified NP or wh-NP, the handle will be the variable that is quantified over. If it is a pronoun or kind term the handle will be of the form a_index(X), where X is the variable that is used in the a_term translation of the pronoun.

Note that the sense entry for *want* also passes the handle feature to the VP complement. This is done because it might be needed for control inside the complement, as in (19).

There is a difference between the control in (17), (18), and (19) on the one hand, and that in example (20) on the other. In (17), (18), and (19) the subject of the main sentence controls the VP complement; in (20) the direct object NP is the controller. This difference is reflected in the sense entries: in cases of object control the subjval feature of the VP complement is applied to the sense of the NP that is also on the complement list. The translation for (20) then becomes:

```
[past,
    [allow_to_do,
        qterm(<t=quant,n=sing,l=ex>,A,[event,A]),
        john1,
        [apply,
        B^[leave1,
            qterm(<t=quant,n=sing,l=ex>,C,[event,C]),
            B],
        mary1]]].
```

Here apply denotes lambda application (cf. Section 5.2.1). The usual shortcut of directly unifying feature values instead of introducing an explicit apply construct will give wrong results in cases where the VP complement has more than one occurrence of a subjval slot, as for instance the translation of *to pack and leave* would have. *John allowd no one to pack and leave* does not mean the same as *John allowed no one to pack and John allowed no one to leave*. This shows that direct feature unification would give wrong results for this case.

After lambda conversion mary1 will occupy the appropriate argument slot:

```
[past,
    [allow_to_do,
```

```
qterm(<t=quant,n=sing,l=ex>,A,[event,A]),
john1,
[leave1,
    qterm(<t=quant,n=sing,l=ex>,E,[event,E]),
    mary]]].
```

Auxiliary VPs   The example sense entry for an auxiliary VP that
was given in Section 5.1.2 is repeated here with inclusion of the features
under discussion:

```
sense(can,
      v:[arglist=[(A,vp:[eventvar=E,subjval=B,
                          handle=X,semGaps=Gaps,...])],
         eventvar=E,subjval=B,handle=X,
         mainv=n,semGaps=Gaps,...],
      [can1,A]).
```

The entry shows that all the features on the VP complement are carried
over to the auxiliary, after which the semantic rule `vp_v_comp_Normal`
ensures that these features are carried up to the mother VP.

VP coordination   The following sentences give examples of VP coordination.

> *The man pushed and pulled.*   (21)

> *Which woman wanted John but chose Mary?*   (22)

The semantic rules handle coordination of complete VPs only, as in
examples (21) and (22). Examples like the following are not handled:

> *She hated or despised every politician.*   (23)

> *What did John want but Mary despise?*   (24)

> *John sold or gave the book to someone.*   (25)

Semantically, the problem with the coordination in (23), (24), and (25)
is that unifying the nonempty argument lists of the two VPs does not
give the right results. Sentence (23), for instance, is not equivalent to

> *She hated every politician or despised every politician.*   (26)

but rather to

Every politician was either hated or despised by her.   (27)

What this means is that *hated* must take *every politician* as its argument but *despised* must not; rather, the argument to *despised* must be interpreted as a variable linked to *every politician.* The semantic problems with (24) and (25) are similar. These cases cannot be dealt with by the current mechanism for semantic gap threading. Obviously, the correct approach would be to allow the formation of coordinated incomplete verb phrases by higher type coordination of lambda expressions representing the incomplete verb phrases. Still, it is interesting to see how far a restricted approach where the lambda abstraction over the argument slots is left implicit, already gets us.

Coordination of complete VPs is handled by rules such as:

```
sem(vp_vp_conj_vp,
   ([Conj,Vp1,Vp2],
    vp:[subjval=A,handle=X,agentval=Agent,
        fullGaps=Fg,semGaps=Gaps,...])
   -->
   [(Vp1,vp:[subjval=A,handle=X,agentval=Agent,
             fullGaps=Fg,semGaps=Gaps,...]),
    (Conj,conj:[conjtype=prop,...]),
    (Vp2,vp:[subjval=X,handle=X,agentval=Agent,
             fullGaps=noFullGaps,semGaps=Gaps,...])]).
```

Note that the subjval feature of the second VP daughter is not linked to the subjval of the mother but to its handle. The feature specification conjtype=prop indicates that a propositional conjunction operator is employed. The translation of (22) is:

```
[and,
 [past,
    [want1,qterm(<t=quant,n=sing,l=ex>,A,[event,A]),
           qterm(wh,sing,B,[woman_female_human,B]),
           john1]],
 [past,
    [choose1,qterm(<t=quant,n=sing,l=ex>,[event,C]),
             B,
             mary1]]].
```

After scoping, the subject positions of both VP predicates will be bound by the wh-quantifier and the verb phrase events will be existentially quantified over:

```
quant(wh,A,
  [woman_female_human,A],
  [and,
    [past,quant(exists,B,[event,B],
        [want1,B,A,john1])],
    [past,quant(exists,C,[event,C],
        [choose1,C,A,mary1])]]).
```

The feature `fullGaps`, with values `fullGaps` and `noFullGaps`, is used to ensure that gaps inside the right daughter of a coordinated structure are never expanded to full quantified phrases.

A woman was liked by John but despised by Mary.   (28)

A woman was liked by John and a woman was despised by Mary. (29)

The translation as a variable of the passive gap inside the second VP conjunct of (28) prevents this example from turning out equivalent to (29). After scoping, (28) translates as:

```
quant(exists,A,
  [woman_female_human,A],
  [past,
    [and,
      quant(exists,B,[event,B],[like1,B,john1,A]),
      quant(exists,C,[event,C],[despise1,C,mary1,A])]]).
```

Sentence coordination, as in (29), (30), and (31), is handled by rules that are similar to the VP coordination rules.

John will leave and I will be angry.   (30)

If John leaves, then I will be angry.   (31)

5.3.3 Adjective Control Phenomena

The semantic treatment of adjectives is very similar to that of VPs. Notably, adjectives are subcategorized-for as well, and in predicative use they exhibit control phenomena, as in:

John is likely to want to talk.   (32)

Here the sense entry for *likely* has to ensure that the subject of the
sentence is taken as the subject of *to want* (and, as explained above,
the sense entry for *want* ensures that the VP *to talk* is controlled by the
subject of *want*). The translation for (32) is:

```
[pres,
  [be,
     qterm(<t=quant,n=sing,l=exs>,S,[state,S]),
     [likely_prop,
        [want1,
         qterm(<t=quant,n=sing,l=ex>,B,[event,B]),
         john1,
         [talk1,
            qterm(<t=quant,n=sing,l=ex>,C,[event,C]),
            john1]]]]]
```

which results from the following sense entry for *likely*:

```
sense(likely,
      adj:[subcat=[vp:_],
           arglist=[(B,vp:[subjval=A,handle=X,
                           semGaps=(Gin,Gout),...])],
           subjval=A,handle=X,
           semGaps=(Gin,Gout),...],
      [likely_prop,B]).
```

Note that the subject of *likely* is passed to the **subjval** feature of the
VP complement. The **handle** is also passed. This is needed to handle
the control inside the complement, as in the case of (32).

We also want (33) to receive the same translation as (32):

That John wants to talk is likely.   (33)

This is ensured by a separate sense entry for the "extraposed" sense of
likely, as opposed to the "normal" sense, a distinction is made by the
feature **vtype**. Note the use of **semGaps=(G,G)** to indicate that no gaps
are consumed within the constituent.

```
sense(likely,
      adj:[subcat=[],arglist=[],gradable=gradable,
           graded=nonGraded,vtype=extrap,
```

```
                subjval=B,semGaps=(G,G),...],
          [likely_prop,B]).
```

The following sentence should get the same translation as (32) and (33):

It is likely that John wants to talk.   (34)

This is accomplished by relating (34) to (33) by an "extraposition movement" rule that interprets the constituent *that John wants to talk*, considered to be extraposed to the right, as the subject of the sentence.

5.3.4   Nbars

Basic Nbars   Sense entries for basic Nbars have a feature **arg** to mark their free argument slot:

```
sense(book,
        nbar:[arg=A,semGaps=(G,G),...],
        [book1,A]).
```

The feature `semGaps=(G,G)` indicates that the gap list coming in equals the gap list going out; in other words, the constituent does not dominate any semantic gaps.

Partitive Nbars   Partitive Nbars are the constituents in square brackets in:

At least three [of those men] have died.   (35)

Some [of the wine] was drunk.   (36)

The semantic constraint on this construction is that the noun phrase following 'of' is a descriptive quantifier, that is, its translation before scoping will be a `qterm` of the form `qterm(<t=ref,...>,V,...)`. Example (35), where the noun phrase following 'of' is a count NP, is given an translation of the form

```
X^[subset,X,Description].
```

The translation of (35) is:

```
[pres,
 [perf,
   [die1,
    qterm(<t=quant,n=sing,l=ex>,A,[event,A]),
    qterm(<t=quant,n=B^C^[geq,C,3]>,E,
         [subset,E,
             qterm(<t=ref,p=dem,l=those,n=plur>,F,
                  [man_male_human,F])])]]]].
```

Example (36) is slightly different in that the noun phrase following 'of' is a noncount phrase. For this reason, its translation employs a relation part_of rather than subset:

```
[past,
  [drink1,
   qterm(<t=quant,n=sing,l=ex>,E,[event,E]),
   qterm(<t=quant,l=some>,B,[entity,B]),
   qterm(<t=quant,l=some>,C,
        [part_of,C,
            qterm(<t=ref,p=def,l=the,n=mass>,D,
                 [wine1,D])])])].
```

Compound nouns Compound nominals, like *computer message* or *education bill*, are formed by a syntactic rule that strings two Nbars together. The semantic counterpart of this rule introduces an a_form expression as an indication of an unresolved relation between the second Nbar and the kind of things denoted by the first Nbar:

```
sem(nbar_nbar_nbar_ComplexN,
    (a_form(<t=pred,p=nn>,R,
           [and,Nbar2,[R,kind(V,Nbar1),W]]),
     nbar:[arg=W,semGaps=(G,G),...]) -->
    [(Nbar1,nbar:[arg=V,...]),
     (Nbar2,nbar:[arg=W,...])]).
```

Nonclausal Nbar modification The following examples exhibit prenominal and postnominal nonclausal Nbar modification.

John discovered a hidden grave.   (37)

Three companies in Cambridge were sold to an American firm.   (38)

Prenominal modifiers can be adjectival phrases (as in *American firm*) or participle verbs (as in *hidden grave*). As an example of the kind of rule for these cases, here is the semantic rule that combines a passive participle with an Nbar:

```
sem(nbar_v_nbar_PreNom,
  ([and,Nbar,V],
    nbar:[arg=A,semGaps=Gaps,...]) -->
  [(V,v:[vform=(ing\/passive),subjval=A,
        agentval=qterm(<t=quant,l=some>,B,[entity,B])],
   (Nbar,nbar:[arg=A,semGaps=Gaps,...])]).
```

The sense of the verb argument is linked to the **arg** features of the mother and daughter Nbars. Furthermore, an existential quantification over the agent position is put in, and the senses of the Nbar and the modifier are conjoined. This gives the following translation for (37):

```
[past,
  [discover1,
    qterm(<t=quant,n=sing,l=ex>,E,[event,E]),
    john1,
    qterm(<t=quant,p=det,n=sing,l=a>,A,
          [and,
            [grave1,A],
            [hide1,
              qterm(<t=quant,n=sing,l=ex>,F,[event,F]),
              qterm(<t=quant,l=some>,B,[entity,B]),
              A]])]].
```

Nonclausal Nbar modifiers in postnominal position can be prepositional phrases, adjectival phrases, or verb phrases. Except for genitive PPs, which are handled separately, these are all taken care of by the rule:

```
sem(nbar_nbar_pred_PostNom,
    ([and,Nbar,Pred],
     nbar:[arg=A,fullGaps=Fg,semGaps=Gaps,...]) -->
    [(Nbar,nbar:[arg=A,...]),
     (Pred,pred:[agentAbove=notAbove,subjval=A,
                fullGaps=Fg,semGaps=Gaps,...])]).
```

The translation of (38), after scoping, is as follows:

```
quant(exists,A,
    [and,[firm1,A],[american1,A]],
    quant(B^C^[eq,C,3],D,
        [and,
        [company1,D],
        quant(exists,E,[state,E],
            [be,E,[in_location,D,cambridge1]])],
        [past,
        quant(exists,F,[event,F],
            quant(exists,G,[entity,G],
                [sell1,F,G,D,A]))])).
```

Nbar modification by means of genitive PPs, as in

The queen of Holland is rich.   (39)

is handled by a special rule that introduces an **a_form** expression to
indicate an unresolved genitive relation (see Section 2.3.4).

Relative clause formation   Nbar modification by means of relative
clauses is exhibited in:

John designed a house to live in.   (40)

The house that John designed was extraordinary.   (41)

Relative clauses are analyzed as sentences having a feature **arg** that is
linked to a gap inside the relative clause (see Section 5.2.2). The senses
of the Nbar and the relative clause are combined by logical conjunction
and their **arg** features are unified. For (41) this gives:

```
[past,
    [be,
    qterm(<t=quant,n=sing,l=exs>,S,[state,S])
    [extraordinary1,
        qterm(<t=ref,p=def,l=the,n=sing>,B,
            [and,
            [house_building,B],
```

```
[past,
    [design1,qterm(<...>,C,[event,C]),
        john1,B])]]])]]].
```

5.3.5   Noun Phrases

Sense entries for proper names are completely straightforward. The use of the **handle** feature is described in Section 5.3.2. The **handle** of a proper name is just a copy of the proper name sense.

Quantifier NPs are the NPs that translate into quantifier-forming **qterms**. They have feature **quantform** set to **quant**, like the determiners that they are formed with. Their **handle** feature is linked to the variable bound in the **qterm**. Wh-NP noun phrases are translated just like quantifier terms, except for the fact that they have quantifier sense **wh**.

Definite descriptions get translated into **qterms** of type **ref**. The main distinction between **qterms** of type **quant** and those of type **ref** is that the latter have a list of possible intrasentential antecedents inside. The handling of these antecedent lists is described in Section 5.2.3.

Possessive determiners like *John's* form descriptive NPs of a special kind: the **qterms** they translate into contain **a_form** expressions to indicate an underspecified relation. An example, with its translation, is:

I designed John's garden.   (42)

```
[past,
    [design1,
        qterm(<t=quant,n=sing,l=ex>,A,[event,A]),
        a_term(<t=ref,p=pro,l=i,a=[]>,B,[personal,B]),
        qterm(<t=ref,p=def,n=sing,a=[-B]>),C,
                a_form(<t=pred,p=poss>,D,
                        [and,[garden1,C],[D,john1,C]]))])].
```

Pronouns translate into **a_terms** and have their **handle** feature set to **a_index(X)**, where **X** is the variable bound in the **a_term** (see also Section 2.3.3). The translation of (42) gives an example of a pronoun translation.

The 'dummy' NPs *it* and *there* always occur in the subject position of sentences with a VP that has all its argument slots filled already. Dummy 'it' and 'there' are combined with their subject by special semantic rules that ignore the translation of the subject.

The basic treatment of gap NPs is discussed in Section 5.2.2 above. A refinement is the distinction between full gaps and "shadow" gaps. The "shadow" translation of gaps—that is, unifying the sense of the gap with the `handle` of the filler instead of the filler itself—is necessary to avoid copying the `qterms` acting as gap fillers in cases of coordination with gapping; see the discussion of (28) above.

Sentential NPs are exhibited in the following examples:

[To live in Cambridge] is nice. (43)

[For John to design a computer] is easy. (44)

The translations are different. The sentential NP in (43) is translated as a property, and niceness is predicated of this property, by means of a predicate `nice1_property`. In (44) *John* is taken to be the subject, and ease is predicated of a proposition, by means of a predicate `easy1_proposition`. The CLE assigns the same meaning to (45) as it does to (44).

```
[pres,
  [be,qterm(<t=quant,n=sing,l=exs>,S,[state,S]),
    [easy1_proposition,
      [design1,
        qterm(<t=quant,n=sing,l=ex>,E,[event,E]),
        john1,
        term(<t=sing,l=a>,C,[computer_thing,C])]]]].
```

It is easy for John to design a computer. (45)

Sentence (45) is the extraposed version of (44), and the extraposition rule inserts the sense of *for John to design a computer* in the same slot as the normal $S \rightarrow NP\ VP$ rule.

The following sentences give examples of NP coordination:

John, Mary and I bought a house. (46)

John designed a house or a garden. (47)

Every man and every woman voted. (48)

The semantic rule that leads to the distributive readings of these examples looks like this:

```
sem(np_np_conj_np,
    (term_coord(<op=Conj>,X,Np1,Np2),
     np:[handle=X,conjval=Conj,semGaps=Gaps]) -->
    [(Np1,np:[semGaps=Gaps]),
     (Conj,conj:[conjval=V,conjtype=term,...]),
     (Np2,np:[conjval=V,semGaps=Gaps])]).
```

The feature conjval is used to pass the value of a coordination operator up; this is needed for a correct analysis of commas in coordination constructions. See Section 8.4.2 for the treatment of term_coord in quantifier scoping.

Noun Phrase Determiners

Noun phrase determiners are of two kinds: determiners that form (unscoped) quantifiers and determiners that form (unscoped) definite descriptions. They are distinguished by the feature quantform, which is set to quant for quantifier determiners and to ref for descriptive determiners.

The syntax of the determiner system for English in the CLE is to a large extent based on semantic considerations. For instance, numerals are taken to belong to the determiner rather than the Nbar for semantic reasons: the numerals contribute to the cardinality predicates that are used to interpret quantifier determiners.

There is a special category for possessive determiners, such as *Mrs. Thatcher's* in the following example:

[Mrs. Thatcher's] idea was interesting.   (49)

The rule that forms the possessive determiner out of a noun phrase and a possessive morpheme introduces an a_form expression to indicate that the possessive relation is underspecified.

The use of cardinality predicates to interpret a quantifier determiner as a constraint on the cardinalities of two sets was explained in Section 2.2.3. These determiners are conjoined by ordinary logical conjunction of their cardinality predicates.

5.3.6 Prepositional Phrases

Semantically, five types of prepositional phrases are distinguished. First, there are the prepositional phrases that act as ordinary modifiers; they have semantic feature pptype set to normal. Next, there are the prepositional phrases that are subcategorized-for in the context of specific constructions, such as *to Mary* in the complement of a ditransitive verb; they have semantic feature pptype set to subcategorized. Third, there are the prepositional phrases that occur in relational noun constructions such as *the queen [of Holland]*. These have semantic feature pptype set to relational. Then, there is the special non-subcategorized use of *by* in postnominal modifiers, as in *a college by Wren*. This PP has pptype set to agent. Finally, there is the special use of *of* in measure expressions like *five pounds of butter*. This use of of has pptype set to partitive.

Prepositional phrases with pptype set to normal or agent are translated as properties of the form X^[Prep,X,Np], where Prep translates the preposition and Np the noun phrase inside. PPs with pptype set to subcategorized or relational are interpreted as noun phrases, that is, the sense of the preposition is discarded. PPs with pptype set to partitive are interpreted as Nbars.

Gap PPs are employed in the treatment of unbounded dependencies involving wh-PPs. Consider:

Where did he live?   (50)

For which company did he want to design a computer?   (51)

The translation of (50) is as follows:

```
[past,
 [and,
  [live1,
   qterm(<t=quant,n=sing,l=ex>,E,[event,E]),
   a_term(<t=ref,p=pro,l=he,n=sing>,C,
          [and,[male,C],[personal,C]])],
  [in_location,A,qterm(<t=quant,l=wh>,B,[place,B])]]].
```

The rule for wh-movement of propositional phrases is completely analogous to the one for noun phrases that was discussed in Section 5.2.2. The rule for discharging a PP gap is similar to the rule for NP gaps.

Where did he live and work?   (52)

As in the case of NPs, gaps can be interpreted either as full gaps or as shadow gaps. The second gap in (52) is interpreted as a shadow gap.

We have not discussed comparative constructions in this chapter, but a semantic analysis of comparatives in English will be presented in Chapter 13.

6 Lexical Analysis

David Carter

This chapter describes the way in which the CLE groups its input character stream into tokens and then recognizes and segments those tokens for subsequent processing. The problems addressed include:

- How should the stream of characters accepted as input be grouped into words and other tokens for subsequent analysis?

- How can words that are not explicitly defined in the lexicon, but are predictable inflectional variants of others, be processed?

- What should be done about special forms such as dates and serial numbers?

- How should the system react when it encounters a token that it cannot interpret?

Lexical analysis in the CLE consists of several phases that operate essentially in series. There is a well-defined interface between each pair of interacting phases; this facilitates both debugging and possible extensions of the system to other kinds of input such as the word or morpheme lattices that might be produced by a speech processor.

The phases are shown diagrammatically in Figure 6.1; optional ones are shown in dashed boxes. The phases can be summarized as follows:

- A sequence of characters is *read* from an input device.

- The character sequence is split into a sequence of *tokens* (Section 6.1).

- The CLE attempts to *segment* each token (Section 6.2)—that is, to analyze it as a sequence of one or more morphemes, or as a "special form" such as a date.

- If any token cannot be analyzed, a variety of *recovery procedures* (Section 6.3) are tried. These can include asking the user to retype the token or to define a new lexical entry, attempting automatic spelling correction, and attempting to construct a lexical entry automatically from an external lexical database. (Another optional recovery procedure, proper name inference, operates before segmentation, for reasons given in Section 6.3.1).

- Negotiation between segmentation and recovery continues until the process either succeeds (all tokens can be analyzed) or fails (some

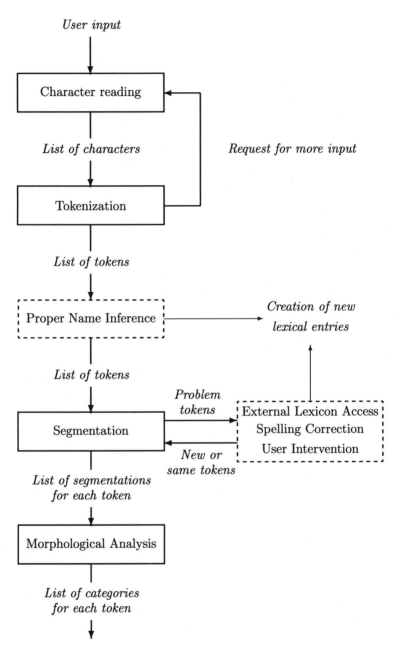

Figure 6.1
The phases of lexical processing

tokens cannot be analyzed, or the user abandons the sentence). If it succeeds, *morphological analysis* (described in Section 7.3) is carried out on each segmented token to derive a set of lexical categories for each one. These categories provide the input to the parser.

6.1   Tokenizing the Input

In the interests of simplicity and efficiency, the tokenization phase is deterministic, in the sense that it produces from a given input a unique sequence of tokens, rather than a lattice representing alternatives.

The basic rule for grouping the input character stream into tokens is that white space characters (spaces and newlines) indicate token boundaries, with additional boundaries being inserted before punctuation characters, as long as they in turn are immediately followed by white space. However, two kinds of modification to this rule are made.

First, some words are more naturally treated in the grammar as two lexical items; these include possessive forms, which are tokenized specially, and words like *nothing* and *everybody*. The latter type of words are specified in the lexicon by entries such as

```
joined_word(everybody,[every,person]).
```

which allows constructions like *everybody that you met today* to be analyzed in such a way that *every* and *person* are part of different constituents.

Second, strings in double quotes need to be made into single tokens even if they contain white space; this allows a rudimentary treatment of quotations as special forms (see below) and the definition of other special forms containing white space that, because tokenization is deterministic, could not otherwise be handled.

6.2   Segmenting the Tokens

The tokenization phase is based on knowledge only about the linguistic usage of characters and operates without reference to any higher linguistic level. Knowledge at the lexical level is brought to bear by the segmentation phase, which applies a number of strategies to analyze each token created by the tokenizer. Every strategy is applied to every token, and a list of the successful analyzes, or segmentations, is created for each token. Each segmentation later triggers the application of one kind of morphological process to derive one or more categories for the token.

Analysis of tokens that appear explicitly in the lexicon, either as root forms or as irregular morphological derivations, is straightforward; the relevant entry is accessed, and its morphological type(s) remembered. Analyses of regular and irregular explicit forms are exemplified, respectively, by:

```
seg(john,[john],lexicon)
seg(gave,[give,ed],irreg(v_v_ed_Past)).
```

In the second case, `v_v_ed_Past` is the name of the morphological rule (see Section 7.3) to be used in deriving syntactic and sense entries for the word. A lexical entry for an irregular word form follows the pattern

irreg(⟨*word*⟩,⟨*segmentation*⟩,⟨*morphology_rule*⟩).

where ⟨*segmentation*⟩ is a list consisting of the stem and affixes, for example:

```
irreg(gave,[give,ed],vp_vp_ed_Past).
```

A word may also be recognized as occurring explicitly in the grammar, though not (necessarily) in the lexicon; an example would be

```
seg(as,[as],literal).
```

Segmentation of regular morphological derivations is performed using a set of segmentation rules. These rules specify the spelling changes, such as elision and gemination, that take place for particular affixes, but they are not constrained by the category of the stem. A successful analysis of this type results in a record such as

```
seg(designed,[design,ed],regular).
```

Segmentation rules apply to either suffixes or prefixes. Suffix rules have the form suffix(⟨*added*⟩,⟨*removed*⟩,⟨*suffixes*⟩)

which says that a known word from which the characters in ⟨*removed*⟩
are deleted and the characters in ⟨*added*⟩ are appended can be analyzed
as the known word followed by ⟨*suffixes*⟩. ⟨*removed*⟩ can be an atom or
[] for the empty string. Example rules are:

```
suffix(ies,y,[s]).
suffix(ments,[],[ment,s]).
suffix(c1c1er, c1, [er]).
```

Prefix rules have the form

prefix_(⟨*added*⟩,⟨*prefixes*⟩)

for example:

```
prefix_(un,[un]).
```

In these segmentation rules, variables (written as a letter followed by a
digit) ranging over groups of letters can be used after declarations such
as:

```
letter_set_var(c1,"bdfglmnprstz").
```

The last suffix rule shown above, that covers gemination cases for *er*,
uses this variable.

In the current English-only version of the CLE, segmentation rules are
not applied recursively. This is because informal experiments indicated
that it was more efficient to list all affix combinations covered explicitly
in the set of segmentation rules. For some languages, listing affix combinations explicitly is impractical, making it preferable to apply binary
segmentation rules recursively. This has been achieved by a trivial modification to the CLE segmentation code for a version of the system that
processes Swedish.

The final possibility for token recognition is that a token is identified
as a special form. Every special form in the lexicon is defined in terms
of a regular expression that is matched against every token; a successful
match will result in one or more subparts of the token being assigned to
various fields of a structure that later, during word parsing, are checked
for validity and assembled into a complex constant for use in the logical

form. A special form also has associated with it a "prototype" pseudoword whose syntax, sense, and sortal entries in the lexicon are used for all special forms of that type.

Regular expressions were selected as the means for defining special forms because they can be specified fairly simply and applied very efficiently to tokens, while still offering sufficient flexibility to capture the basic structure of most forms that users might need to define. For example, the core lexicon contains the following entry:

```
spec_form('\([0-9]+\)\([/:]\)\([0-9]+\)\2\([0-9]+\)',
          [Day,_,Month,Year],
          date(Day,Month,Year),
          'DATE',
          date_semantics).
```

The first field of this entry is a regular expression that defines a date as a sequence of three strings of digits delimited by slashes or colons. When this expression matches a token, each of the variables Day, Month, and Year is instantiated to one of the component digit strings, which serves to instantiate fully the structure date(Day,Month,Year). This structure is handed to the Prolog predicate date_semantics, which checks that the values of day and month are legal for either American order (month/day/year) or British (day/month/year). The resulting constant (either the original date(Day,Month,Year) then represents the date in question in any resulting logical forms. The DATE field of the definition is a word "prototype" for which the core lexicon contains syntactic, sense, and sortal entries that all instances of dates inherit. This prototype has, as far as the CLE is concerned, nothing to do with the definitions of the English word *date*.

If all the tokens in the sentence can be analyzed in some way, the results are passed on to the morphology phase (Section 7.3). If some tokens are unrecognized, some or all of the recovery procedures described in the next section may be applied; if they produce results, segmentation is tried again, and otherwise, the sentence is abandoned as uninterpretable.

6.3   Recovering from Unknown Tokens

In any serious application, the CLE will often encounter tokens that it cannot analyze either as a known word or as a special form. When this occurs, a range of optional strategies is available to remedy the situation. The strategies, in the order that they are applied by the CLE, are

- *proper name inference:* where one or more capitalized unknown words occur in sequence, to assume that they form a proper name, and to infer the appropriate CLE entries.

- *external database access:* to look for the token in some large external database such as a machine-readable dictionary, and to infer a CLE entry from whatever information is found there.

- *correction:* to hypothesize that the token contains a spelling or typographical error, and to try to derive from it another, typographically similar one that can be analyzed.

- *user intervention:* to ask the user to type a replacement word, or to enter the lexical acquisition component of the system (Chapter 11) to create the relevant entries.

- *the cautious approach:* to abandon the attempt to process the current sentence.

There are advantages and disadvantages to all these actions, and which of them is appropriate will depend on characteristics of the application. User intervention requires that the system is running interactively rather than in batch mode, and that there is a user available who is competent to define the relevant words and to make whatever other additions are needed to the application back end. Correction can be performed automatically but carries with it the risk of making the wrong change, which may or may not have serious consequences. External database access, too, may lead to errors, since the database in question may not contain all the information needed to construct the required CLE entries; even if it does, the process of converting between formalisms will be far from trivial (Boguraev and Briscoe 1989); and even if the conversion is carried out correctly, the back end may also need to be extended, and the knowledge needed to do this may not be found in a general-purpose dictionary. Similar remarks apply to inferring proper names, with the added caveat that this strategy is only appropriate when the casing of the input is reliable.

Because of these risks and limitations, each of the recovery procedures
may be turned on or off using CLE commands. Nevertheless, there are
situations where they will be useful: user intervention during the development of an application, and correction, external database access,
and proper name inference in applications, perhaps in areas like machine
translation and information gathering, where it is better to risk producing an analysis that may be partly or totally erroneous than to reject a
sentence altogether, and where the task is basically linguistic in nature.

The construction of new lexical entries using the VEX subsystem is
described in Chapter 11. Here, we describe the proper name inference,
external database, and spelling correction capabilities. When switched
on, proper name inference is tried first, because when casing is reliable,
a capitalized non-sentence-initial unknown word is probably functioning
as (part of) a proper name, even if the same word is defined in the
external lexicon in some other way. Similarly, external database access
will be tried before spelling correction, because it is assumed that an
unrecognized token that happens to be an English word is more likely to
have been intentionally entered than to have been an erroneous version
of a word in the CLE's lexicon.

6.3.1   Inferring Proper Names

If the appropriate switch is set, then the CLE selects apparent unknown
proper names and asserts the relevant lexicon entries in main memory
only. This process occurs before any segmentation is attempted on a
sentence and is applied to the sentence as a whole, rather than (merely)
to individual words in it. In contrast, the other recovery strategies are
applied to each individual word on which segmentation initially fails.
This is because proper name inference results in definitions of sequences
of words selected according to their context in the sentence; the other
strategies apply only to single words and are context-independent.

The algorithm for proper name inference is:

1. If the first word in the sentence is already defined as something
   other than a proper name, make the second word the current word;
   otherwise make the first word the current word.

2. Look for a proper name sequence starting at the current word: a
   sequence of tokens each of which is either capitalized (first letter
   upper case, others lower case) or upper case (in every letter). If

this sequence is not already defined as a proper name, define it as one.

3. If a proper name sequence was found in step (2), set the current word to be the word after the end of the sequence, if any. Otherwise, set the current word to be the word after the current word, if any. If all words have been consumed, exit; otherwise go to step (2).

Step (1) ensures that in a sentence like *Has Fred Bloggs arrived?*, the phrase *Fred Bloggs*, and not *Has Fred Bloggs*, is defined as a proper name. Steps (2) and (3) ensure that maximal strings of suitable words are defined as proper names, since when two proper names occur in sequence, they almost always function as a single, multiword proper name; an exception would be something like *The receptionist told Mary Fred had arrived.*

It is worth noting that proper name inference can succeed even when every word in a sequence is known to the CLE, as long as the sequence itself is not defined as a name.

6.3.2   Using an External Lexicon

An interface procedure (Section 10.3) is provided by the CLE, which, if defined, will be handed an unrecognized token and expected to succeed if and only if it manages somehow to create lexical entries that will allow the token to be recognized. A suite of code has been written that defines this predicate to access the MRC psycholinguistic database (Coltheart 1981) and create entries on the basis of what it finds there. Although this code is not part of the CLE, we discuss its design here to illustrate the issues involved in interfacing to other external lexicons.

The MRC database contains a range of information about some 75,000 distinct words, excluding those that are marked as derivational variants of others. None of this information is semantic, and the only syntactic information is parts of speech. This means that the process of guessing CLE entries is inevitably of limited accuracy and specificity. Nevertheless, a useful set of deductions can often be made. For example, proper names are distinguished from other nouns by being marked in the database as capitalized; and a large majority of names in the language are those of either people or places. Most of the common exceptions, such as day and month names, are already in the core lexicon. Thus when a name is retrieved, it is assigned a sortal restriction (see Chapter 9) of physical object. (The same applies to predicates constructed by the proper name inference strategy).

Although the MRC database contains many derivational variants, the CLE does not attempt to construct entries from these if it can avoid doing so; instead, it computes the set of possible root forms for a token and queries the database for these. This means that the CLE can apply its own morphological knowledge to such words, and also that occurrences of different inflections of the same root should map onto the same (automatically generated) predicate name.

This whole process is open to the objection that the predicates produced are worthless because they are uninterpreted. Although in some applications this is the case, in others it will not be. For example, in a machine translation application, the external database could be some existing bilingual lexicon. From such a lexicon one could generate not only English entries for analysis but also target language entries for the equivalent word(s) or phrase(s), and also define a mapping between the two. Also, even in applications where the predicates generated are not associated with any other knowledge, they can still serve as hooks for some kinds of inference and intelligent retrieval. Given the input *The management described the union's demand as outrageous*, questions such as *What did the management say about the union?* and *Who thought that something was outrageous?* could be answered without any prior knowledge of the meanings of *management, union, demand*, or *outrageous*.

Another possible drawback of using an external lexicon is that the entries created are likely to be very general, both syntactically and semantically, and hence may give rise to a large number of readings. Selecting the correct one may be difficult, especially since each will contain uninterpreted predicates.

6.3.3 Spelling Correction

The spelling corrector used by the CLE is fairly simpleminded. Given an unrecognized token, it derives from it a set of possible corrections involving one or (if necessary) two letter insertions, deletions, transpositions, or substitutions. These corrections are found by applying the token in a "sloppy" manner to a discrimination net constructed from the words in the currently loaded lexicon, taking account of morphological inflections. Each possible correction is handed to the segmenter and rejected if segmentation fails. Spelling correction is deemed to have succeeded if and only if exactly one candidate survives this process.

Experience with the spelling corrector suggests that it almost never produces incorrect results. This is due largely to its cautious strategy of only considering the possibility of one or two errors in a token, and of giving up when more than one possible correction can be segmented. The same characteristics mean, however, that the correction process will sometimes fail to produce any result even when the intended word is recognizable by the CLE, especially when the error is one of spelling rather than typing.

More recently, spelling correction has been made context-dependent. The system will, optionally, attempt to parse and interpret a lattice containing the various correction possibilities, and discard those that do not allow a complete interpretation before the user is queried. If only one possibility remains then, again optionally, recovery will be fully automatic and the user will not be queried at all. Because of the way sentence analyses are packed (Section 7.4), a sentence containing alternative corrections for several unrecognized tokens can be parsed relatively quickly. Initial observation suggests that the procedure often results in a major reduction in the number of candidate corrections a user needs to consider.

7 Syntactic and Semantic Processing

Robert C. Moore and Hiyan Alshawi

This chapter describes the syntactic and semantic processing performed by three components of the CLE: the morphological analyzer, the parser, and the semantic analysis component. The later processing stages of sortal filtering, quantifier scoping and reference resolution are discussed in separate chapters. In some respects, morphological processing in the CLE is the word-level counterpart of sentence parsing and semantic analysis so these two are discussed first.

7.1 Parsing

7.1.1 The Basic Parsing Algorithm

The parser in the CLE uses a "left corner" parsing strategy with top-down filtering (Rosenkrantz and Lewis 1970, Aho and Ullman 1972). This is primarily a bottom-up strategy, but it does a limited amount of top-down processing in order to use the left context to decide whether a particular constituent could occur at a given position in the input. The idea is that, having parsed a constituent bottom-up, the system selects a syntax rule (Section 3.9) in which that constituent could be the leftmost daughter, and it postulates that this rule provides the analysis of the immediately following input, predicting the remaining daughters in the rule top-down. In parsing the next segment of the input, it considers only analyses that are consistent with the selected rule, by checking that each constituent it builds bottom-up could be a "left corner" of the next daughter needed to satisfy the rule. (For our purposes, a left corner of a constituent is either the constituent itself or a left corner of the constituent's leftmost daughter.)

The motivation for using this algorithm is that it seems to be the simplest parsing method that avoids the major problems of pure top-down or pure bottom-up search schemes. Pure top-down parsing has the problem that left-recursive rules (e.g., nbar → nbar rel) lead to infinite recursion. Pure bottom-up parsing has the disadvantage, in a formalism such as ours that permits empty categories (gaps), that every possible empty category has to be proposed at each point in the input string, since the parser cannot tell from the input string where gaps exist.

A left-corner parser avoids the left-recursion problem because it is fundamentally bottom-up, and it can be made to solve the gap-proliferation problem by using the top-down filtering to make sure that gaps are proposed only in places where they can actually occur. In the grammar presented in Chapter 4, the gap-threading mechanism ensures that, whenever a constituent proposed top-down cannot have a gap as its left corner, it will have a feature, `gapsSoughtIn`, set to the empty list, but every empty category will have its `gapsSoughtIn` feature set to a list whose first element is that category, e.g., `np:[gapsSoughtIn=[np:[]|X]]`. The top-down check, that the constituent proposed bottom-up is a possible left corner of the constituent proposed top-down, will fail unless the `gapsSoughtIn` feature of the first is unifiable with the `gapsSoughtIn` feature of the second (another consequence of the gap-threading mechanism). Hence, an empty category will never be proposed as the left corner of a constituent that cannot start with, or be, a gap.

The basic parsing algorithm is embodied in the nondeterministic procedure presented in Figure 7.1. Since several rules can be selected at any one time, representing hypotheses about the analysis of the sentence at several different levels, the parser must maintain a stack in which each frame records, for a selected rule, the mother category of the rule, the daughters found so far, and the remaining daughters needed to satisfy the rule. The CLE's implementation of the algorithm handles the non-determinism by Prolog backtracking and explores all possible analysis paths. As is discussed in Section 7.4.3, the parser creates "constituent" and "analysis" records in the Prolog database for all the constituents it successfully analyzes, instead of building explicit parse trees. Parse trees can easily be reconstructed from these records but in practice this is unnecessary, because later stages of processing simply operate directly on these records.

An Example   The basic parsing algorithm can be illustrated, bringing out the role of top-down filtering, by looking at how *John likes Mary* might be parsed with a simple context-free grammar containing the rules

```
sigma → s
s → np vp
np → det n
vp → v np
```

Start. To initialize the parser:

- let the mother category be the start symbol **sigma**, let the list of daughters found be the empty list, and let the list of daughters needed be the right-hand side of a **sigma** derivation,
- apply Shift or Create Gap.

Shift. If the list of daughters needed is not empty:

- remove the next lexical item from the input,
- find a possible category C of the item, and form a constituent of category C analyzed as the lexical item,
- apply Predict or Match based on C.

Create Gap. If there can be an empty constituent of category C, and C can be a left corner of the first category in the list of daughters needed:

- form a constituent of category C analyzed as a gap,
- apply Predict or Match based on C.

Reduce. If the list of daughters needed is empty and C is the mother category:

- form a constituent of category C analyzed as the list of daughters that have been found,
- if the stack is not empty, pop the previous mother category, list of daughters found, and list of daughters needed from the stack, and apply Predict or Match based on C,
- if the stack is empty and there is no remaining input, then C is the topmost constituent of a complete parse of the sentence.

Predict. If a constituent of category C_1 has just been found, and there is a rule $C_0 \rightarrow C_1 \ldots C_n$ such that C_0 can be a left corner of the first category in the list of daughters needed:

- push the mother category, the list of daughters found, and the list of daughters needed onto the stack,
- let C_0 be the mother category, let the list of daughters found contain C_1, and let the list of daughters needed contain $C_2 \ldots C_n$,
- apply Reduce, Shift, or Create Gap.

Match. If a constituent of category C has just been found, and C is the first category in the list of daughters needed:

- move C from the list of daughters needed to the list of daughters that have been found,
- apply Reduce, Shift, or Create Gap.

Figure 7.1
Left-corner parsing algorithm

Step	Constituent Found	Mother Category	D'ghters Found	D'ghters Needed	Stack
Shift	[np [john]]	sigma	[]	[s]	—
Predict	—	s	[np]	[vp]	(sigma,[],[s])
Shift	[n [likes]]	s	[np]	[vp]	(sigma,[],[s])
Shift	[v [likes]]	s	[np]	[vp]	(sigma,[],[s])
Predict	—	vp	[v]	[np]	(s,[np],[vp]) (sigma,[],[s])
Shift	[np [mary]]	vp	[v]	[np]	(s,[np],[vp]) (sigma,[],[s])
Match	—	vp	[v np]	[]	(s,[np],[vp]) (sigma,[],[s])
Reduce	[vp [v np]]	s	[np]	[vp]	(sigma,[],[s])
Match	—	s	[np vp]	[]	(sigma,[],[s])
Reduce	[s [np vp]]	sigma	[]	[s]	—
Match	—	sigma	[s]	[]	—
Reduce	[sigma [s]]	—	—	—	—

Figure 7.2
Parsing *John likes Mary*

with *John* and *Mary* entered into the lexicon as nps, and *likes* entered both as an n (as in *his likes and dislikes*) and as a v. sigma is the distinguished 'accept' category. Figure 7.2 summarizes the trace of the parser analyzing this sentence.

The parser starts with sigma as the mother category, the empty list as the list of daughters found, and s as the only thing on the list of daughters needed. The parser next does a shift, removing *John* from the input and finding that it is an np. It then tries to execute a prediction step, looking for a rule that has np as the leftmost daughter category and whose mother category can be a left corner of an s. The rule s → np vp is such a rule, so the previous mother category and daughter lists are saved on the stack, the mother category is set to be s, the list of daughters found is set to contain np, and the list of daughters needed is set to contain vp.

The parser then shifts again, removing *likes* from the input. At this point it can choose either n or v as the category of *likes*. If the parser chooses n, it will not find any suitable rule in the predict step—because an n cannot be a left corner of a vp—nor can it match, so it has to backtrack and choose v as the category of *likes*. It can then select the rule **vp** → **v np**, saving the previous mother category and daughter lists on the stack and setting the mother category to be **vp**, the list of daughters found to contain **v**, and the list of daughters needed to contain **np**.

The parser shifts again, removing *Mary* from the input and finding that it has the category **np**. The parser can then match the **np** constituent just created with the first (and only) item on the list of daughters needed, so **np** is moved from this list to the list of daughters found. The list of daughters needed is now empty, so the parser can reduce, creating a **vp** constituent analyzed as **v np** and restoring the previous mother category and daughter lists. The same sequence of matching and reducing is repeated twice more, with the **vp** constituent matching the **vp** needed to complete the **s**, and the **s** constituent matching the **s** needed to complete the **sigma**. At this point the stack is empty and there is no more input, so the parse is complete.

7.1.2   Elaborations of the Basic Algorithm

An important feature of our parser, compared with standard context-free parsers, is that categories can be arbitrary Prolog terms rather than simply atoms. In the basic algorithm described above, all that is required to handle this is to use unification where a standard context-free parser would check for identity.

The major modification to the basic algorithm made by our parser is to use records of constituents found in the course of parsing as a "well-formed substring table", to avoid reanalysis of already parsed constituents after backtracking. This is more complicated in a left-corner parser than in either a pure top-down or pure bottom-up parser, because of the effect of top-down constraints on bottom-up parsing. In our parser, the first time a given category is predicted top-down starting at a particular point in the input, a record is stored in the Prolog database indicating that this has occurred. Then, whenever any category is predicted top-down, the database can be checked to see whether a constituent of that category (or a more general category) has previously been predicted at that point in the input. If it has, then any constituent of the predicted category that can be parsed at that point would already be recorded in the database. Thus, no bottom-up parsing needs to be performed, and the database is simply checked for records of constituents of the predicted category.

If there have been no previous attempts to parse a constituent of the
predicted category at a given point in the input, then bottom-up parsing
has to be tried. As a result of previous attempts to predict a different
category, some constituents may have been found that would contribute
to an analysis of the predicted category, but they may not include all
relevant constituents because of differing top-down constraints. Our
approach is to treat all the previously parsed constituents as if they
are "shifted" from the input string, as alternatives to the lexical items
they span, in attempting to build an analysis of the predicted category
bottom-up. If in the course of a parse a constituent is produced for a
category that already has a constituent in the database, that parse can
be aborted because the same parse would be found when the previous
constituent is retrieved. An alternative approach would be to ignore
the previously found constituents when parsing bottom-up and simply
reparse everything. However, this would lose the benefits of packing
(Sections 1.2, 7.4), since we would be separately pursuing equivalent
parses based on constituents that have different analyses but the same
category.

Another modification of the parsing algorithm that improved performance was the addition of a test that there is sufficient input remaining
to satisfy parsing predictions. This test is used to cut off parsing paths
in which the number of nonempty daughter categories still to be found
exceeds the number of remaining words in the input. Although this test
only comes into operation for the last few words of input, the increase
in parsing paths towards the end of a sentence (for purely syntactic
parsing) means that the test is effective even for longer sentences.

7.1.3 Grammar Compilation

The set of syntactic rules is preprocessed in order to compute a "reachability" relation which states that one constituent can be a left corner
of another constituent. This relation is a similar to Aho and Ullman's
(1977, 186–189) FIRST sets, but our relation holds between a pair of
grammatical categories rather than between a category and a lexical
item. The reachability relation is composed with the rules to produce
two relations that form the actual tables used, respectively, by the 'predict' and 'create gap' steps of the parser:

rule($\langle index \rangle$, $\langle found \rangle$, $\langle goal \rangle$, $\langle mother \rangle$, $\langle needed \rangle$, $\langle rule\_id \rangle$)
gap($\langle goal \rangle$, $\langle empty\_cat \rangle$, $\langle rule\_id \rangle$)

where $\langle goal \rangle$ is the category being sought just before application of the rule, $\langle index \rangle$ is a symbol used to improve efficiency of access to the table, $\langle rule\_id \rangle$ is an identifier used to tie semantic rules to syntax rules, and the other arguments are as described in Section 7.1.1 above.

Two points concern the compilation of the reachability relation. Ideally, this relation would be computed simply by generating the reflexive transitive closure of the set of ordered pairs (C_1, C_2) such that there is a rule of the form $C_1 \rightarrow C_2 \ldots C_n$, taking into account the effects of unification. The need for this last qualification, however, leads to the possibility of an infinite list of (C_1, C_2) pairs being generated. Since categories can be arbitrarily complex terms, the effects of unification in a left-recursive derivation in the grammar can lead to an infinite number of entries in the rule tables if the rules manipulate features in certain ways. For example, a rule such as

```
syn(cat1_cat1_cat2,
    cat1:[feature1=X] -->
    [cat1:[feature1=f(X)],cat2:[]])
```

would result in an infinite number of pairs in the reachability relation:

```
(cat1:[feature1=X], cat1:[feature1=f(X)])
(cat1:[feature1=X], cat1:[feature1=f(f(X))])
(cat1:[feature1=X], cat1:[feature1=f(f(f(X)))])
    ...
```

To avoid the possibility of generating an infinite reachability relation, we impose a cutoff after two nested occurrences of the same functor in a feature specification, substituting new unique variables for the arguments of the inner occurrence of the functor, so that any constituent with a more complex feature description will be accepted. In the example presented, the reachability relation would contain only the following two entries:

```
(cat1:[feature1=X], cat1:[feature1=f(X)])
(cat1:[feature1=X], cat1:[feature1=f(f(Y))]).
```

The second entry would subsume all of the additional entries that would have been generated without the cutoff, so that no parses will be missed.

It is possible that the left-corner check carried out by the parser will be more generous than necessary as a result of the cutoff, but this will not lead to spurious parses, because the left-corner check affects only the efficiency of the parser and not its correctness.

The second point about the reachability relation is that often features on the leftmost daughter in a rule are used to control what constituents can follow that daughter, rather than to restrict what that daughter itself can be. In that case, there may be multiple rules covering all possible values for a feature on the leftmost daughter, which will in turn result in multiple entries in the reachability relation, although a single entry giving the feature a variable value would do just as well. This can cause a substantial increase in the size of the rule tables and significantly slow down parsing. Since this situation would be extremely difficult for the system to recognize automatically, we give the grammar writer the facility to make declarations of the form

   not_filtered_on(⟨feature⟩)

which ensures that the constraints imposed by the feature in question are ignored when the reachability table is computed.

Another parser based on Prolog unification and a bottom-up strategy is the BUP system (Matsumoto et al. 1983). Our parser is an extension of this in that its top-down filtering uses feature values as well as major categories, and its well-formed substring table construction is sound since it is based on subsumption checking.

7.2   Semantic Analysis

The process of applying semantic analysis rules to produce QLFs is much simpler than parsing. The system merely traces the syntactic analyses down from the start symbol **sigma** to look up the word senses of all the lexical items and apply the semantic rules to all the complex constituents that appear in complete sentence analyses. This phase of processing puts into the database "semantic constituent" and "semantic analysis" records, as described in Section 7.4.3, which encode a packed representation of the QLFs for the sentence.

To process a constituent, the system finds a syntactic analysis for the constituent in the database and recursively computes a semantic analysis (QLF) for all the daughter constituents in that analysis. It then looks for a semantic rule (Section 3.10) that corresponds to the syntax rule for the analysis and is compatible with the semantic analyses of the daughter constituents; the identifiers for the syntactic and semantic rules must be the same and the categories built recursively must unify with those in the semantic rule. If there is such a semantic rule, the mother category and its QLF are extracted from the rule and added to the database as a semantic constituent record and a semantic analysis record. The system generates all possible semantic analyses of the constituent by backtracking. In addition to applying semantic rules to a constituent, the system may also use the QLFs from any applicable phrasal sense entries.

One important point about this procedure is that, in processing a constituent, the system produces semantic analyses of the constituent's most general variant compatible with a syntactic analysis of the constituent, without applying any top-down constraints that might be encoded in the features of the constituent being processed. In some cases, this results in superfluous semantic analyses being generated for the constituent, but these never get incorporated into semantic analyses for the complete sentence. There are overriding advantages that outweigh the possibility of doing extra work of this sort, however. One advantage is that we are guaranteed that each syntactic analysis record need be processed only once and then it can be removed from the database to prevent it being reprocessed in case the same constituent is encountered again, for example, as a result of an attachment ambiguity.

A second advantage is that we cut down on the number of different semantic analysis records we would otherwise produce because of our technique of unifying one logical form into an argument position of another. With a rule like

```
sem(s_np_vp,
    (Vp,s:[]) -->
    [(Np,np:[]), (Vp,vp:[subjval=Np])])
```

taking the constraint subjval=Np into account when we interpret the vp would produce distinct semantic analysis records for the vp for each semantic constituent record for the np. By processing the vp before top-down constraints are applied, we avoid multiplying the number of vp semantic analysis records by the number of np semantic constituent records. Each vp record produced has a variable for its subject argument

that is unified with a particular np QLF when different QLFs for the
sentence are being constructed for later stages of processing.

7.3 Morphological Processing

Lexical Analysis Subphases

Lexical processing in the CLE takes place in three subphases, the last
two of which we refer to as morphological processing:

- orthography (tokenizing and segmentation)
- word parsing
- sense derivation

The first subphase, described in detail in Chapter 6, operates on the
string of input characters taking into account the segmentation rules
for regular affixes (Section 3.9), punctuation marks, definitions of special forms such as dates and serial numbers, proper name identification,
and spelling correction. The result is a set of possible segmentations
for each token (roughly speaking, a word) identified in the input. Each
segmentation specifies a list of subword components but without associated syntactic or semantic features, so a word like *covers* is segmented
into [cover,es] without regard to whether this corresponds to plural
formation or the third person singular verb inflection.

The category and feature information is computed by the next two
subphases, which apply context free (or more general) rules that are
similar to the syntax rules and semantic analysis rules applied at the
sentence level. Nevertheless morphological analysis in the CLE is reasonably efficient; it represents only a small fraction of the time taken by
morpho-syntactic processing. Our approach also has the advantage that
relatively transparent rules are used, which do not need compilation into
large finite state transducers (cf. Koskenniemi 1984).

7.3.1 Word Parsing

Word parsing applies word structure rules to the segmentation of a morphologically complex word, giving an analysis tree that is similar in kind
to the syntax tree for a sentence. The root node of this tree gives the
syntactic category to be used by the sentence parser. For example, the
word structure tree produced for *designers* is:

```
word(nbar_nbar_es,
    nbar:[agreement=plur, lexform=L ...]
    [word(nbar_vp_er_Agentive,
        nbar:[agreement=sing, lexform=L ...]
        [stem(design,vp:[lexform=L ...]),
        affix(er)]
    affix(es)]).
```

This says that the word *designers* is analyzed as applying morphology rules for agentive *er* (nbar_vp_er_Agentive) and for the plural morpheme (nbar_nbar_es) to the verb stem *design*. Morphological rules (Section 3.9) typically constrain some feature values of the word to be the same as those on the stem (e.g., lexform above) while other feature values (e.g., **agreement** above) are altered to capture the relevant inflection.

The parsing procedure used to apply morphology rules is a simple nondeterministic left corner parser. Because the number of possibilities that are explored during word parsing is small, this parser does not incorporate the techniques of top-down prediction and packing that are used to improve the efficiency of the sentence parser.

Before passing the categories generated for a word to the parser, a subsumption check is used to remove duplicated or subsumed categories. These arise, for example, when different stem categories corresponding to different subcategorizations of a verb like *teach* (it can take one or two noun phrases, or a *that* complement) result in the same syntactic category for the nominalization *teacher*. However, the word-analysis trees corresponding to these alternative derivations of *teacher* are all retained, since they can give rise to different senses during semantic analysis.

Morphological rules are also applied according to irregular form lexical entries (Section 3.11) such as:

```
irreg(went,[go,ed],vp_vp_ed_Past).
```

This results in word-analysis trees having the same format as those produced for regular inflections, so that sense derivation does not need to distinguish between regular and irregular cases.

7.3.2   Sense Derivation

Sense derivation is not applied immediately after word parsing in order
to avoid deriving senses from morphological analyses that are ruled out
by syntactic constraints during sentence parsing. Instead, sense derivation is applied as needed during the semantic analysis phase when a
QLF needs to be derived for a syntax tree leaf node that corresponds to
a morphologically complex word. The category on this syntax tree node
is used to constrain the extraction of word-analysis trees to which sense
derivation is then applied.

Sense derivation rules (Section 3.10) are similar in format to semantic
rules and they are applied similarly, except that the process is simpler
since no packed structures are involved. Thus the rule identifier in a
word-analysis node is used to select one or more sense derivation rules
that are applied to word sense entries for the stem or to intermediate
derived senses. Applying the rule corresponding to the top node of the
word-analysis tree results in the derivation, by unification, of a QLF
and a (semantic) category for the word. These are then used to continue the semantic translation of the sentence syntax tree in the normal
way. For example, the application of a suitable sense derivation rule
corresponding to the morphological rule `nbar_vp_er_Agentive` would
result in deriving the following category and logical form for *designer*
(the rule actually used by the CLE gives a different logical form):

word:	`design`	`designer`
category:	`vp:[subj=A,obj=O]`	`nbar:[arg=A]`
QLF:	`[design,A,O]`	`[design,A,`
		`qterm(...,O,[entity,O])]`

Although the example above is a case of derivational morphology,
most of the morphology and sense derivation rules for English used by
the CLE are concerned with inflectional morphology such as those for
the past tense, plural, and superlative morphemes. This is because of
the problems inherent in derivational morphology rules: they are often
nonproductive (e.g., *prettify* is acceptable but not *sillify*), and they can
involve complex semantics (e.g., possibility in the case of *breakable* and
causality in the case of *beautify*).

There can be lexicalized senses for morphologically complex words,
and these are used as additional alternatives to the derived senses. This

can be regarded as a special case of the CLE treatment of lexicalized phrases, whereby sequences of words can be given a sense entry consisting of a category and a QLF (Section 3.11). If such an entry is present for a phrase that has been analyzed as a syntactic constituent of the appropriate category, then the QLF is used as an alternative to those produced by the compositional semantic analysis of the constituent.

7.4 Ambiguities and Packing

7.4.1 Representing Local Ambiguities

When there are multiple analyses of a natural language sentence, they often have a large proportion of their structure in common. This happens because ambiguities are frequently localized to one part of a sentence. At the syntactic level, examples of this are prepositional phrase attachment and the internal structure of compound nominals, and at the semantic level, word sense ambiguity and, again, prepositional phrase modification.

It is possible simply to ignore the locality of these types of ambiguities and generate all the possible analyses as separate structures. However, the combinatorics involved can lead to an unacceptably large number of structures. It can also lead to duplication of the same work several times over, such as semantic processing of the syntactic analysis of a prepositional phrase being repeated for each of its various attachment possibilities. Alternatively, a natural language processing system could recognize each of the construction types that give rise to such ambiguities and produce special representations indicating multiple senses, attachment possibilities, and the like. Rather than follow either of these courses, we have adopted a systematic approach to the representation of alternative structures for local ambiguities. This treatment is based on the use of packed structures mentioned in Chapter 1. As explained there, the packing technique was a significant factor in our choice of a staged architecture for the CLE.

7.4.2 A Structure Sharing Method

Packing is a particular type of structure sharing appropriate to representing local ambiguities. For example, in the sentence *Two liter bottles of wine were delivered to a customer from France*, there are two local ambiguities: there could have been two one-liter bottles or several two-liter bottles, and the customer may have been from France or the wine may have been delivered from France. Thus four different structures for the entire sentence would be created by a conventional chart parser. Using packing, however, only one sentence-level structure is created, with two subanalyses for the subject and two for the predicate.

Although packing was suggested to us by Tomita's work, the technique is implicit in standard polynomial-time context free parsing algorithms such as Earley's algorithm and the CKY algorithm. (Our use of the term "packing" subsumes the techniques called "packing" and "subtree sharing" by Tomita 1985.) We have generalized it, however, so that it can be used with categories represented by arbitrary term structures including variables, rather than just atomic symbols, and we have applied it in semantic as well as syntactic analysis.

Packing can be implemented for a context-free grammar simply by indexing each subtree by the segment of the input it covers and its atomic mother category and replacing each occurrence of an indexed subtree by its index. This not only means that each subtree need be represented only once, but also that equivalent subtrees (those with the same index) can be treated as identical for purposes of generating larger structures, so that fewer of those structures need to be built. The situation we face is more complicated than this because our categories can be general Prolog terms with variables. This means that when we generate complete structures from the indexed subtrees we have to perform unifications to check that all constraints on the variables are compatible, and it also means that to keep the representation as compact as possible we must make sure that when two subtrees cover the same segment of the input and the category of one subsumes the category of the other, only the most general one is retained.

7.4.3   CLE Packed Structures

Each analysis of a constituent can be thought of as having three components: the segment of input text spanned by the constituent, a category, and an internal structure. This applies to both syntactic and semantic analyses; in syntax, the internal structure is a list of daughters and, in semantics, it is a QLF. The basis of the packed representation is that we can abstract away from alternative internal structures of constituents that have the same category. This is possible because the application of our syntactic and semantic rules depends on only the categories of constituents and not their internal structure.

Syntactic analysis records   A local ambiguity creates multiple analyses for the same segment of text. Thus the prepositional phrase attachment ambiguity in the sentence *Wren designed the library in Trinity* yields two analyses for the verb phrase following *Wren*. Simplified phrase structure trees for the sentence might be the following:

```
[s,s_np_vp,
  [[np,Wren],
   [vp,vp_v_np,
      [[v,designed]
       [np,np_np_pp,
          [[np,np_det_n,[[det,the],[n,library]]],
           [pp,pp_p_np,[[p,in],[np,Trinity]]]]]]]]]]
[s,s_np_vp,
  [[np,Wren],
   [vp,vp_vp_pp,
      [[vp,vp_v_np,
          [[v,designed],
           [np,np_det_n,[[det,the],[n,library]]]]],
       [pp,pp_p_np,[[p,in],[np,Trinity]]]]]]]].
```

Instead of building explicit trees such as these during parsing, the CLE parser maintains two types of records. "Constituent" records state that a particular segment of input has been analyzed as a particular category. These records are of the form

con($\langle from \rangle$, $\langle syntactic\_category \rangle$, $\langle to \rangle$)

where $\langle syntactic\text{-}category \rangle$ is the category of the constituent in internal format (Section 3.7), and $\langle from \rangle$ and $\langle to \rangle$ are numbers indicating where in the input sentence the constituent begins and ends. "Analysis" records give possible local syntactic structures of such constituents. These records are of the form

ana($\langle rule\text{-}identifier \rangle$, $\langle mother \rangle$, [$\langle daughter_1 \rangle$, ..., $\langle daughter_n \rangle$])

where the $\langle mother \rangle$ and each of the $\langle daughter \rangle$ items are of the same form as constituent records, and $\langle rule\text{-}identifier \rangle$ comes from the syntax rule that caused the analysis record to be built.

In the example above, assuming the positions in the input sentence are numbered as follows:

```
wren designed the library in trinity
 0   1        2   3       4  5      6
```

the constituent record for the whole sentence would be con(0,s,6) and the single analysis record for the sentence would be:

ana(s_np_vp,con(0,s,6),[con(0,np,1),con(1,vp,6)]).

The point is that, at a given level, only the constituent records play a role in building analysis records at the next level, so regardless of how many different analyses there are of *designed the library in Trinity* as a vp, they do not lead to multiple analysis records being built for the whole sentence as an s. In this example, there would be two analysis records for the vp:

ana(vp_vp_np,con(1,vp,6),[con(1,v,2),con(2,np,6)])

ana(vp_vp_pp,con(1,vp,6),[con(1,vp,4),con(4,pp,6)]).

Since they contain the same mother constituent item, they have the same corresponding constituent record.

Semantic analysis records The CLE also builds packed semantic structures using two additional record types, "semantic constituent" records, which are of the form

sem_con(⟨*index*⟩,con(⟨*from*⟩,⟨*category*⟩,⟨*to*⟩))

and "semantic analysis" records, which are of the form:

sem_ana(⟨*index*⟩,con(⟨*from*⟩,⟨*category*⟩,⟨*to*⟩),⟨*QLF*⟩).

Categories in semantic constituent and analysis records differ from those in the syntactic records in that the values of semantic features can be instantiated (a difference not exhibited by the atomic categories we are using in this example). Semantic analysis records have a QLF expression for the constituent instead of the list of daughter constituents present in syntactic analysis records. In this QLF, constituent records occurring in the place of normal QLF subexpressions stand for (possible) QLFs for the constituents. In our example sentence, a simple semantic rule (see Section 3.10), which applies the QLF of the verb phrase to that of the noun phrase

```
sem(s_np_vp,
    ([apply,Vp,Np],s) --> [(Np,np), (Vp,vp)])
```
would produce the semantic analysis record:

```
sem_ana(0_6,
        con(0,s,6),
        [apply,con(1,vp,6),con(0,np,1)]).
```

In the semantic rule, the QLF for the verb phrase is represented by the variable Vp without regard for its internal structure. The alternative semantic analyses of the verb phrase (predicate) would be expressed with multiple semantic analysis records.

In early versions of the CLE, sortal information (Chapter 9) was associated directly with each semantic constituent in the packed representation with the aim of ruling out spurious interpretations as early as possible. However, it turned out to be more efficient, on average, to apply sorts to QLFs after extracting them from the packed structure. This was because as sort expressions became larger and more refined the overhead of maintaining sorted packed semantic records increased, especially since differences between word sense sorts often prevented the packing of local semantic alternatives. The modularity gained from separating sorts from the semantic analysis phase also reduced compilation dependencies and improved analysis failure reporting.

Non-atomic categories So far we have shown how packing works in the case of atomic categories. In order to handle the more general case of CLE categories that contain arbitrary terms as feature values, more complex management of the records implementing packing is necessary. In the general case, in order to check that two or more analysis records can be 'packed' under a single constituent record, it is no longer sufficient to test that their mother categories are identical. Instead, we must check whether the category in the constituent record subsumes the mother categories in each of the analysis records in question. Thus we might have assertions with the following information (for readability, categories are shown in ⟨feature⟩=⟨value⟩ format rather than the actual internal format):

```
con(7,np:[f1=X,f2=r],10)
ana(np_det_nbar,con(7,np:[f1=X,f2=r],10),...)
ana(np_det_nbar,con(7,np:[f1=a,f2=r],10),...).
```

Table 7.1
Syntax structure packing for *Wren built a chapel (in a college)^n*

prep phrases	parses	explicit nodes	packed nodes
0	1	10	10
1	2	33	21
2	5	116	38
3	14	414	62
4	42	1481	94
5	132	5306	135
6	429	19043	186

There may, in addition, be other analyses for the same segment of text,

```
con(7,np:[f1=a,f2=Y],10)
ana(np_det_nbar,con(7,np:[f1=a,f2=Y],10),...)
```

where the categories in the constituent records are unifiable, but neither
subsumes the other, so packing does not occur. The CLE ensures that
the constituent and analysis records are maintained in their most general form. This is done by not asserting records that are subsumed by
existing ones and by removing records that are subsumed by newly created ones. Unification is then used at the later stage of selecting records
for constructing complete syntactic or semantic analyses for a sentence.

Analysis trees   Table 7.1 compares the number of nodes that would
be required to represent separately all parse trees of a set of sentences
with the number of nodes required by the packing scheme. The numbers
shown are for the syntactic analyses produced by an early version of the
CLE grammar for the phrase *Wren built a chapel* followed by zero to
six occurrences of the prepositional phrase *in a college*. This illustrates
that, as ambiguity increases, the number of records used by the packed
representation grows much more slowly than the number of nodes needed
to represent explicit syntax trees.

Syntax trees can be recovered easily from the packed representation,
but in fact such trees are not required by the semantic analysis phase
that operates directly on the packed analysis records, producing packed
semantic records. A QLF for the whole sentence can be recovered by
starting with the QLF for a semantic analysis record spanning the sentence and recursively replacing each occurrence of a constituent term

in that expression with a QLF corresponding to the relevant subconstituent.

7.4.4 Parallel Parsing

Our use of the structure sharing technique discussed above is mainly motivated by the need for increasing the efficiency of sentence analysis, and in particular parsing. (The factoring of ambiguities provided by packing may also prove useful in interactive applications involving cooperative disambiguation, but that is another matter.) It is therefore reasonable to ask whether we could use parallel processing as an alternative route to improving efficiency.

The efficiency question arises from the potentially large number of paths that need to be explored during parsing; packing effectively merges some of these paths together. However, our basic parsing algorithm is purely nondeterministic in the sense that the alternative parsing paths can be explored independently. When the basic algorithm described in Section 7.1.1 is coded in Prolog, this nondeterminism corresponds directly to choices between different clauses of the parser, parsing table, and lexicon during parsing. It was thus possible to carry out an experiment in which this algorithm was run using a nondeterministic OR-parallelism model for executing Horn clauses.

This experiment, the particular execution model used, and results of timing tests are presented in Alshawi and Moran (1988). Briefly, this involved executing the basic parsing algorithm on a set of nonshared memory computers that would independently explore different parts of the search space. Load balancing was carried out by dynamic redistribution of possible continuations of parsing paths by communicating numerical encodings of the choice points corresponding to particular paths. This method had the advantage that the original algorithm could be used without reprogramming. With the hardware available at the time of the experiment, Alshawi and Moran demonstrated that it was possible to break even with a serial implementation by the use of four processors connected by a local area network.

The effectiveness of this technique at achieving improved performance during parsing is strongly dependent on the relative speed of processing units and the communication network. Given the speed of current workstations, it is probably fair to say that parallel processing is not necessary for parsing in interactive applications. However, such techniques may still have a role to play in real-time speech processing where uncertainty in the input leads to increased nondeterminism during parsing.

8 Quantifier Scoping

Douglas B. Moran and Fernando C. N. Pereira

This chapter discusses constraints on the scope of quantifiers in English and an algorithm for deriving scoped representations from unscoped quasi logical forms. The discussion of scoping constraints is adapted from that presented in Moran 1988.

8.1 The Quantifier Scoping Problem

One of the major sources of ambiguity in sentences results from the different scopes that can be assigned to the various quantified noun phrases in the sentence. Part of the problem in determining the preferred scopings of quantifiers is the number of factors involved. For example, consider these three sentences:

John visited every house on a street.	(1)
John visited every house on a square.	(2)
John visited every patient in a private room.	(3)

Each of these sentences has two quantifier scopings: in one, *every* has wider scope over *a*, while in the other, *a* has the wider scope. However, the readings that most people obtain for these sentences are quite different. In (1), the reading in which *a* has wider scope is highly preferred; in (3), the reading in which *every* has wider scope is highly preferred; in (2), the reading with wide-scope *every* is preferred, but wide-scope *a* is also acceptable. A plausible explanation for the difference between (1) and (2) is that, since the typical house is located on a street but not on a square, the default preference represented by (2) is overridden by a conversational maxim of quantity—if *a street* has narrow scope, *on a street* would contribute too little information to justify its presence. A plausible explanation for the difference between (2) and (3) is based on the relationship among the components. The reading of (3) in which *a* is given wider scope is improbable because the domain of quantification for *every* would then be the single patient in the selected room—an infelicitous use of *every*, whereas there is no similar problem in (2) because there are normally multiple houses on a square. Similarly, in

John visited a person on every committee.	(4)

John visited a house on every street.   (5)

the reading in which *a* has wider scope is reasonable for (4) but not for
(5)—it is conceivable that, for the committees in the domain of discourse,
there is a person who is on all of them, but it is highly improbable that
the streets are in a configuration such that a single house could be located
on all of them.

In (1), (3), and (5), discourse criteria and domain information seem to
be the primary factors in determining the preferred quantifier scopings,
whereas when multiple scopings correspond to plausible interpretations,
as is arguably the case for (2) and (4), other factors, which we assume
to be linguistic, come into play.

Our approach presumes that the determination of a sentence's preferred scoping can be divided into two phases, the first of which is the
subject of the algorithm described in this chapter. In this initial phase,
linguistic information is used to generate the possible quantifier scopings in order of preference. The relevant linguistic information consists
of surface position, syntactic structure, and the relationship among the
function words (determiners, modals, and negation). In the second phase
(future work), domain and discourse information is applied successively
to these scopings, modifying the scores produced by the first phase. We
expect that the modifications will be only penalties, thus making it possible to identify the best choice when it is encountered (cutting off the
processing of remaining scopings generated by the first phase).

The primary study of quantifier scoping preferences was done by Van-
Lehn (1978). The experimental data reported therein was of limited
usefulness in developing the algorithm described here—it was gathered
and evaluated under assumptions arising from a different linguistic theory. However, we will make reference to some of his conclusions in our
discussion.

The semantic analysis phase of the CLE produces unscoped logical
forms (QLFs) in which quantifier expressions are represented by *q-terms*
(Chapter 2). In this chapter, we will show simplified q-terms in which
the surface determiner appears instead of the q-term category. The
relationship between q-term categories for determiners and their corresponding quantifiers is explained in Section 10.2.4. Event variables and
some operators are also omitted from logical forms.

A sample unscoped logical form is the following for the sentence *John saw a student*:

`[see,john,qterm(a,X,[student,X])]`.

Since the only permissible scope for the quantified expression is the whole sentence, the q-term is left in *store* (Cooper 1983) until it can be *unstored* as a quantifier with the whole expression as its scope. The resulting scoped logical form is

`quant(exists,X,[student,X],[see,john,X])`.

A q-term expression can best be thought of as a quantified expression before its scope has been established. In the above q-term and quantified expressions, `[student,X]` is the *restriction* of the quantified variable X; that is, it specifies a set of the possible values of X over which the quantifier ranges. In the above quantified expression, `[see,john,X]` is referred to as either the *body* or the *scope* of the quantifier. This treatment of the logical form of quantifiers follows that employed in many previous systems (Woods 1978, Moore 1981, Barwise and Cooper 1981, Hobbs and Shieber 1987).

Keeping a quantifier in store has the effect of *raising*[1] the quantifier from where it occurs as a q-term to its ultimate position in the scoped logical form.

8.2   Scoping Rules and Preferences

Many of the following rules have appeared in various forms in multiple places in the literature, and several natural language processing systems include some mechanism for selecting a preferred quantifier scoping. However, the published descriptions of many of those systems' capabilities tend to be cursory, with the scoping rules utilized in the LUNAR system (Woods 1978) still among the best descriptions in the NLP literature.

Rule 1 A quantifier A that is not in the restriction of quantifier B and occurs within the scope of B cannot outscope any of the quantifiers in the restriction of B.

---

[1]We use this term informally, without subscribing necessarily to the notion of quantifier raising (QR) from transformational grammar (May 1985).

Rule 2 If a quantifier is raised past an operator, so its scope will include the operator, any quantifier that occurs within its restriction must also be raised past that operator, and thus its scope will also include the operator.

These rules, presented by Hobbs and Shieber (1987), can best be explained with examples.

A bishop visits every chapel by a river.   (6)

has an unscoped logical form of

```
[visit,
  qterm(a,B,[bishop,B]),
  qterm(every,C,[and,[chapel,C],
                     [by,C,qterm(a,R,[river,R])]])].
```

The following is one of the possible permutations of the quantifiers, but according to rule 1 it is not a valid scoping because the restriction of *every* (*chapel by a river*) has been fragmented:

```
*quant(forall,C,[chapel,C],
    quant(exists,B,[bishop,B],
       quant(exists,R,[and,[river,R],[by,C,R]],
             [visit,B,C]))).
```

Similarly, for the sentence

John did not visit a chapel by a river.   (7)

the quantifier permutation

```
*quant(exists,C,[chapel,C],
    [not,quant(exists,R,[and,[river,R],[by,C,R]],
               [visit,john,C])])
```

is blocked by rule 2 as a possible scoping of the unscoped logical form

```
[not,[visit,john,
          qterm(a,C,[and,[chapel,C],
                        [by,C,qterm(a,R,[river,R])]])]].
```

Rule 3 For a set of quantifiers, which quantifier receives wide-scope preference can be determined by a pairwise comparison of the determiners. This comparison is based upon a *combination* of factors that include their relative strengths and surface positions, and whether or not either quantifier was raised.

In many systems, determiners are assigned numerical strengths and these values are compared to determine what scope should be assigned to each quantifier. Such a ranking is implicit in our preference rules and can be viewed as a first approximation of the relationships represented in our rules.

Preference 3.1 There is a strong preference for *each* to outscope other determiners.

That *each* is the strongest determiner is a common feature of most quantifier-scoping treatments. However, the evidence for the relative strengths of the remaining quantifiers is much less clear—our current ranking of them is an *ad hoc* blending of those in TEAM (Grosz et al. 1987) and in VanLehn 1978.

Preference 3.2 There is a strong preference for wh-terms to outscope all determiners except *each,* which outscopes wh-terms.

In the unscoped logical forms currently produced, wh-words (*which, who, what*) and phrases are represented as q-terms. Our scoping preference rules assign wide scope to *each* in

> *Which exams did each student pass?*   (8)

However, there are subtle interactions between quantifier scoping and wh-constructions (May 1985, 38-52), which could, in principle, be described by suitable preference rules for our algorithm.

Preference 3.3 A logically weaker interpretation is preferred. This preference is strong when it maintains surface order, weak when it inverts surface order.

VanLehn proposes a more general form of this preference—that, when comparing two quantifiers within the same general group, the "more numerous" one will have a preference for wider scope. For example, *many* would take wider scope over *few.* However, for everything except *every/a,* such preferences appear to be very slight.

The quantifier order $\forall\exists$ is weaker than $\exists\forall$, accounting for the preferences in

> *A man loves every woman.*   (9)

> *Every man loves a woman.*   (10)

In both sentences, the reading with wide-scope *every* is the preferred one; the reading with wide-scope *a* is possible for (9) but is very strained for (10).

Rule 4 Raising a quantifier past certain syntactic constituents changes the strength of its determiner.

VanLehn presents an "embedding hierarchy" of the probability of a quantifier in the modifier of an NP being raised to have wider scope than the quantifier in the NP's head

> *Prepositional phrase > Reduced relative clause > Relative clause.*

A method frequently proposed to account for this distinction is to use, as a measure of the cost of raising, a count of the number of nodes of certain types (e.g., maximal projections) in the syntactic structure over which the quantifier is raised. Empirical evidence on this issue is scarce, but the following preference has proved useful in our applications.

Preference 4.1 A quantifier cannot be raised across more than one major clause boundary.

A common rule in the quantifier-scoping literature is "quantification is generally clause bound." While it is possible to generate sentences with acceptable readings when a quantifier has wider scope than the clause in which it occurs, we have been unable to find any examples showing that it can be raised out of two clauses.

Preference 4.2 A quantifier cannot be raised out of a relative clause.

This is a common restriction in many quantifier-scoping algorithms. In our system, this is not a special rule, but one of the preferences. Consequently, this could easily be modified from never being permitted to being "highly unpreferred."

Rule 5 In unscoped logical form, quantifiers can occur within the scope of an *opaque* operator. Whether or not to raise such a quantifier outside that operator is determined by a pairwise comparison between the operator and the determiner in the quantifier, as well as by their relative surface position.

Preference 5.1 There is a strong preference for *some* to outscope negation.

Preference 5.2 There is a preference for negation to outscope *every*. This preference is strong when it maintains surface order, weak when it doesn't.

Different scopings of *some* and *every* under negation produce equivalent readings ($\exists\neg$ is equivalent to $\neg\forall$). The preferred scopings for the two sentences

John did not see someone.   (11)

John did not see everyone.   (12)

have equivalent logical forms

    quant(exists,P,[person,P],[not,[see,john,P]])
    [not,quant(forall,P,[person,P],[see,john,P])].

Similarly, the preferred scopings of sentences

Someone did not see John.   (13)

Everyone did not see John.   (14)

have equivalent logical forms

    quant(exists,P,[person,P],[not,[see,P,john]])
    [not,quant(forall,P,[person,P],[see,P,john])].

Any is treated as being potentially ambiguous between the usual universal quantifier, free-choice *any*, and a second form, polarity-sensitive *any*, which occurs in conjunction with negative-polarity items. Polarity-sensitive *any* is treated as a narrow-scope existential quantifier (Ladusaw 1980). The reading of (11), which would assign narrow scope to *some* is produced by substituting *any* for *some*:

John did not see anyone.   (15)

This has the following logical form (no other scopings exist):

`[not,quant(exists,P,[person,P],[see,john,P])]`

which is logically equivalent to

`quant(forall,P,[person,P],[not,[see,john,P]])`

which corresponds to the strongly "unpreferred" readings of (11) and (12). Similarly, the sentence

Noone saw John. (16)

which has a scoped logical form of

`quant(forall,P,[person,P],[not,[see,P,john]])`

corresponds to the "unpreferred" scoping for (13) and (14).

One of LUNAR's scoping rules was that in the antecedent of *if-then* statements, the quantifiers *some* and *any* should be assigned wide scope, and *a* and *every* should be given narrow scope. If such antecedents were treated as a negative environment (or equivalent thereto), the foregoing preferences could produce this effect.

Preference 5.3 There is a strong preference for free-choice *any* to have wider scope than modals. There is a preference for all other determiners that occur within the scope of a modal to have narrower scope than that modal.

Did some student take every test? (17)

Does some student take every test? (18)

Some student took every test. (19)

Some student takes every test. (20)

Some student is taking every test. (21)

For sentences (18), (20), and (21), there are two acceptable quantifier scopings. However, for (17) and (19), the scoping in which *every* is assigned narrower scope seems to be strongly preferred. We ascribe this to the presence in the logical form of a modal operator corresponding to the past tense.

Rule 6 If polarity-sensitive *any* occurs within a clause in which its trigger does not occur, it must be raised out of that clause.

Nonrule *There is a strong preference for a noun phrase in a prepositional phrase complement to outscope the head noun.*
This criterion is used in many quantifier scoping mechanisms. It is a good heuristic, but it is not a reliable rule. In

> *John visited every house on a street.*   (22)
>
> *John visited every house with a dog.*   (23)

the heuristic correctly predicts the preferred scoping for (22), but fails for (23).[2] This heuristic is *not* part of our scoping algorithm; we believe that its effects are part of the processing that we have consigned to the second phase of quantifier scoping (domain and discourse factors).

De Dicto/De Re

Another ambiguity associated with quantifier terms is whether or not the referent is required to exist. In *PTQ* (Montague 1974), the sentence

> *John wants to find a unicorn.*   (24)

is assigned a *de dicto* reading (which does not require that any unicorns exist),

`[want,john,quant(exists,X,[unicorn,X],[find,john,X])]`

and a *de re* reading (which requires the existence of some unicorn)

`quant(exists,X,[unicorn,X],[want,john,[find,john,X]]).`

In *PTQ*, this distinction is produced by syntactic rules. Cooper (1975, 1983) demonstrated that a mechanism using a store could produce both readings from a single logical form.

Our scoping mechanism obtains similar results. Starting from the unscoped logical form

`[want,john,[find,john,qterm(a,X,[unicorn,X])]]`

with the verb *want* treated as an operator that allows a quantifier to keep narrow scope with respect to the operator or to gain wide scope (see Section 8.5 for details). The two readings correspond to the only two sites with the correct semantic type (proposition) to be the scope of a quantifier.

---

[2]This was brought to our attention by Richard Crouch.

8.3   The Scoping Algorithm

The purpose of the scoping algorithm is to transform unscoped logical
forms (QLFs) into scoped logical forms. As discussed in the preceding
section, the basic elements in an unscoped logical form that need to
be assigned scope are the q-terms that provide the semantic analysis of
quantified noun phrases. In the simplified representation used in this
chapter, a q-term has the form $\mathtt{qterm}(D, X, R)$ where D represents a
natural-language determiner or the analysis of quantifier phrase, X is the
bound variable for the quantification, and R is a formula restricting X
(see Section 2.3.2). Informally, a q-term is given a scope by finding some
formula containing the q-term that will be the scope of the quantification
introduced by the q-term. We represent the quantification corresponding
to a q-term $\mathtt{qterm}(D, X, R)$ by an expression $\mathtt{quant}(Q, X, R, S)$, where
Q is the quantifier corresponding to determiner D and S is the chosen
scope of the quantification (Section 2.2.3).

More formally, we can understand the operation of the scoping algorithm in terms of an *unstoring rule* that rewrites a formula containing a
q-term into one in which the q-term has been given a scope as a quantifier. By unstoring all the q-terms in an unscoped logical form in all
possible ways we obtain all possible scopings for the initial form.

To define precisely the unstoring rule, consider an unscoped logical
form F containing an occurrence of the q-term Q. F can be seen as the
formula $F'[X/Q]$ that results by replacing Q for new variable X in a
suitable *matrix* formula F', the *abstraction* of Q from F. For example,
abstracting the q-term from the unscoped formula

$$F = [\mathtt{not}, [\mathtt{own}, \mathtt{john}, \mathtt{qterm}(\mathtt{a}, \mathtt{X}, [\mathtt{car}, \mathtt{X}])]] \tag{25}$$

for *John does not own a car* we get the matrix formula

$$F' = [\mathtt{not}, [\mathtt{own}, \mathtt{john}, \mathtt{X}]].$$

Now consider any subformula S of F containing the given occurrence of
Q. Clearly, there is a formula S' and a *context* formula F'' such that
$S = S'[X/Q]$ and $F' = F''[T/S']$ for some new variable T, that is, S'
is the abstraction of Q from S and F'' is the abstraction of S' from
F'. Then the *unstoring* of Q with scope S is the formula $F''[T/Q'(S')]$,
where Q' is the translation of Q as a logical form quantifier. Continuing
our example, selecting the scope

$S = [\texttt{own}, \texttt{john}, \texttt{qterm}(\texttt{a}, \texttt{X}, [\texttt{car}, \texttt{X}])]$

we get

$S' = [\texttt{own}, \texttt{john}, \texttt{X}], \quad F'' = [\texttt{not}, \texttt{T}].$

Then the unstoring of the q-term with scope S is the scoped formula

$$[\texttt{not}, \texttt{quant}(\texttt{exists}, \texttt{X}, [\texttt{car}, \texttt{X}], [\texttt{own}, \texttt{john}, \texttt{X}])] \qquad (26)$$

meaning "it is not the case that there is a car that John owns". If instead the chosen scope were the whole formula (25) the resulting scoped formula would be

$$\texttt{quant}(\texttt{exists}, \texttt{X}, [\texttt{car}, \texttt{X}], [\texttt{not}, [\texttt{own}, \texttt{john}, \texttt{X}]]) \qquad (27)$$

meaning "there is a car that John does not own".

Several issues complicate the application of unstoring. We classify those issues under three headings: soundness, constraints, and irredundancy.

8.3.1 Soundness

The simpler soundness question is that of which terms are allowable as the scope of an unstored quantifier. In terms of the generalized quantifier view of quantified noun phrases, the meaning of a noun phrase (e.g., *a car*) is a function from properties (e.g., the property of not being owned by John) to propositions (e.g., the proposition that there is a car that is not owned by John). In our representation above, the property to which the noun phrase meaning is being applied is represented by an open formula S' with a free variable X that will ultimately be bound by the quantification introduced by the noun phrase. Since a property is a function from individuals to propositions, which in this case we can represent explicitly by the lambda abstraction $\lambda X.S'$, the logical type of S' (and hence of the scope S) is that of a proposition. Thus, allowable scopes for a q-term Q are those subterms containing Q that express propositions. Ideally, we should rely on a full typing of unscoped logical forms to determine those allowable scopes. However, a less principled but more practical scheme is possible given the restricted nature of our logical forms: unless otherwise specified, all function symbols in the logical form are assumed to return a proposition type; that is, they are assumed to represent predicates. The operator declarations discussed in Section 8.5 can override this default.

The main soundness problem with the application of unstoring comes from the fact that a q-term $Q_1 = \mathtt{qterm}(D, X, R)$ may itself contain q-terms in its restriction component R. If X occurs free within a q-term Q_2 in R, Q_2 cannot be unstored from within Q_1, because otherwise the free occurrence of X in Q_2, which was bound in Q_1, would result in an ill-formed logical form (Hobbs and Shieber 1987, Pereira 1990). This problem generalizes to other binding operators in logical form besides $\mathtt{qterm}$: a q-term Q cannot be unstored from inside a term U headed by a binding operator binding X if X occurs free in Q. To enforce this constraint, the scoping algorithm must keep track of the free variables in the terms it attempts to unstore.

8.3.2 Constraints

Exhaustive application of the unstoring rule in all possible ways would generate all possible sound scopings. However, linguistic and pragmatic constraints, discussed earlier, block certain alternatives or suggest a preference ranking among alternatives. For example, (26) is preferred to (27). As explained in Section 8.1, the scoping constraints we consider are always *local* in that they express whether a particular type of q-term must, may, or may not be raised past another operator in the logical form. If the unstoring is possible, it may be preferred or unpreferred.

Scoping constraints fall into two categories: those between a q-term being raised and the operators past which it is being raised, and those between two stored q-terms. These two types of constraints are expressed by two distinct types of scoping rules, which we shall discuss later.

The task of the scoping algorithm with respect to scoping constraints is to enforce obligatory constraints and choose between alternatives in order of preference. This is carried out just on the basis of local information as stated by Rule 3 in Section 8.1. Thus, an obligatory constraint is only applied if a q-term satisfying the preconditions of the constraint is being considered for unstoring over an operator also satisfying the constraint's preconditions. The same applies to preferences, only ensuring that if the unstoring under consideration is preferred, all the scopings resulting from the preferred outcome will be generated before those resulting from the unpreferred outcome.

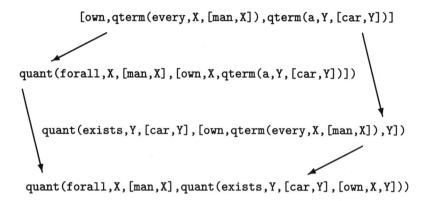

Figure 8.1
Redundant derivations

An important application of obligatory constraints is the enforcement of 'island' constraints that prevent a q-term from being raised outside a particular scope. For instance, readings in which a quantified noun phrase is raised from within a full relative clause are very rare if not impossible. To block such readings, the logical forms of relative clauses are wrapped in the operator island, which is logically the identity function but is declared to forbid unstoring of any q-term past itself. To avoid unnecessary clutter in the final logical forms, the scoping algorithm takes into account operator rewriting rules (discussed below) that allow an operator such as island to be totally removed or otherwise rewritten when the output logical form is being created.

8.3.3   Irredundancy

If the scoping algorithm tried all the possible ways of applying the unstoring rule, the same scopings would be generated in many different ways, as can be seen by comparing the two derivations of a particular scoping for *Every man owns a car* in Figure 8.1. To avoid the redundancy, instead of applying the unstoring rule to separate q-terms independently, the scoping algorithm collects the stored q-terms, generates all of their possible sound orderings satisfying the scoping constraints, and scopes the q-terms in the chosen order. The ordered list of q-terms to be scoped forms the *quantifier store* (Cooper 1983), and the open formula to be quantified over is the *matrix*. Continuing with the above example, the two possible scopings for *Every man owns a car* are given by the application of the two alternative orderings of the set

{qterm(every,X,[man,X]),qterm(a,Y,[car,Y])}

to the matrix [own,X,Y].

8.3.4   The Basic Algorithm

We will start our discussion of the scoping algorithm by presenting a simplified version that illustrates the basic ideas in an uncluttered form. The logical forms for some of the examples are also slightly simplified for expository purposes from those produced by the CLE.

The simplified algorithm can be understood as a nondeterministic program that implements a ternary relation $\text{pull}(U, S, M)$ between unscoped logical forms U, ordered stores S, and scoped logical forms M, which holds when S is a possible ordering of some subset R of the set Q of q-terms in U, and M is the result of unstoring and scoping all the q-terms in $Q - R$ and replacing all those in R by the corresponding variables. The idea is that when applied to an unscoped logical form, pull nondeterministically generates all pairs of an ordered store and a matrix arising from scoping some of the q-terms in the unscoped logical form and leaving the others in the store. Different store orderings correspond to different relative scopes for the q-terms in the store, with the earlier q-terms having wider scope. We also use the auxiliary function $\text{app}(S, M)$, whose value is the scoping of the q-terms in S, in order, over the matrix M. Then F is a fully scoped version of an unscoped logical form U if and only if there is a store S and a matrix M such that $\text{pull}(U, S, M)$ and $F = \text{app}(S, M)$.

The relation pull is defined inductively on the structure of its first argument. The basic idea is that the store of each immediate subformula of pull's first argument is nondeterministically split into two sublists, one of q-terms to keep in storage and another of q-terms to be scoped over the appropriate subformula. The q-terms to be kept in storage, derived from each of the n immediate subformulas, must then be combined nondeterministically into alternative ordered stores for the whole formula. This combination is done by a $n+1$-ary nondeterministic merge

A student from each class read a report

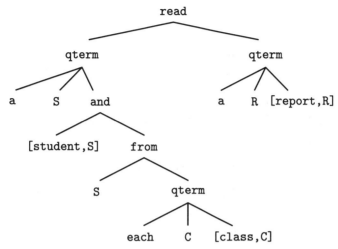

Figure 8.2
Logical form tree

relation $\text{merge}(S_1, \ldots, S_n, S)$ that generates all possible shuffles S of the sequences $S_1, \ldots, S_n$.

An intuitive way of understanding the above ideas is to view the unscoped logical form as a tree (Figure 8.2) in which each node supplies a nondeterministic sequence operator that uses nondeterministic split and merge to combine the sequences of unscoped q-terms produced by the node's daughters into a sequence of unscoped q-terms for the whole node. That is, the tree for an unscoped logical form can be understood as a dataflow graph operating on q-term sequences (Figure 8.3). For a given node U, $\text{pull}(U, S, M)$ holds if S is a possible output of the node seen as a sequence operator, and M is the formula left after all of U's q-terms have been unstored outside U (making S) or scoped within U. The definition of pull has four main cases, corresponding to a four-way distinction between unscoped logical forms:

- *simple terms* (constants and variables): clearly, $\text{pull}(U, \langle \rangle, U)$ for any simple term U.

- *application of a function or predicate*: pull is applied to each argument of the application. If the logical type of the argument is

A student from each class read a report

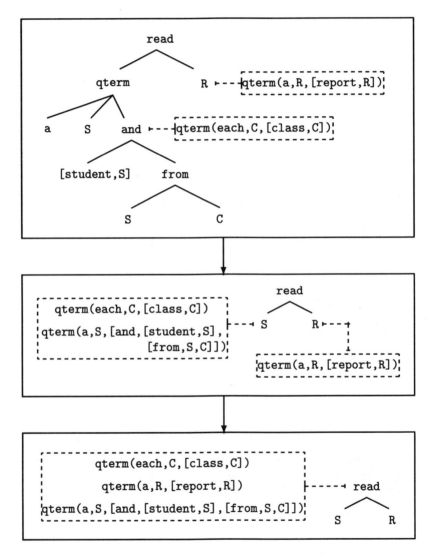

Figure 8.3
Q-term flow

proposition, the store for the argument is split nondeterministically into two parts, a prefix to be kept in store and a suffix to be applied to the argument's matrix. Otherwise, the store for the argument is kept intact. We thus have a final store and a final matrix for each argument. The stores are nondeterministically merged into a store for the application, and the function or predicate symbol is applied to the matrices. Examples of this case can be seen at the top node of Figure 8.3 and in Figure 8.4.

- *application of a binding operator*: the rule is just as for a function or predicate symbol, except that the variable bound by the operator is not allowed to occur free in any q-terms left in store.

- *q-term*: q-term Q is seen as a binding operator, and its restriction argument is treated just like a binding operator argument, yielding a store and a matrix. A revised q-term Q', with the new matrix as its restriction, is built and appended to the end of that store, yielding a new store for the whole term. The corresponding matrix is just the variable bound by Q'. The fact that the q-terms unstored from the restriction precede Q' in the store ensures that Rules 1 and 2 of Section 8.1 will be followed. Several instances of this operation are shown in Figure 8.3.

8.4   Refinements to the Basic Algorithm

The basic algorithm described above does not deal with preferences, and the treatment noun phrase coordination is yet to be discussed. Finally, there are various refinements that improve the algorithm's performance.

8.4.1   Preferences

Preferences are applied at the two nondeterministic steps in the algorithm, that is, when the store of a subformula is split and when stores from several subformulas are merged. The preferences used in a split are those between the operator at the root of the formula and the q-terms in the store being split; the preferences used in a merge are those between q-terms from the different stores being merged. Thus, splitting and merging are modified to carry out preference checks and to generate preferred alternatives before unpreferred ones.

The ordering of the stores means that if a q-term Q in a store S is

John believes that every man owns a car

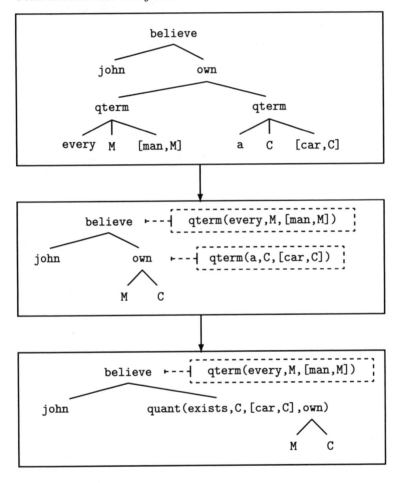

Figure 8.4
Pulling from applications

given smaller scope than an operator or q-term Y, all other q-terms in S that appear after Q will also be given smaller scope than Y. This method does not lead to incompleteness, since the demoted q-terms may still be given larger scope than Y by appearing ahead of Q in alternative permutations of S (if they are possible).

The scoping rules provided with the algorithm described here implement most of the rules and preferences discussed in Section 8.1 except for rules involving changes of determiner strength (Rule 4 and Preference 4.1). Preference 4.2 is implemented with the island operator as discussed in Section 8.3.2.

8.4.2 Coordination

The unscoped logical forms and scoping mechanisms discussed so far in this section are not sufficient for dealing with noun phrase coordination. For this purpose, we introduce an additional type of q-term with the form term_coord$(C, \mathtt{X}, Q_1, Q_2)$ where $\mathtt{X}$ is a variable, C is a conjunction operator (for instance and), and Q_1 and Q_2 are q-terms (including possibly other coordinations). For example, the unscoped logical form for *Most men and some women own a car* would be

```
[own,term_coord(and,X,
          qterm(most,V,[man,V]),
          qterm(some,W,[woman,W]))),
     qterm(a,C,[car,C])].
```

The application of pull to a q-term coordination

term_coord$(C, \mathtt{X}, Q_1, Q_2)$

returns the variable $\mathtt{X}$ as matrix and a store containing a single term

coord$(\mathtt{X}, C, \langle M_1, M_2 \rangle, \langle S_1, S_2 \rangle)$

where pull(Q_i, S_i, M_i) for each i. A simple argument shows that M_1 and M_2 must be variables.

The purpose of coord store elements is to keep stores for the conjuncts parallel, rather than having them shuffled inappropriately. Thus, when

coord$(\mathtt{X}, C, \langle M_1, M_2 \rangle, \langle S_1, S_2 \rangle)$

is applied to a matrix M, the result is the application of the conjunction C to two formulas obtained by applying each store S_i to a copy of M in which M_i has been substituted for $\mathtt{X}$:

$[C, \text{app}(S_1, M[X/M_1]), \text{app}(S_2, M[X/M_2])]$.

For instance, the coordinated store element for the previous example would be

```
coord(X,and,⟨V,W⟩,
              ⟨⟨qterm(most,V,[man,V])⟩,
              ⟨qterm(some,W,[woman,W])⟩⟩))
```

and one of the scopings would be

```
[and,
    quant(most,V,[man,V],
          quant(exists,Y,[car,Y],[own,V,Y])),
    quant(exists,W,[woman,W],
          quant(exists,Y,[car,Y],[own,W,Y]))].
```

8.4.3   Equivalent Logical Forms

Although the scoping algorithm will not generate the same scoping in more than one way, it can still generate several alternative scopings that are logically equivalent, such as

```
quant(exists,X,[man,X],
              quant(exists,Y,[car,Y],[own,X,Y]]))
quant(exists,Y,[car,Y],
              quant(exists,X,[man,X],[own,X,Y]]))
```

for *Some man owns some car*. While avoiding such redundancies altogether would require a (not-always-terminating) test for logical equivalence, it is possible to detect easily some special cases that account in practice for many logical redundancies in scoping. Following the discussion of scoping rules in Section 8.1, the algorithm uses scoping rules that state sufficient conditions for certain alternative scopings to be equivalent. One type of redundancy rule applies to pairs of q-terms that are cousins (neither was originally a subterm of the other) in the unscoped logical form and that have been ordered such that one of them is to outscope the other immediately. Another type of redundancy rule applies to a q-term Q and the widest scope q-term chosen to be applied to Q's restriction. In either case, a standard ordering for the q-term pair under consideration is allowed, and the alternative ordering is blocked.

Because the equivalence rules apply only to pairs of q-terms, one of which would immediately outscope the other, they must be invoked when the full store for a subformula has been determined and no further q-terms can be merged into that store. Thus, the rules can only be applied to block a possible store immediately before the store is to be applied to a scope.

8.4.4   The Full Scoping Relation

Surface and logical form position   Some of the scope preferences described in Section 8.1 depend on the surface order of the phrases whose logical forms are being compared. It is thus necessary to associate with subformulas of the unscoped logical form information about their surface position. A *position tree* whose structure parallels that of the unscoped logical form carries at each node the start position of the corresponding phrase in the input sentence. The start positions of q-terms are carried with them into store and are thus accessible to scope preference rules.

For use in the redundancy rules of the previous section, it is also necessary to keep track of the formula-subformula relationships in the unscoped logical form. This is most easily achieved by associating with each subformula a tree address consisting of a sequence of integers identifying which branches are taken in a path from the root of the tree representation of the formula to the subformula.

Free variables   Since the scoping algorithm must in any case traverse the whole unscoped logical form, it is more efficient to keep track of the free variables in subformulas than to determine the free variables when checking the variable binding condition of Section 8.3.1. Boolean operations on variable sets are used to derive the set of free variables of a formula from the sets for its subformulas.

From the above discussion, we derive a seven-place `pull` relation

$$\text{pull}(U,T,A,M,L,V,S)$$

that holds if U is an unscoped logical form, T the corresponding position tree, A the tree address of U in the containing logical form, M a scoped matrix, L its logical type, V its free variables, and S a store of q-terms from U not scoped in M, satisfying all soundness and preference constraints. This is the relation actually implemented by the full algorithm.

8.5 Implementation

The implementation follows the foregoing discussion closely, with all the nondeterministic choices mapped directly into Prolog's nondeterminism. The main remaining question is the representation as Prolog terms of the various objects considered above.

First, sequences are as usual represented as lists. Second, as we have seen earlier, we need to distinguish expressions of propositional type, represented by the constant t for truth values, from expressions of individual type, represented by the constant e for entities.

The Prolog representation of logical forms involves four kinds of terms: Prolog constants representing logical form constants, Prolog variables representing logical form variables, lists representing applications in which the first element represents the operator (normally a predicate) being applied, and other compound terms in which the principal functor represents a special logical form operator. During the execution of the algorithm, the Prolog variables representing logical form variables are instantiated to unique constants to facilitate operations on sets of variables. The special logical form operators include qterm and quant, already discussed, and others specified by appropriate declarations of the form discussed below.

Store elements have two possible forms, already discussed in simplified form:

- store(d, x, r, V, s, a) represents a q-term in store with determiner d, bound variable x, and restriction r. List V contains the variables free in r, s is the surface position of the phrase translated by the original q-term, and a the tree address of the original q-term in the logical form being scoped.

- coord$(x, [c \mid M], S, s, a)$ is a stored q-term coordination, with bound variable x and conjunction operator c. List M contains the matrices for the coordinated formulas, and S the corresponding stores. Again, s is the surface position of the phrase translated by this q-term and a the q-term's tree address.

Parameters of the Algorithm

The scoping algorithm is parameterized by several tables, some corresponding to scoping rules, that specify such information as the preferred

relative scopes of determiners and other logical operators, the quantifiers corresponding to various determiners, and what special operators
appear in the logical forms produced by the semantic analysis rules.
These tables are represented by Prolog predicates.

Scoping preferences   Scoping preferences are specified by the tables
det_det for scoping preferences among determiners and det_pred for
scoping preferences between determiners and other operators in logical form. In comparing two objects d_1 and d_2, the resulting preference should always be one of the four constants **always**, meaning that
d_1 should always outscope d_2, **never**, meaning that d_1 should never
outscope d_2, **pref** meaning that it is preferred that d_1 outscope d_2 (but
the other scoping is possible), and **unpref** meaning that it is preferred
that d_2 outscope d_1 (but the other scoping is also possible).

Preferences between two determiners are specified by clauses for

$$\text{det\_det}(d_1,\ d_2,\ s_1,\ s_2,\ p)$$

where d_1 and d_2 are the determiners being compared, s_1 and s_2 their
respective input string positions, and p is the preference value.

Preferences between a determiner and function symbols are specified
by clauses for

$$\text{det\_pred}(d,\ f,\ i,\ s_d,\ s_f,\ p)$$

where d and s_d are the determiner and its surface position, f and s_f are
a function symbol and its surface position, i is the argument position
from which d is being unstored, and p is the resulting preference.

Specifying known logical redundancies   As discussed in Section
8.4.3, certain quantifier-ordering alternatives are logically redundant in
the sense that all the alternatives are logically equivalent. It is important to specify as many of these redundancies as possible to reduce the
number of equivalent scopings being generated. Two tables are used to
give this information.

$$\text{quant\_order\_equiv}(q_1,\ q_2)$$

specifies that the two formulas

$$\text{quant}(q_1,\ x_1,\ P_1,\ \text{quant}(q_2,\ x_2,\ P_2,\ R))$$

and

$$\text{quant}(q_2,\ x_2,\ P_2,\ \text{quant}(q_1,\ x_1,\ P_1,\ R))$$

are logically equivalent.

$$\text{quant\_order\_equiv\_restrict}(q_1,\ q_2)$$

specifies that

$$\text{quant}(q_1,x_1,[\text{and},P_1,\text{quant}(q_2,x_2,P_2,Q)],R)$$

is logically equivalent to

$$\text{quant}(q_2,x_2,P_2,\text{quant}(q_1,x_1,[\text{and},P_1,Q],R)).$$

Special logical form functors Finally, there are two tables that specify how the scoping algorithm should deal with various special functors in the logical form, such as those representing anaphoric terms or syntactic islands.

Logical-form rewrite rules: In logical form, an application p of a functor f to some arguments is normally represented as a Prolog list $p = [f,a_1,\ldots,a_n]$. However, in some cases f carries information for the scoper that should be modified or removed for the final logical form. Such logical-form rewrites are specified by

$$\text{rewrite\_lf\_op}(f,\ a,\ r,\ t)$$

where f is the functor being applied, a is the list of arguments, r is the resulting term in the final logical form and t is the logical type of the result.

Binder definitions: Certain functors, the binding operators, introduce bound occurrences of variables in the logical form. Such functors are declared by

$$\text{binder\_def}(e,\ p_e,\ b,\ p_b,\ v,\ a,\ p_a,\ t)$$

where e is a binder application, p_e its position tree, b the binder, p_b the position of the application, v a list of the variables bound by the binder, a the arguments of the application, p_a the corresponding list of position trees, and t the logical type of the whole application.

9 Sortal Restrictions

Hiyan Alshawi and David Carter

Sortal restrictions encode constraints on the sorts of objects that can fill argument positions of specified relations. These constraints allow spurious ambiguities to be ruled out. The fact that a river is not the kind of object that can build things can be used to disallow the interpretation of *Trinity was built by a river* in which the river is taken to be the agent of the building event. Sortal restrictions have been used, in some form or other, for disambiguation in natural language systems for a long time (Wilks 1975, 1977).

Since sortal restrictions largely depend on what is possible in the world or in some domain of discourse, they fall into the realm of pragmatics rather than semantics. Most of the sortal restrictions we use can be regarded as meaning postulates about word senses; what distinguishes them from arbitrary rules of inference for disambiguation is that they can be applied very efficiently. Because of this it is practical to apply sortal restrictions twice during sentence processing. This takes place just after the initial semantic analysis in order to rule out spurious readings at an early stage and again during the plausibility checking phase to resolved logical forms (Section 10.4). Before describing how the sortal restrictions for a domain are specified, we explain how they are applied to logical form expressions.

9.1 Applying Sortal Restrictions

When checking that a given LF or QLF obeys the current set of sortal restrictions, the restrictions are applied recursively to subexpressions of the logical form, a sort being computed for each subexpression. When the logical form involves the application of a predicate (or other functor) to its arguments, then sort restrictions can come into play; it is ensured at that point that the restrictions imposed by the predicate on each argument are compatible with the sorts of the arguments. It is also ensured that the sorts imposed on variables are compatible over the whole logical form by replacing them with "sorted variables" during sort checking, as explained shortly.

For example, assuming for the moment that the sorts associated with entities are simply atoms, so that the argument of `river1` has the sort inanimate and the arguments of build1 have the sorts event, human, and object, respectively, then the following LF will be ruled out:

```
quant(exists,R,
     [river1,R],
     quant(exists,E,
          [event,E],
          [build1,E,R,trinity])).
```

On its own, the subexpression [build1,E,R,trinity] would obey sortal restrictions if trinity has the sort object. However, checking the sorts of the whole LF involves applying them to [river1,R], and this has the side effect of unifying R with a sorted variable having the form (V;inanimate). When sort checking reaches the build1 predication it has become

```
[build1,(U;event),(V;inanimate),trinity]
```

which fails to obey the restriction on the second argument. Sorts for entity classes used in the CLE are more complex than the atomic ones shown in the build1 example, and the compatibility of sorts is checked by unification rather than equality. This generalization, explained in Section 9.2, allows finer and nonhierarchical classification of entities.

To enable a sort to be assigned recursively to subexpressions of a logical form all functors, including those that are part of the LF and QLF languages, are given appropriate sorts. The sort associated with a functor of arity n is an ordered pair consisting of a list of sortal restrictions on the arguments and a sort for the expression resulting from the application of the functor to its arguments:

$$([\langle sort_1 \rangle, \ldots, \langle sort_n \rangle], \langle expression\text{-}sort \rangle).$$

We therefore have the following sorts for the predicate build1 in the above example, which says that build1 is a function taking an event, a human, and an object and returning a truth value:

```
([event,human,object],truthvalue).
```

Similarly, the logical form functor for lambda abstraction returns a function from the sort of its variable to that of its body:

([ArgSort,BodySort],([ArgSort],BodySort)).

The sort for the QLF functors a_term and qterm are the same as the
sort for the variables they introduce.

Arguments standing for collectives pose a special problem for applying
sortal restrictions. Unifying the sorts of the members of a collection (i.e.,
taking the conjunction of the sortal constraints) would be overrestrictive.
For example, assuming that sorts include gender information, this would
cause the collective reading of *John and Mary met* to be ruled out. On
the other hand, taking the generalization of the sorts of the members is
not restrictive enough because, for example, it might allow a reading of
John and the printer met in which the printer refers to a machine.

In the CLE this problem is tackled by treating the "union terms" used
to represent collectives specially in that sortal constraints are applied
separately to each member. For example, when applying sorts to the LF

quant(exists,E,[event,E],[meet1,E,'U'([john,mary])]),

a separate copy, with renamed variables, of the sort specified for the
second argument of meet1 is unified with each of the sorts for john and
mary, so conflicts between the sorts of these constants will not cause
unification failure.

9.2 Encoding Sorts as Terms

Argument sorts are represented internally as terms encoding the sort
of a class of individuals according to a classification hierarchy. They
are specified externally, in the lexicon files, using a more perspicuous
constraint-based scheme. This scheme and its mapping onto the internal
encoding are described in Section 9.3.

To see how the internal encoding works, consider the schematic representation of a sort hierarchy in Figure 9.1. This hierarchy is a simplified
version of the general one provided with the system and described in
Section 9.5 below.

In the figure, branching indicates mutually exclusive classification. For
example, according to this classification scheme animate objects cannot
also be inanimate. The terms encoding sorts use different functors to
ensure that the sorts for mutually exclusive classes do not unify:

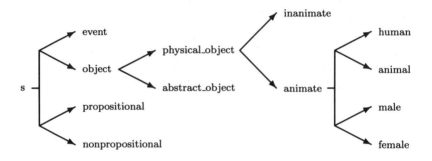

Figure 9.1
Representation of a sort hierarchy

```
animate(_,_)
inanimate.
```

Further instantiation of these terms gives finer degrees of classification. If we want to define *Selwyn* as a proper name that can refer either to a college or to a bishop, we can specify that those senses have the sorts "inanimate physical object" and "human" with the following sort declarations:

```
of_sort(selwyn_college,
    s(object(physical_object(inanimate)),_)).
of_sort(selwyn_bishop,
    s(object(physical_object(animate(human,_))),_)).
```

In the term encoding, functors with more than one argument (such as the functor **animate** above) represent classes having non-exclusive subclassifications. These subclassifications are indicated by vertical lines in the diagram. For example, objects in the class **animate** can be classified with respect to sex or humanity. The two-argument functor **animate** has **human** and **animal** as possible values for its first argument, and **male** and **female** as possible values for its second argument. A more specific sort for the bishop sense of *Selwyn* can therefore be encoded by the sort declaration:

```
of_sort(selwyn_bishop,
    s(object(physical_object(animate(human,male))),_)).
```

To summarize, the term encoding of sorts allows nonexclusive classification, but ensures that the unification of two sorts succeeds only in case the sorts do not violate an exclusive classification restriction imposed by the hierarchy. This encoding and related techniques for implementing classification constraints by unification are discussed by Mellish (1988).

In Section 9.1 we gave a simplified sort for the predicate `build1`. According to the sort hierarchy in Figure 9.1 and the term encoding for sortal information described here, the sort encoding for `build1` would be the following:

```
of_sort(build1,
    ([s(event,_),
      s(object(physical_object(animate(human,_)))),_),
      s(object(physical_object(inanimate)),_)],
    s(_,propositional))).
```

A sort associated with the prototype of a special form (see Section 6.2) will be inherited by all instances of that form. Sorts can also be specified on the fly by an application, typically for new (application-created) constants (see Section 10.3).

If there is no sort specified for a word sense or constant, its sort is set to be a unique uninstantiated variable that will unify with any sortal restriction.

9.3   The External Representation for Sorts

The internal encoding of sort terms is unsuitable for use in "external" lexicon entries, written by hand or using the lexicon acquisition tool, for two reasons. It is somewhat redundant, in that when any node from the hierarchy occurs in a term, all its mother nodes must do so too. It is inflexible, in that a sort term exactly reflects the current shape of the hierarchy, so that any changes to the hierarchy necessitate changes to many sort terms, making it impractical for large lexicons.

Thus instead of using the internal of_sort predicate, sort restrictions
in external lexicon entries are expressed in terms of a predicate sor. The
arguments of sor correspond to those of of_sort; however, selectional
restrictions on each individual entity are expressed not as a complex term
but as a constraint or list of constraints, and the sort hierarchy itself is
defined elsewhere. A list of constraints is interpreted conjunctively.

A constraint in a sor assertion will typically be the name of a node
in the hierarchy, in which case its occurrence implies the presence in
the corresponding internal sort term both of that node and of all its
ancestors. Thus the restriction for build1 above could be expressed by

sor(build1,[event,human,inanimate]=>propositional).

Here, the "=>" symbol expresses the relationship between the domain,
corresponding to a triple of constraints, and the range (a single constraint).

This representation is clearly much more readable than the internal
one. It is also quite tolerant to changes in the sort hierarchy itself.
Problems will arise only if the hierarchy is changed in a way that alters
the mutual consistency of existing nodes. For example, if human in Figure 9.1 were to be promoted to a sister node of animate instead of a
daughter, then any constraint list containing both human and animate
would become uninterpretable. However, no problems will arise if parts
of the hierarchy are simply deleted, or if new nodes are added, either at
existing leaves or by interpolation into branches.

A constraint may refer not only to a node in the hierarchy but also to
part or all of the restriction on some other word sense. This can both be
more succinct and make it easier to change one's mind later about what
sortal restrictions are appropriate for a group of related predicates. For
example, an alternative way of specifying the sort for selwyn_college
is to state that it is the same as the sort for the first argument of the
predicate college1, if this is a sense for the common noun *college*. This
can be expressed with the sor predicate as follows:

sor(selwyn_college,arg(college1,1)).

The range of another predicate can be referenced by range(*predicate*),
and an entire sort term can be expressed by sort(*predicate*), as for
example in

```
sor(selwyn_college,sort(trinity_college)).
```

The CLE translates these references to other predicates into the internal
format by taking advantage of the fact that of_sort is an ordinary
Prolog predicate for which one can assert clauses such as:

```
of_sort(selwyn_college,S):-of_sort(college1,([S],_))
```

or alternatively

```
of_sort(selwyn_college,S):-of_sort(trinity_college,S).
```

Constraints of both types may be mixed in a list, so that it is legal to
say

```
sor(selwyn_college,[arg(college1,1),area]).
```

A constraint on one argument of a predicate may refer to the restriction on another argument. There are two ways of doing this:

```
sor(resemble1,
    [event,physob,arg(resemble1,2)]=>propositional).
sor(resemble1,
    [event,physob,myarg(2)]=>propositional).
```

The first of these definitions just results in the constraint physob being
placed on the third argument as well as on the second; physob could
have been written instead of arg(resemble1,2) . However, the second
definition is much more restrictive: the use of myarg(2) results in the
same variable occurring in both positions in the internal representation

```
of_sort(resemble1,([s(...),R,R],s(...)))  :-
                           R=s(...physob...)
```

so that any two entities that "resemble" each other must have compatible
sorts (e.g., [resemble1,E,john1,mary1] would violate sorts if there
were a male/female distinction in the sort hierarchy).

9.4   Specifying the Sort Hierarchy: Notation

The top node in the hierarchy is, by convention, always the atom s, representing the class of all possible entities. The position in the hierarchy
of every other class is specified by assertions such as the following, which
define part of Figure 9.1:

```
disjoint_subclasses(s,
                    [[event,object],
                     [propositional,nonpropositional]]).

disjoint_subclasses(physical_object,
                    [[inanimate,animate]]).
```

The second argument of each `disjoint_subclasses` assertion is a list of lists of classes. Each inner list specifies, independently from every other inner list, a set of mutually exclusive classifications.

The hierarchy can be extended beyond a strict tree structure by specifying additional dependencies with the use of assertions such as

`subclass(nonpropositional,human).`

This constrains all sort containing `human` to contain `nonpropositional` as well; thus all `human` entities would then be `nonpropositional`, just as they are `animate`, and a constraint list such as `[human,propositional]` would be inconsistent.

The final type of hierarchy-defining assertion is `ignore_sort_class`, which takes a single class as argument, causing any occurrence of that class in a `sor` assertion to be ignored. This allows classes in the hierarchy assumed for the core lexicon to be removed without `sor` assertions in the core lexicon that reference those classes giving rise to error messages as apparent misspellings.

When the sort hierarchy is loaded (e.g., during CLE compilation or hierarchy development) it is examined to ensure that

- no class appears in the second argument of a disjoint-subclasses assertion more than once (either in different sublists of the same assertion or in sublists of different assertions),

- no class appears as the first argument of a disjoint-subclasses assertion more than once,

- each class appearing as either argument of a `subclass` assertion appears in the second argument of a disjoint-subclasses assertion,

- no class has mutually exclusive superclasses (this can occur through the incorrect use of subclass assertions).

Any violations of these rules are reported, with a trace of the relevant part of the hierarchy where necessary.

9.5   Specifying the Sort Hierarchy: An Example

The sort hierarchy provided with the CLE English core lexicon is a general, language-oriented one. Tailoring the CLE to applications will normally involve modifying the hierarchy: adding more detail to areas particularly relevant to the domain and disabling any parts that assume constraints that do not hold in the domain. As stated above, if the hierarchy is simply expanded or shrunk, rather than being rearranged, the core lexicon will continue to be usable.

The purpose of sortal restrictions is to rule out sentence readings that are incoherent in the domain in question. The hierarchy should be chosen with such specific tests in mind, rather than attempting to make it model aspects of the domain that have no direct linguistic correlates. To illustrate this principle, we now describe the general hierarchy, which is shown in Figure 9.2. This hierarchy is intended to provide a basis for encoding the selectional preferences of as wide a variety of word senses as possible and is used for this purpose in the core lexicon. However, there are several reasons why such use inevitably results in both some acceptable readings being rejected and some unacceptable ones being allowed. First, any attempt to encode preferential, pragmatic information as absolute meaning postulates can at best only be an approximation. Second, not every desirable distinction can be captured without making the hierarchy unreasonably large; for example, using the hierarchy as it stands there is no way for the system to recognize that *a letter to Mary* is an acceptable noun phrase whereas *a newspaper to Mary* is odd, because letters and newspapers are classified identically. Third, the imposition of any hierarchical structure, while reflecting as many similarities and differences as possible, will inevitably cut across others and prevent them from being expressed. Finally, the applicability of sortal constraints to sentences depends strongly on discourse context, for which no allowance is made in the current system. With these caveats in mind, however, the rationale behind the general hierarchy may be appreciated.

The distinctions at the top level each reflect primarily the possibility of attaching particular kinds of qualifying phrases.

- **spatial** is for entities that exist or take place in a particular physical location, and can thus be qualified by locational adverbial phrases.

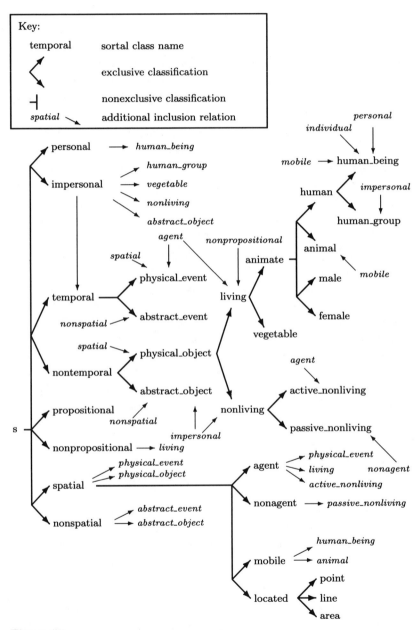

Figure 9.2
Representation of the general sort hierarchy

Thus the main senses of *rock*, *celebration*, and *speak* are spatial or physical: one can say *"the rock beside the tree"*, *"the celebration in the house"*, and *"John spoke at the conference"*. Nonphysical (abstract) entities like years and theorems are **nonspatial**: thus *"1988 beside the tree"* and *"Fermat's last theorem in Cambridge"* are anomalous. (Noun phrases such as *"one night in Paris"* are rejected on these assumptions; however, they may represent ellipsis from phrases like *"spending one night in Paris"*).

- **temporal** is for entities that are temporally bounded or qualified, and can thus be qualified by temporal adverbial phrases. One can say *"the* battle *during the morning"* and *"John* spoke *for two hours"*, but not (as single, clearly nonelliptical noun phrases) *"the* rock *for a week"* or *"the* theorem *at midday"*. Thus **temporal** entities are events, and **nontemporal** ones are objects.

These two distinctions give us four classes: **physical_objects**; **abstract_objects** such as numbers and facts; **physical_events** such as battles; and **abstract_events** such as days, which are temporally but not (at least naively) spatially bounded.

- **propositional** is for entities that have some cognitive or propositional content, and therefore can be qualified by phrases with prepositions like *about* or *concerning*. Thus the verb *speak* is **propositional**, but *eat* is not; *book* is **propositional** but *rock* is not. The ranges of all predicates are **propositional**.

- **personal** is for entities that cannot (when singular) be referred to by the pronoun *it*; **impersonal** entities are those that cannot, when singular, be referred to be *he* or *she*. Human beings are personal, and animals are unspecified, to allow both kinds of reference; all other entities are impersonal. As the definition suggests, this distinction is intended for use mainly in pronoun resolution.

Two further distinctions apply to **spatial** (physical) entities, both events and objects:

- An **agent** is an entity that can in some sense independently bring about changes in the world. Thus many verbs constrain their subjects to be **agents**. All **spatial** entities are agents except for some **nonliving** ones.

- A `mobile` event is expressed by a verb like *travel* or *raise*: one that can be qualified by a directional phrase introduced by a preposition like *from* or *towards*. `located` events cannot be so qualified: thus *John lived to Cambridge* is disallowed.

  A `mobile` object is one that can move. Thus Selwyn the man is mobile, but Selwyn the college is located. *"Selwyn went to Cambridge"*, under the literal sense of *went*, must refer to the man. Verbs of motion normally constrain their patients to be `mobile`.

  `located` objects may be further subdivided into `points`, `lines`, and `areas`. Adjectives like *narrow* demand a `line` argument, although this constraint should ideally be preferential rather than absolute.

The rest of the hierarchy, below `physical_object`, is fairly self explanatory. The distinction between `male` and `female` is of use mainly in pronoun resolution, while that between the classes `active_nonliving` and `passive_nonliving` distinguishes nonliving entities that are agents from those that are not.

9.6   Recent Developments

More recently, the mechanism for applying sortal restrictions by unifying terms has been developed in two ways. First, restrictions may be applied preferentially: a failure to unify the sort terms imposed by two occurrences of a variable does not immediately cause the logical form in question to be rejected, but causes it to be dispreferred. After all competing logical forms have been assessed in this way, those with the fewest failures are considered for further processing. This is useful in applications such as dialogue translation, where strict interpretation of the input is less important than providing *some* output.

Second, a capability for cooperative response to sortal restriction failure has been added. When two sort terms fail to unify, the predicates and argument positions from which they originate are recorded. If no sortally correct QLFs result from semantic analysis, the system generates English sentences expressing the various reasons for failure. For example, if only the literal sense of *drink* were defined, the input *My car drinks petrol* might produce the response *A car cannot drink anything!*

In addition to the sortal constraints expressed explicitly in the lexicon, sortal restrictions can now be derived automatically from meaning postulates that form part of the knowledge base for a CLE application. For example, a meaning postulate of the form

$$\forall x, y.S(x,y) \leftarrow R(x,y),$$

where S is a word sense predicate and R is a relation in the application domain, can be used to place sortal restrictions (specified for the arguments of S) on all domain objects for which R is known to hold. Work is also under way to allow application developers to construct sortal hierarchies through English statements about relationships between sortal classes, rather than by writing terms of the kind described in Section 9.4 above.

10 Resolving Quasi Logical Forms

Hiyan Alshawi

10.1 Deriving LFs from QLFs

This chapter describes the intermediate and resolved logical form representations of sentences involving referring expressions, and a reference resolution process for mapping between these representations. It is therefore concerned with the relationship between the linguistic analysis of sentences and their interpretation in context: the intermediate representation, QLF, is the result of applying declarative rules for morphological, syntactic, and semantic analysis independently of the influence of context. Formally, it may be possible to regard the resolution process as defining a function from ⟨QLF,context⟩ pairs to LFs. In practice, however, since the contextual information exploited by the CLE resolution process is incomplete, a particular QLF expression may correspond to several LF expressions. The material presented here is a revised version of that in Alshawi 1990.

QLFs may contain unresolved terms corresponding to anaphoric noun phrases covering bound variable anaphora, reflexives, and definite descriptions. Implicit relations arising in constructs such as compound nominals appear in QLF as unresolved formulae. QLFs are also neutral with respect to quantifier scope, and the collective/distributive and referential/attributive distinctions. Collective and attributive readings are viewed as resolution to suitable quantifiers in a manner explained below. Reference candidates are proposed according to an ordered set of "reference resolution rules" producing possible resolved logical forms to which linguistic and pragmatic constraints are then applied.

The process of resolving QLFs involves quantifier scoping as well as reference resolution, the former has already been described in Chapter 8.

10.1.1 QLF Constructs

As explained in Chapter 2, the QLF language is a superset of the logical form (LF) language used in the CLE. The additional QLF constructs relevant to reference resolution are a_terms (anaphoric terms), qterms (quantified terms), and a_forms (anaphoric formulae). In general, the first two arise from anaphoric and quantified noun phrases, while a_forms arise from linguistic expressions that embody implicit relations or ellipsis. a_terms, qterms and a_forms are composed of a variable, a restriction (a QLF formula), and linguistic information represented as a "QLF category":

a_term(*Category*, *EntityVar*, *Restriction*).
qterm(*Category*, *EntityVar*, *Restriction*).
a_form(*Category*, *PredicateVar*, *Restriction*).

In a_terms and qterms the variable stands for a referent or is simply the variable of an LF quantification, and the formula is a restriction on that variable. In a_forms the variable appears in predicate position in the restriction.

All three QLF constructs are introduced explicitly by the semantic analysis rules. For example, the sentence *She met a friend of John* has the following QLF representation in which the a_term is the semantic analysis of *she*, the qterm is the analysis of the quantified noun phrase *a friend of John*, and the a_form is the analysis of *friend of John*[1]:

```
[meet,
    a_term(<t=ref,p=pro,l=she,n=sing,a=[]>,
           Y,
           [female,Y]),
    qterm(<t=quant,n=sing,l=a>,
          X,
          a_form(<t=pred,p=genit>,
                 R,
                 [and,[friend,X],[R,john,X]]))]]).
```

The QLF expressions corresponding to various linguistic phenomena are described in Section 10.2.

10.1.2   QLF Resolution

Basically, the process of QLF resolution involves determining possible LF terms to replace each QLF a_term or definite description, possible quantifiers to replace the determiners for qterms, and possible formulae to replace each QLF a_form. The quantifier scoping phase determines

---

[1]For expository purposes, most formulae are shown simplified in this chapter. In particular, we will often omit tense operators and Davidsonian-style event variables.

the scope, or *body*, for each qterm producing scoped expressions that
employ a four-part generalized quantifier notation (Chapter 8):

quant (*Quantifier, Variable, Restriction, Body*) .

In the example above, QLF resolution leads to the following LF in
which the a_term is replaced by an intersentential referent mary, the
noun phrase determiner is replaced by the quantifier exists, and the
a_form is simply replaced by a formula involving the relational noun
predicate friend_of taken from the lexicon:

```
quant(exists, X,
      [and,[friend,X],[friend_of,john,X]],
      [meet,mary,X]).
```

Proposing resolutions for a QLF is followed by the application of
plausibility constraints, both linguistic and nonlinguistic (Section 10.4).
These constraints are applied to a version of the QLF that includes proposed resolutions of referring expressions. This "resolved quasi logical
form", or RQLF, thus implicitly represents a QLF, an LF, and the correspondence between them. If the proposed RQLF fails to obey the
constraints, then reference resolution will generate other possibilities for
resolving the QLF; if all such proposed RQLFs fail the tests, other QLFs
for the sentence will be considered. Once an RQLF is accepted, the CLE
updates its model of currently salient discourse entities used for resolving
intersentential references (Section 10.3). The LF implicit in the RQLF
is then extracted to become the final output of the reference resolution
and plausibility phases. To summarize, we can view a QLF as giving
a *semantic analysis* for an utterance, an RQLF as a representation of
its *interpretation* in context, and an LF as a representation of its *truth
conditions*. The process of QLF resolution can be viewed schematically
as follows:

QLF —*scoping and reference*→ RQLFs —*constraints and plausibility*→ LF.

A general property of RQLFs is that they are formed by adding information to the QLFs from which they were derived; intuitively, this
corresponds to fleshing out the QLFs in context. Thus referents are
shown in-place in an RQLF, that is, the variables for resolved a_terms
and definite descriptions are unified with their referents, and resolved

a_form relations are unified into the a_form restriction. qterms also remain in the RQLF, so the information about quantified noun phrases from the original (unscoped) QLF is preserved. This does mean that an RQLF can contain redundancies, but these will be removed when the final LF is extracted from it, though, for brevity, we will usually not show qterms in scoped expressions. The RQLF interpretation leading to the LF shown above is

```
quant(exists, X,
      a_form(<t=pred,p=genit>,
             friend_of,
             [and,[friend,X],[friend_of,john,X]]),
      [meet,
       a_term(<t=ref,p=pro,l=she,n=sing,a=[]>,
              mary,
              [female,mary]),
       qterm(<t=quant,n=sing,l=a>,
             X,
             a_form(...friend_of...))]).
```

This representation shows mary unified into the a_term for the pronoun, and friend_of unified with the relation variable in the a_form body.

In the final section of this chapter, we briefly describe a later version of the RQLF representation that more directly models the idea of resolving QLFs monotonically by further instantiation. For the purposes of the present discussion, the important thing about RQLF representations is that they include, and show the relationship between, unresolved expressions and their referents.

10.1.3   Reference Resolution Rules

The motivation for having a set of rules for reference resolution is that this allows the basic resolution algorithm to be independent of the details of how anaphoric expressions are categorized and how different approaches to their resolution are ordered. This is in contrast to approaches (e.g., Hobbs 1976 and Carter 1987) in which these details are encoded in the algorithm, leading to different success rates for different algorithms depending on the type of text (Walker 1989 compares the performance of two such algorithms). Our approach should make it possible to write different sets of resolution rules for different natural languages, or sublanguages, without changing the mechanism applying these rules.

In the CLE, an ordered set of "reference resolution rules" determines the order in which proposed resolved LFs are derived from a QLF. Unresolved QLF expressions can be nested, so before the rules are applied to an unresolved expression, they are applied recursively to its restriction. Each rule specifies a "resolution method" that can be used to suggest a referent for an unresolved expression that matches a QLF expression specified in the rule:

refrule(*QLF_expression*, *Method*).

The resolution method corresponds to a relation between QLF expressions, contexts, and referents. In the CLE implementation, a method is the name of a Prolog predicate that takes an unresolved expression and returns candidate referents in a preference order by backtracking, so the method may succeed zero, one, or several times. The contextual information handed to the resolution method is in the form of an ordered list of discourse entities (Section 10.3) together with the whole QLF for the sentence being processed.

The QLF expression appearing in a rule can unify with either an a_term, a qterm, or an a_form; a rule is taken to be applicable to the resolution of a QLF expression if the expression unifies with the left-hand side of the rule. In general, it is the category in unresolved QLF expressions that plays the major role in selecting resolution methods to be applied. The information represented in these categories is, in principle, open-ended in the same sense that holds for categories appearing in rules in unification grammar formalisms.

As well as the main reference resolution rules just described, the resolution process makes use of lexical declarations specifying, for example, the predicate corresponding to relational nouns or the quantifier cardinality predicate corresponding to determiners:

lexref(*WordSense*, *Category*, *Predicate*).

Examples of these "lexical reference declarations" will be given in Section 10.2.

The implementation of our QLF resolution model in the CLE uses a set of rules covering a range of reference phenomena that occur in English including pronouns (Sections 10.2.1, 10.2.2 and 10.2.7), definite descriptions (Sections 10.2.3 and 10.2.7), quantifiers and collective readings (Sections 10.2.4 and 10.2.5), one-anaphora (Section 10.5.3), implicit nominal relations (Section 10.5.1), temporal relations (Section 10.5.4), and ellipsis (Chapter 13).

The possibilities available for resolving QLF expressions are governed by the set of reference rules and the context from which the rules propose referents. Choosing between these possibilities to arrive at a final LF depends on the constraints applied during the plausibility phase and on heuristic factors such as rule ordering and the salience weights associated with discourse entities. We will not be discussing these heuristic factors much but instead will focus primarily on illustrating how a wide range of semantic and pragmatic phenomena can be viewed as QLF resolution (Section 10.2), and secondarily on the application of constraints on resolution to resulting RQLF interpretations (Section 10.4).

One way of viewing a QLF expression is as a conditional interpretation in the sense of Pollack and Pereira 1988. To take the simplest case, we can regard an a_term representing a pronoun in a QLF as an assumption that the variable for the a_term can be resolved by a matching reference rule. Our framework for QLF resolution can then be seen as a modular approach to representing and discharging such assumptions in a way that does not require their interactions, or the constraints on resolution, to be specified in the semantic interpretation rules of the system. It may be a consequence of the resulting simplicity of description that we have been able to cover a wide range of English constructions in the CLE implementation.

We now turn to the particular cases for noun phrase anaphora, and then to the constraints on resolution that are mainly relevant to such anaphora. We conclude the chapter with a section on the use of a_forms for relation and formula anaphora.

10.2 Anaphoric Terms

Various anaphoric phenomena handled by the CLE are considered in separate sections for expository purposes, but this does not correspond to a disjoint classification; bound variable anaphora, for example, overlap with both reflexive and nonreflexive pronouns. The same features introduced in Chapter 2 appear in the reference categories in this section:

t for the *type* of anaphoric expression (e.g., `ref`, `ell`); p for the *phrase* type (e.g., `pro`); l for *lexical* form; n for *number*; and a for intrasentential *antecedents*.

10.2.1   Pronouns

The QLF representation of a pronoun is an a_term. For example, the translation of *him* in *Mary expected him to introduce himself* is as follows:

`a_term(<t=ref,p=pro,l=him,n=sing,a=[mary]>,X,[male,X])`

The QLF category states that the a_term is for a nonreflexive pronoun, with surface form him, expecting a singular referent, and that mary is a possible referent from within the sentence. The logical form restriction on the variable X constrains the referent to be male in this case. In the case of *there* and *then* it ensures that the referent is a place or time, respectively, this information being specified in the sense entries for the pronoun.

Intersentential reference possibilities are not included on the list of antecedents, since this list is built by the sentence-level semantic analysis rules. The list contains indices to the denotations of other noun phrases in the sentence. In the semantic rules, the list is built up by unification by accumulating it in a pair of features that are "threaded" through the daughters of each constituent in a manner similar to the threading of long distance dependency gaps (Pereira 1981, and Chapter 4). Consequently, a pronoun cannot co-refer with a nonpronominal noun phrase following it in the order in which antecedents are threaded, unless this co-reference is made through an intersentential reference of the pronoun.

The threading order can be varied for different semantic rules but tends to correspond to a recursive traversal of the nodes in the syntax tree in the order: mother, left-daughter, right-daughter. For semantic analysis rules covering topicalization, however, indices of noun phrases in the preposed constituent are threaded as though there were no topicalization, allowing a treatment of a common type of cataphoric reference. For example, in both the sentences:

Mary heard a dog behind her
Behind her, Mary heard a dog

`mary` is on the antecedents list for *her* because in the second case *Behind her* is analyzed as preposed.

Several CLE reference rules cover pronouns, including the following:

```
refrule(a_term(<t=ref,p=pro,l=i>,_,_),
        hearer_speaker_ref).
refrule(a_term(<t=ref,p=pro>,_,_),
        intra_sentential).
refrule(a_term(<t=ref,p=pro>,_,_),
        inter_sentential).
```

The ordering of the rules shown above means that precedence is given to the method `hearer_speaker_ref` when the pronoun is *'I'*, and that intrasentential pronoun referents (taken from antecedents lists) are proposed before intersentential ones (discourse entities from the context model).

Reflexive Pronouns

Reflexive pronouns are also translated into `a_terms` in QLF, the only difference being that the phrase type feature is `refl` instead of `pro`, the main reference rule being

```
refrule(a_term(<t=ref,p=refl>,_,_),
        intra_sentential).
```

Again taking the sentence *Mary expected him to introduce himself*, the `a_term` for *himself* is

```
a_term(<t=ref,p=refl,l=him,n=sing,a=[-X,mary]>,
       Y,[male,Y]).
```

The antecedents list for this reflexive pronoun includes `mary` as well as the variable from the other pronoun `a_term`, that is, the variable that will eventually be unified with the referent of *him*.

The QLF level of representation does not take account of the linguistic constraints on co-reference for reflexive and nonreflexive pronouns. Instead, these constraints are handled separately (see Section 10.4), so the antecedent lists for reflexive and nonreflexive pronouns are the same. Another possible approach is for the semantic rules to maintain two lists, one for reflexive and one for nonreflexive pronouns, but there are disadvantages to this: it adds considerable complexity to the semantic analysis rules, it is difficult to implement by unification (since it can involve moving items between the two lists), and it is also arguable that the constraints on reflexives are not purely linguistic (Section 10.4).

10.2.2 Bound Variable Anaphora

In the QLF category of the example a_term just given in the previous section, we saw that the antecedent list for a pronoun may contain variables. Resolving one pronoun to the variable corresponding to another one ensures that they co-refer. In the case of *Mary expected him to introduce himself*, this means that both a_terms will be replaced by the same constant from outside the sentence. Bound variable anaphora, on the other hand, involves replacement of the a_term by a variable bound by a logical form quantifier (Partee 1978). A simple example is *Every bishop admires himself*, which has the following scoped QLF:

```
quant(<t=quant,p=det,l=every,n=sing>,X,
      [bishop,X],
      [admire,X,
       a_term(<t=ref,p=refl,l=him,n=sing,a=[-X]>,Y,
              [male,Y])]).
```

In the resolved LF, the a_term is replaced by the variable X giving [admire,X,X] as the scope of the quantification over X. Further examples of resolving pronouns to variables are given in Sections 10.2.3, 10.2.8, and 10.5.2.

In the antecedents list, the item -X indicates that the variable X comes from a singular noun phrase antecedent (it would have been +X for a plural antecedent). This information is included in the QLF category of the a_term rather than in its restriction, because it is relevant, for intrasentential reference, to syntactic agreement as opposed to constraining what the logical form variable can be bound to. This can be seen by comparing the sentences *Every bishop admires himself* and *All bishops admire themselves*. In both cases the logical variable ranges over individual bishops, while there is number agreement between the pronoun and the singular and plural subject noun phrases, respectively.[2]

---

[2]It would perhaps be more consistent with our overall framework not to represent this agreement information on antecedent lists, but to apply an agreement constraint together with the other constraints on pronominal reference to be discussed later.

10.2.3   Definite Descriptions

Definite descriptions are represented as qterms in QLF and as such
are scoped by the CLE quantifier scoping mechanism in the same way
as other quantified noun phrases. The scoping of definite descriptions
is motivated by the possibility of their resolution to quantifiers (Section 10.2.6). The scoped QLF and unscoped QLFs for *the small dog
slept* are, therefore, respectively:

```
[sleep,
    qterm(<t=ref,p=def,l=the,n=sing,a=[]>,
          X,
          [and,[dog,X],[small,X]])]

quant(<t=ref,p=def,l=the,n=sing,a=[]>,
      X,
      [and,[dog,X],[small,X]],
      [sleep,X]).
```

If the referent of the definite description here is fido, say, then the
resolution of the description is effected by replacing the above quant
formula with its body after replacing occurrences of the variable X in the
body with fido. In simple cases such as this, the same effect could have
been achieved by representing the definite description with an a_term to
be replaced by fido in the resolved LF.

The rules for handling such referential readings of definite descriptions
include methods for proposing referents from the external application
context as well as the CLE context model:

```
refrule(qterm(<t=ref,p=def,l=the,n=sing>,_,_),
             salient_satisfying_restriction).
refrule(qterm(<t=ref,p=def,l=the,n=sing>,_,_),
             reference_candidate_applic).
```

In the second rule, the resolution method is an application-dependent
method for singular definite descriptions. Typically, such a method
will attempt to check that candidates it proposes satisfy the restriction (though not necessarily the body) of the definite quantifier, this
checking done by simple database lookup or inference from a knowledge
base. For example, it might propose a salient entity john as the referent
for *the sailor that Mary loves* if it managed to prove that the LF

`[and,[sailor,john],[loves,mary,john]]`

holds in the knowledge base. We will return to definite descriptions when discussing plurals and attributive readings below.

10.2.4   Determiners and Quantifiers

Resolving QLFs covers phenomena that are often handled by the semantic analysis and quantifier scoping components of language processing systems (including earlier versions of the CLE). Some of these, such as the correspondence between determiners and quantifiers and the derivation of collective and attributive readings of noun phrases, are handled as "quantifier resolution". The basic idea will be given in this section; other cases are discussed in Sections 10.2.5 and 10.2.6.

As mentioned earlier, the QLF representation of a quantified noun phrase or definite description is a `qterm` for which the scoping algorithm proposes possible scopes (body expressions). This process takes into account scoping preferences, in particular those associated with the determiner appearing in the category of the `qterm`. In the resulting scoped QLF, there will be a `quant` formula for each `qterm` as follows:

> `qterm(`*Category*, *Variable*, *Restriction*`)`
> `quant(`*Category*, *Variable*, *Restriction*, *Body*`).`

In earlier versions of the CLE scoping algorithm, the `qterm` was replaced with its variable. Currently this information is only removed from the body when a final LF is extracted from an RQLF, so that it can be taken into account by the constraints applied to RQLF interpretations.

After scoping, reference resolution fixes the interpretation of determiner categories as quantifiers yielding:

> `quant(`*Quantifier*, *Variable*, *Restriction*, *Body*`).`

The mapping of determiner categories to quantifiers depends on lexical reference declarations. For example, the following two declarations allow resolution of the determiners in *some dog* and *all dogs* to `exists` and `forall` respectively:

> `lexref(some,<t=quant,p=det,n=sing,l=some>,exists)`
> `lexref(all,<t=quant,p=det,l=all>,forall).`

Quantifiers (in the distributive case) are taken to be predicates on two cardinalities, the number of entities, R, satisfying the restriction, and the number of entities, I, satisfying the conjunction of the restriction and the body. Abbreviations for these predicates are used for common cases, so, for example, `forall` abbreviates $\lambda r \lambda i.r = i$, which in our notation is `R^I^[eq,R,I]`. Other examples of the declarations for distributive quantifiers are:

```
lexref(N,<t=quant,p=det,n=number(N),lex=N>,
        R^I^[geq,I,N])
lexref(several,<t=quant,p=det,n=plur,lex=several>,
                R^I^[geq,I,3])
lexref(bare,<t=quant,n=plur,l=bare>,forall)
lexref(bare,<t=quant,n=plur,l=bare>,R^I^[geq,I,2])
lexref(bare,<t=quant,n=plur,l=bare>,most).
```

The first of these is for numeral determiners, so this declaration treats *3* as *at least 3* (geq is the $\geq$ relation).[3] The last three declarations allow "empty determiners" for bare plurals like *dogs* to be resolved as a universal, as in *dogs are animals*, or some number greater than one, as in *she could hear dogs barking*, or `most` as in *dogs eat meat*.

10.2.5 Collective Readings

Our treatment of quantifier resolution covers collective/distributive distinctions. As explained in Section 2.2.9, quantifiers in the LF language can be of the form `set(Q)`, in which case the variable ranges over sets of individuals (or, more precisely, the variable is not restricted to ranging over singleton sets). For example, the LF representation of the collective reading of *Two boys carried John* is:[4]

```
quant(set(R^I^[geq,I,2]),
      B,
      [boy,B],
      quant(exists,E,[event,E],[carry,E,B,john])).
```

---

[3]Another possibility is to treat *3* as *exactly 3*. We take the contextual dependence of the plausibility of these interpretation possibilities to support the "quantifier resolution" approach.

[4]In discussing collective and distributive readings, we explicitly show the quantification over event variables to make clear the number of events involved.

For such a quantification to be true, Q must hold of the cardinality of the union of sets satisfying the restriction and the cardinality of the maximal subset of this union which satisfies the body.

The QLF for the sentence, before scoping, is:

```
[carry,
  qterm(<t=quant,n=sing,l=ex>,E,[event,E]),
  qterm(<t=quant,p=det,n=number(2),l=2>,B,[boy,B]),
  john],
```

in which the determiner is resolved to the set quantifier according to the first of the following declarations:

```
lexref(N,<t=quant,p=det,n=number(N),l=N>,
          set(R^I^[geq,I,N]))
lexref(several,<t=quant,p=det,n=plur,l=several>,
          set(R^I^[geq,I,3])).
```

The interaction of scoping alternatives with the collective/distributive readings allowed by the declarations matching **several** and 2 gives several possible LFs for a sentence like *2 girls met several boys* of which the following involves two (or more) girls, a meeting event for each girl, each event involving three or more boys.

```
quant(R^I^[geq,I,2],G,[girl,G],
      quant(exists,E,[event,E],
            quant(set(R^I^[geq,I,3]),B,[boy,B],
                  [meet,E,G,B]))).
```

10.2.6   Attributive Descriptions

In addition to the referential readings of definite descriptions discussed in Section 10.2.3, attributive readings expressed as quantified LF expressions are also proposed during QLF resolution. Since definite descriptions are represented in QLF as qterms, the analysis of *Mary met the minister from France* is:

```
[meet,
  mary,
  qterm(<t=ref,p=def,l=the,n=sing,a=[mary]>,
        M,[and,[minister,M],[from,M,france]])].
```

After scoping, determiner resolution (Section 10.2.4) takes place according to a lexical declaration:

```
lexref(the,<t=ref,p=def,l=the,n=sing>,exists),
```

producing the following LF:

```
quant(exists,M,
      [and,[minister,M],[from,M,france]],
      [meet,E,mary,M]).
```

If uniqueness of the description referent is required (e.g., if presuppositions are being derived from the sentence) a more appropriate lexical declaration might be one giving the predicate R^I^[eq,R,1] (exactly one) as the quantifier.

In the case of parametrized definite descriptions, only attributive readings are allowed. An example of a description parametrized by a free variable can arise in the resolution of a sentence such as *Every dog buried the bone that it found* for which the QLF, shown here after scoping, is:

```
quant(<t=quant,p=det,l=every>,
      X,[dog,X],
      quant(<t=ref,p=def,l=the,n=sing,a=[-X]>,Y,
            [and,[bone,Y],
                 [find,
                      a_term(<t=ref,p=pro,l=it,
                                n=sing,a=[-Y,-X]>,
                             W,[impersonal,W]),
                      Y]],
            [bury,X,Y])).
```

One of the possibilities for resolving the pronoun *it* in this sentence is to treat it as a bound variable anaphor, that is, to replace the a_term with X, the variable ranging over dogs. (This resolution is proposed because X is on the a_term antecedents list, see Section 10.2.1. Y is also proposed but this possibility is eventually ruled out by sortal constraints). If this resolution is made, then the definite description variable, Y, cannot be resolved to a constant because the variable X is free in its restriction. This constraint is checked along with other binding constraints on resolution (Section 10.4). After resolution of the pronoun, quantifier resolution takes place giving:

```
quant(forall,X,[dog,X],
   quant(exists,Y,
      [and,[bone,Y],[find,X,Y]],
      [bury,X,Y])).
```

10.2.7   Plural Pronouns and Descriptions

Plural Pronouns

Plural pronouns that are bound variable anaphora are treated in the
CLE in the same way as singular cases, but taking number agreement
into account as was illustrated in Section 10.2.2 above by the example
All bishops admire themselves. This gives us a collective or distributive
reading depending on whether the variable replacing the a_term is bound
by a **set** quantifier or a normal quantifier (Section 10.2.5).

Plural pronouns, including plural reflexives, can also be resolved to
collections (i.e., sets of entities) taken from the antecedents list in reference categories or from the context model (Section 10.3). These referents
may be proposed by either intrasentential or intersentential resolution
methods, including application-specific methods. At the QLF level, a
plural pronoun such as *they* is represented as a qterm for quantifying
over subsets S of a collection corresponding to an a_term:

```
qterm(<t=quant,l=all>,
   S,
   [subset,S,
      a_term(<t=ref,p=pro,l=they,n=plur>,
         X,[entity,X])]).
```

This QLF representation covers the possibilities of a distributive or collective reading depending on whether the qterm is resolved to a normal
or **set** quantifier. In other words, the use of the two QLF constructs in
the pronoun analysis factors out the distributivity and reference aspects
of its interpretation.

As an example, the QLF representation for *John and Mary met after
they graduated* is:

```
[and,
   [meet,
      qterm(<t=quant,n=sing,l=ex>,E,[event,E]),
      U([john,mary])],
```

```
[after,E,
 [graduate,
  qterm(<t=quant,n=sing,l=ex>,F,[event,F]),
  qterm(<t=quant,l=all>,S,
        [subset,S,
         a_term(<t=ref,p=pro,l=they,n=plur,
                 a=[U([john,mary]),mary,john]>,
                 X,[entity,X])])])]].
```

In this example, the collection U([john,mary]) is the subject of the (collective) meeting event and it also appears on the antecedents list for *they*. If the pronoun a_term is resolved to this collection and its qterm is resolved to the normal (distributive) forall, we get the following LF:

```
quant(exists,E,[event,E],
      [and,
       [meet,E,U([john,mary])],
       [after,E,
        quant(forall,S,
              [subset,S,U([john,mary])],
              quant(exists,F,[event,F],
                    [graduate,F,S]))]]).
```

Since the variable S is interpreted distributively, the restriction will bind it to singleton subsets of U([john,mary]), ensuring that there are graduation events for each of John and Mary. We are thus able to capture an interpretation in which the same set of entities is treated both distributively and collectively, as required for this reading of the sentence.

Plural Definite Descriptions

Plural definite descriptions are handled in a parallel fashion to their singular counterparts except that the restriction employs subset in a similar way to plural pronouns. The QLF representation for a noun phrase like *the three dogs* is thus:

```
qterm(<t=quant,n=plur,l=all>,
      S,
      [subset,S,
       qterm(<t=ref,p=def,l=the,n=number(3)>,
             X,[dog,X])]).
```

If the lower `qterm` is resolved to an explicit set, this gives a referential reading. Otherwise the determiner can be resolved to a quantifier with the declaration:

```
lexref(the,<t=ref,p=def,n=number(N)>,set(R^I^[eq,I,N]))
```

giving an attributive reading. The collective/distributive distinction arises from the resolution of the quantifier for the variable S to `forall` or `set(forall)` as explained in the case of plural pronouns (Section 10.2.7).

The formation of discourse entities for plural referents is a major problem for language processing systems since it requires identifying salient criteria, which are often pragmatic, for grouping entities together. This is reflected in the CLE in that the current coverage of English plural reference is far from complete. In particular, none of the current built-in resolution methods in the CLE produce new collections from the set of entities present in the context model, which is required for handling discourses like *John left. Bill left. They were angry.* However, the CLE external context interface (Section 10.3) allows collections, such as the set of answers to a database query, to be included in the model.

10.2.8 Unbound Anaphoric Terms

When an argument position in a QLF predication must co-refer with a pronoun or definite description, this is indicated as `a_index(X)`, where X is the variable for the antecedent. For example, because *want* is a subject control verb, we have the following QLF for *He wanted to swim*:

```
[want,
    a_term(<t=ref,p=pro,l=he,n=sing,a=[]>,X,[male,X]),
    [apply,
        Y^[swim,Y],
        a_index(X)]].
```

(The unreduced lambda application comes from the infinitive; see Section 10.4.3.) If the `a_index` variable is subsequently resolved to a quantified variable or a constant, then the `a_index` operator becomes redundant and is not included in the final LF. However, in special cases such as the so-called donkey sentences (Geach 1962, Kamp 1981), an anaphoric term may be resolved to a quantified variable V outside the scope of the quantifier that binds V. An example is one reading of *Every farmer who*

owns a dog loves it in which the "unbound dependency" is indicated by
retaining the a_index operator in the final structure:

```
quant(forall,X,
      [and,
       [farmer,X],
       quant(exists,Y,[dog,Y],[own,X,Y]),
       [love,X,a_index(Y)]]).
```

Such structures, which in some sense are not fully resolved LFs, cannot
be given an interpretation using normal variable binding. However, an
interpretation model similar to the one advocated by Groenendijk and
Stokhof (1987) for their "dynamic logic" may be appropriate. In our
own CLE applications, when evaluating an LF like the one above, we
simply ensure that the design of the LF evaluator is such that bindings
of Y remain in force when the body of X is evaluated (taking care that all
variables are suitably renamed to avoid clashes). The more immediate
question of how we recognize that the out-of-scope reference is permitted
is treated in our framework as a constraint on binding (Section 10.4).

10.3   Context Model

Discourse Entities and Salience

The CLE maintains a simple model of context consisting of a set of entities with associated salience weights. These entities, ordered by salience,
are then passed to any reference resolution methods called; methods may
or may not make use of this information when proposing referents. Entities in the salience model are represented as LF expressions. They are
typically constants corresponding to individuals or collections, but they
also include descriptions (predicates on one argument represented as a
lambda abstraction) which are used in one-anaphora resolution (Section 10.5.3). RQLFs corresponding to the interpretation of previous
sentences are also included in the context model for the purposes of
ellipsis resolution.

Updating the context model involves changing the set of items in the
model and updating their salience weights. New items enter the model
when an RQLF expression is derived which is taken to be the correct
interpretation of a sentence. The addition of items to the context model

in response to producing an RQLF interpretation is in many respects a simplification of Webber's approach to the introduction of discourse entities (Webber 1979), so we will not discuss it further here. One difference is that our treatment of bound variable anaphora operates directly on QLFs, so we avoid the need to generate temporary descriptions of entities for resolving such anaphora.

Updating salience weights is very simple in the CLE, weights being decremented as new sentences are processed. It is possible to extend the salience weight mechanism so that it can take into account the influence of syntactic, semantic, and nonlinguistic factors contributing to contextual salience as shown in Alshawi 1987 where it is also argued that notions of global and local focus (Grosz 1977, Sidner 1979) can be viewed as corresponding to salience thresholds.

External Context Interface

When the CLE is used as an interface to application software, the application becomes part of the context within which the interpretation of user utterances takes place. In order that the application may influence the interpretation process, the CLE provides facilities for interfacing the application to CLE processing during the pragmatics phases, that is, reference resolution and plausibility checking. This is done through sortal restrictions (Section 10.4.1) and through the use of "interface procedures".

CLE interface procedures relevant to reference resolution and plausibility are concerned with proposing referents for noun phrase anaphora and implicit relations and for checking the plausibility of interpretations in the context of the application domain. It is easy to add reference rules with application-specific methods. For example, a rule could be added matching the a_term for the deictic pronoun *here*, the method in the rule being a procedure that returned the coordinates of a pointing device. This approach allows simpler or more comprehensive interfaces to CLE pragmatics, according to the effort available for application development.

The CLE external context interface also allows applications to send back constants, such as answers or sets of answers to database queries, for inclusion in the model after logical form evaluation has taken place. This makes it possible for the user to refer to such entities with anaphoric expressions in later exchanges. Sortal information for the new constants can also be provided through this interface.

10.4 Constraints on Resolved LFs

Applying the Constraints

Resolved logical forms proposed by the reference resolution component
are passed to the plausibility checking component. The main role of
this component is to apply both pragmatic constraints on plausibility
in the form of sortal restrictions and any application-specific constraints
defined through the external context interface. Linguistic constraints
on reference are also applied during this phase because they also act as
filters on the output of the reference resolution component.

In earlier versions of the CLE, linguistically motivated preferences,
encoded implicitly in the CLE by ordering lexical entries and rules
and explicitly as quantifier scoping rules, were reflected in the order
in which logical forms were passed to the plausibility component. The
normal mode of operation was to assume that the first proposed logical
form to pass the plausibility constraints was the intended interpretation.
More recently, constraints are not treated as absolute but rather make
greater or lesser contributions to an overall preference measure applied
to RQLFs. This gives a flexible way of arbitrating between conflicting
constraints and allows linguistics constraints to be included even if the
conditions under which they can be violated are not fully understood.

As explained earlier in Section 10.1.2, the RQLF passed to the plausibility phase includes the set of resolutions made, enabling the plausibility
of these resolutions to be evaluated rather than simply the plausibility
of the corresponding final LF. This is particularly relevant to applying
the linguistic constraints on pronoun reference, but it also gives the application a chance to veto resolutions proposed by the CLE. In general,
the reason for passing the RQLF to the plausibility component is that
plausibility, as we view it, is really a function of the interpretation of
an utterance in context rather than simply a function of its truth conditions, as illustrated in the rest of this section.

10.4.1 Sortal Constraints

The sortal restriction mechanism used in the CLE associates sorts with
objects, properties, and relations according to a declaratively specified

sort hierarchy (Chapter 9), giving an efficient way of applying plausibility constraints on domain predicates. It should be possible to extend the sortal restriction mechanism to cover constraints on whether predicates corresponding to word senses take individuals or collections as their arguments in order to rule out distributive or collective readings proposed during QLF resolution, but this has not yet been tried in the context of the CLE.

As with the other constraints, sortal constraints are applied to the RQLF rather than the final LF. This is necessary because QLF subexpressions that do not appear in the final LF, such as expressions for relative clauses in referential definite descriptions, need to be taken into account, and also because reference resolution introduces new predicates and arguments as referents. Applying the sortal check to the RQLF ensures that the constraints arising from the QLF expressions and the resolutions are checked for compatibility.

10.4.2 Binding Constraints

Variable binding constraints on resolved logical forms have already been mentioned in the discussion of definite descriptions and unbound anaphoric terms. Three constraints on variable binding are applied:

1. All variables, other than a_index variables, must occur within the scope of their binders.

2. A definite description whose restriction includes a variable bound outside the restriction must be resolved as a quantified expression.

3. An a_index variable must be "accessible" from a QLF qterm for the variable.

The first of these is the familiar constraint disallowing free variables (Montague 1973, May 1985) and covers variables bound by lambda abstraction as well as quantifiers. The second constraint was discussed with an example in Section 10.2.6. Clearly this constraint must be applied to an RQLF before its conversion into an LF as the restriction of the definite description may not appear in the final LF representation.

The third constraint is the one relevant to unbound anaphoric terms (Section 10.2.8). Various characterizations of the required accessibility conditions relevant to this constraint have been studied, especially in terms of subordination of discourse representation structures in DRT

(Kamp 1981). The accessibility condition in the CLE is rather simplistic and is currently restricted to making variables from an indefinite noun phrase in the restriction of a quantification accessible from its body (or one in the antecedent of an implication accessible in its consequent). This predicts the following for the acceptability of resolving the pronoun *it* in the examples below to the variable ranging over dogs (assuming narrow scoping of this variable):

> *Every farmer who owns a dog loves it*
> *Every farmer who owns no dog loves it**
> *Every farmer who owns it loves a dog**
> *If a farmer owns a dog then s/he loves it.*

10.4.3   Configurational Constraints

The configurational constraints we consider here are basically linguistic constraints on the co-reference of reflexive and nonreflexive pronouns with other noun phrases in a sentence. In the CLE the constraints are expressed at the RQLF level in contrast to some approaches in the linguistics literature (Lasnik 1976, Reinhart 1983), where they are expressed at the level of syntax trees.

Some constraints are implicit in the way semantic analysis rules thread items on the antecedents list for pronouns (Section 10.2.1). In this section we will describe the constraint that applies to the distribution of reflexive and nonreflexive pronouns. A simplified version of the constraint is explained first: A reflexive pronoun whose a_term is an argument to a logical form predicate must co-refer with another argument of that predicate, whereas a nonreflexive pronoun cannot co-refer with such an argument. This rules out the starred sentences below, under the resolutions shown in parentheses, while accepting the others:

> *Mary shot her (Janet)*
> *Mary shot her (Mary)   **
> *Mary shot herself (Janet)   **
> *Mary shot herself (Mary)*
> *Every bishop admires him (John)*
> *Every bishop admires him (that same bishop)   **
> *John's father loves himself (John)   **
> *Bill said that he (Bill) had shot him (John)*

Bill said that he (John) had shot himself (John)
Bill said that he (John) had shot himself (Bill). *

Other possible resolutions of these sentences are also accepted or rejected by the constraint as expected. When applying the constraint, only the RQLF needs to be examined, since this will include the predicate-argument structure, the QLF category for a_terms showing p=pro or p=refl, and the proposed resolutions. In the first and last of the above sentences, the constraint applies to the arguments of the predicates shoot, and say and shoot, respectively:

```
[shoot,
   mary,
   a_term(<t=ref,p=pro,l=her,n=sing,a=[mary]>,janet,
          [female,janet])]

[say,
   bill,
   [shoot,
       a_term(<t=ref,p=pro,l=he,n=sing,a=[bill]>,
              john,[male,john]),
       a_term(<t=ref,p=refl,l=him,
              n=sing,a=[-john,bill]>,
              bill,[male,bill])]].
```

The constraint also gives the expected behavior for comparatives like

John is taller than him (Bill)
John is as tall as him (John) *

because it applies to the arguments of a predicate more used in the LF representation of comparative constructions (Section 2.2.12); the final LF for the second of the examples above includes the predication:

```
[more,E^F^[tall_degree,E,F],john,john,0].
```

The actual constraint that is applied is slightly more complicated than the one stated above because it takes into account (and was part of the motivation for) propositional arguments which are unreduced lambda applications. These are used in the representation of infinitival complements, so, for example, *John expected him (Bill) to shoot himself (Bill)* has the following resolved LF:

```
[expect,john,
    [apply,X^[shoot,X,bill],bill]].
```

The full constraint is as stated before except that it demands that when a predicate P has a lambda application argument:

```
[P, ..., [apply,X^Body,A], ...]
```

then the argument A for the application is treated as though it were also an argument of P, and, furthermore, the constraint is enforced on the lambda body after performing the reduction with a resolved argument. Informally then, the full constraint says how the simpler one should be applied at both clause levels. It accepts or rejects resolutions as shown for the following sentences:

> *John expected to shoot himself (John)*
> *John expected to shoot himself (Bill) ***
> *John believed him (Bill) to be nice*
> *John expected him (Bill) to shoot himself (Bill)*
> *John expected him (John) to shoot himself (Bill) ***
> *John expected him (Bill) to shoot himself (John) ***
> *John expected him (Bill) to shoot him (Bill) ***
> *John expected him (Bill) to shoot him (John).*

Since the constraint is applied at the level of logical form, it can cover sentences with 'picture nouns' to give:

> *John saw a picture of himself (John)*
> *John saw a friend of himself (John) *.*

The implementation requires declarations specifying that relations like picture_of are "representational", and then treats the meaning of the noun phrase *a picture of himself* as though it were co-referential with *John* for the purposes of checking the reflexive constraint. (But see Kuno 1987 for a more complete analysis of picture nouns and reference constraints.)

One weakness in the way the constraint on reflexives is currently applied in the CLE is that it is sensitive to whether prepositional phrases are subcategorized-for or whether they are treated as optional modifiers. Optional arguments do not appear in the predication for the verb, but rather as additional predications involving the event variable.

This means that *John spoke to himself*, for example, will be rejected by the constraint as implemented unless the *to* prepositional phrase is subcategorized-for. Fortunately, for cases like *Mary wrapped a jumper round herself* there is a strong argument that the prepositional phrase is not optional: *Mary wrapped a jumper* means something quite different.

10.5   Anaphoric Relations and Formulae

10.5.1   Implicit Relations

English constructions like possessives, genitives, and compound nominals are translated into QLF expressions containing uninstantiated relations introduced by the a_form relation binder. This binder is used in the translation of *John's house*, which says that a relation, R, introduced implicitly by a possessive phrase, holds between John and the house. Since possessive constructions are treated as definite descriptions, the scoped QLF for *John's house leaks* is as follows:

```
quant(<t=ref,p=def,...>,X,
      a_form(<t=pred,p=poss>,R,
             [and,[house,X],[R,john,X]]),
      [leak,X]).
```

The implicit relation R can then be determined by the reference resolver and instantiated, to owns or lives_in say, in the resolved LF. (The plausibility phase would then be expected to rule out incorrect candidates in order to assign different relations for the two sentences *Where was John's car hired from?* and *John's car broke down three days after he bought it.*)

Relations implicit in (nonlexicalized) compound nouns, possessives, and *have* constructions can often only be determined from detailed knowledge of the domain of discourse (Alshawi 1987). Since this knowledge is not available to the CLE, the CLE depends on application-specific rules such as:

```
refrule(a_form(<t=pred,p=nn>,_,_),
              relation_candidate_applic)
```

for proposing resolutions for these constructions.

Lexicalized Relations

These are treated as a special case of implicit relations and are applicable
to relational nouns and lexicalized compound nominals with rules like:

```
refrule(a_form(<t=pred,p=poss>,_,_),
        relational_sense)
refrule(a_form(<t=pred,p=nn>,_,_),
        lexicalized_compound).
```

At the QLF level, the representation of *John's mother* has an a_form
that is exactly parallel to the one for *John's house*:

```
a_form(<t=pred,p=poss>,R,[and,[mother,X],[R,john,X]]).
```

Lexical reference declarations associated with noun senses in the CLE
lexicon can specify a relation to be used to resolve the a_form analysis
of a noun phrase with a relational noun head. The declarations give
the phrase type (e.g., **poss** for possessive constructions and **genit** for
genitive *'of'* constructions) for which resolution to the relational sense
is applicable. Given such a declaration,

```
lexref(mother,<p=poss>,mother_of),
```

the resolution method **relational_sense** will propose a resolution of
the above a_form in which R is instantiated to the predicate **mother_of**:

```
[and,[mother,X],[mother_of,john,X]].
```

Lexicalized compound nominals like *boat train* are treated similarly in
that the method **lexicalized_compound** in the resolution rule given
above proposes predicates specified in lexical declarations for the relevant noun senses.

10.5.2   Possessive Pronouns

Noun phrases with possessive pronouns acting as determiners are covered
by the rules for pronouns, implicit relations, and definite descriptions.
For example, the noun phrase *his mother* is analyzed in QLF using a
combination of an a_term for the pronoun, a definite description quantifier for the whole noun phrase, and an a_form for the relation between
the noun phrase referent and the pronoun. The scoped QLF representation for *John met his mother* is:

```
quant(<t=ref,p=def,n=sing,a=[john]>,X,
    a_form(<t=pred,p=poss>,R,
        [and,[mother,X],
          [R,a_term(<t=ref,p=pro,l=he,
                        n=sing,a=[john]>,
                      Y,[male,Y]),
           X]]),
    [meet,john,X]).
```

Since resolution proceeds recursively, the a_term is resolved first, to john say, then the a_form to the relational noun predicate mother_of, and finally the definite description is resolved to janet, say, giving [meet, john, janet]. If no appropriate referent corresponding to John's mother is proposed, then an attributive reading will be produced by resolving the definite description to an existential quantification (Section 10.2.6) giving the following LF:

```
quant(exists,X,
    [and,[mother,X],[mother_of,john,X]],
    [meet,john,X]).
```

10.5.3 'One' Anaphora and Ellipsis

'One' Anaphora

The so-called one-anaphora (Webber 1979), which can be complete noun phrases, as in *Mary knitted one*, or modified nominals, as in *John knitted a grey one* are taken to refer to restrictions from a preceding noun phrase, for example, $X^\wedge$[jumper,X] (i.e., $\lambda x.\text{Jumper}(x)$) from the sentence *Is it easy to knit a jumper?* It is therefore appropriate to represent such an anaphor in QLF with an a_form rather than an a_term, so that it matches the rule:

```
refrule(a_form(<t=pred,p=one>,_,_),
            previous_description).
```

Unlike the relation variables used in the representation of implicit relations, the variable bound by the a_form has the type of a one-place predicate. For example, the scoped QLF for *John knitted a grey one* is:

```
quant(<t=quant,p=det,l=a,n=sing>, X,
    [and,a_form(<t=pred,p=one>,P,[P,X]),
```

```
              [grey,X]],
      [knit,john,X]).
```

The resolution process involves replacing the body of the a_form with a resolved conjunct, in this case the one obtained by instantiating P to jumper, giving the following LF for the sentence:

```
quant(exists,X,
      [and,[jumper,X],[grey,X]],
      [knit,john,X]).
```

In the more general case, the resolution must be made to some but not all conjuncts of the preceding noun phrase restriction. For example, after a sentence like *John found a female cat*, the resolved restriction in *Mary wanted a male one* cannot include the contradictory conjunct [female,X]. The resolution method previous_description proposes each of the predicates

```
X^[and,[cat,X],[female,X]]
X^[cat,X]
X^[female,X]
```

as resolution candidates, but only the second of these results in an LF satisfying sortal constraints.

A similar resolution method is used to resolve intrasentential one-anaphora to the restrictions of noun phrases whose variables appear on the list of antecedents employed for bound variable anaphora.

Ellipsis

a_forms are also used in the QLF representation of other kinds of ellipsis. A simple example is the following a_form for verb phrase ellipsis in *Did John?*

```
a_form(<t=ell,p=vp>,P,[P,john1]).
```

We postpone the discussion of ellipsis until Chapter 13.

10.5.4   Tense Resolution

Another significant aspect of QLF resolution that we have started to address is determining the temporal indices implicit in QLF tense and aspect operators. In one approach being explored, an a_form in the restriction of qterms for events replaces the tense and aspect operators. For example, instead of

```
[past,
  [sleep,
    qterm(<t=quant,n=sing,l=ex>,E,[event,E]),
    john]],
```

the QLF for *John slept* becomes the following:

```
[sleep,
  qterm(<t=quant,n=sing,l=ex>,E,
        [and,[event,E],
             a_form(<tense=past,...>,P,[P,E])]),
  john]
```

in which tense and aspect information is represented by features in the a_form category. The predicate P applied to the event may then be resolved to a temporal relation such as before, which links the event to t1, a contextually determined point in time:

```
quant(exists,E,
      [and,[event,E],[before,E,t1]],
      [sleep,E,john]).
```

10.6 Further Work on QLF Resolution

Plausibility   Perhaps the most challenging problem in automatic language processing, that of simulating the role of plausibility in understanding, remains the most difficult part of QLF resolution. Our framework isolates this problem into the more concrete one of assigning plausibility ratings to RQLF interpretations. We will be looking at ways of exploiting inferential and probabilistic reasoning with domain knowledge in developing solutions to this problem.

Generation   We are also exploring the possibility of making resolution rules, including those for tense resolution, reversible so that they can be applied during text synthesis. Reversible resolution methods could then be used, for example during response generation in interactions with knowledge-based systems, to build QLF constructs for anaphoric noun phrases that refer to salient entities; text generation proceeding from QLF representations is described in Section 13.3.

Monotonic Interpretation   With regard to the representations employed in the resolution process, we have recently been using a modified RQLF representation that allows scoping and reference to be carried out monotonically by adding information to a QLF analysis. In this version of RQLF, referents corresponding to the resolutions of a_terms, qterm determiners, and a_forms appear as additional arguments of these constructs. Quantifier scope is indicated by ordered lists of variables associated with formulae (or subformulae) rather than by raising restrictions. For example, in the following RQLF (with abbreviated categories) for *Every boy met her:*

```
[X,E]:[meet,
        qterm(<...>,E,
             [and,[event,E],
                   a_form(<...past...>,R,
                          [R,E],
                          [before,E,'6/2/91'])]),
             exists),
        qterm(<...every...>,X,[boy1,X],forall),
        a_term(<...her...>,Y,[female1,Y],mary1)]
```

the list [X,E] indicates that X outscopes E, the pronoun *her* is resolved to mary1, *every* is resolved to forall, and the temporal a_form corresponding to the past tense is resolved to a formula involving the predicate before.

With this representation, an RQLF is simply the original QLF further instantiated by term, formula, quantifier, and scoping "referents". The resulting monotonicity of the resolution process allows it to be more incremental and less order dependent (Alshawi and Crouch 1991). This in turn leads to an improved treatment of phenomena like ellipsis, where interactions between scoping and reference can be important. It also simplifies the process of generation from resolved interpretations because there are no destructive operations to be reversed.

11 Lexical Acquisition

David Carter

The lexical acquisition tool VEX (Vocabulary EXpander) allows the creation of CLE lexicon entries by users with knowledge both of English and of the application domain, but not of linguistic theory or of the way lexical entries are represented in the CLE. It asks the user for information on the grammaticality of example sentences, and for sortal (selectional) restrictions on arguments of predicates, and writes to disc a set of instructions that can then be used by the CLE to create the appropriate lexical entries automatically. This chapter describes the principles on which VEX works and the motivation behind them. The material given here is an extended version of that presented in Carter 1989.

11.1 The Task of Lexical Acquisition

VEX's task is to aid in the creation of lexical entries that will allow the CLE to map certain English expressions into appropriate logical form predicates. These predicates are expected then to receive further application-specific processing. A crucial factor in designing VEX was that virtually no assumptions can be made about the nature of this subsequent processing or about the representations, if any, into which predicates will be mapped; indeed, the main use of VEX so far, one that suggests its viability, has been to construct the core lexicon, which is intended to be application-independent.

This situation contrasts with that obtaining in, for example, the TEAM system (Grosz et al. 1987). Whereas the CLE is intended to interface to a range of backend systems, TEAM was designed specifically as a front end for databases of a particular kind. This means that lexical acquisition in TEAM is essentially a matter of determining the English counterparts of particular database relations, and that the possibilities for word behaviors are constrained by the kinds of relations that exist. Furthermore, TEAM's coverage of verb subcategorization is rather more limited than that of the CLE. Thus TEAM is able to allow the user to volunteer a sentence from which, with the help of some hard-wired auxiliary questions, it infers the syntactic and semantic characteristics of the way a verb and its arguments map into the database.

However, because of the CLE's wide syntactic coverage and the lack of constraints from any known application, it is too risky to allow the user to volunteer sentences to VEX. Instead, VEX itself presents example sentences to the user and asks whether or not they are acceptable. In addition, the logical forms produced are of a fairly neutral, conservative nature and correspond one-to-one to the individual surface syntactic subcategorization(s) that are identified; for example, related usages like the transitive and intransitive uses of *break* (*John broke the window* vs. *The window broke*) will be mapped onto different predicates, leaving it to the back end to make whatever it needs to of the relationship between them. Thus apart from eliciting sortal restrictions, virtually all of VEX's processing is done at the level of syntax.

11.2   The Strategy Adopted

VEX adopts a *copy-and-edit* strategy in constructing lexical entries. It is provided with pointers to entries in a "paradigm" lexicon for a number of representative word usages and declarative knowledge of the range of sentential contexts in which these usages can occur. For example, it knows that a phrasal verb such as *rely on* that takes a compulsory prepositional phrase complement can be the main verb in a sentence of the form *np* verb prep *np* (e.g., *John* relies on *Mary*) but not in one of the form *np* verb *np* prep (e.g., *John relies *Mary* on). Entries in the paradigm lexicon are distinguished not only by the type and number of arguments they take, but also by phenomena such as "tough-movement" and control. VEX elicits grammaticality judgments from the user to determine which paradigm (or set of paradigms) occurs in the same contexts as the word being defined, and then constructs the new entries by making substitutions in these paradigm entries. Each use of a paradigm will give rise to one distinct predicate.

An alternative to this copy-and-edit strategy would be a more detailed, knowledge-based method in which VEX was equipped with knowledge of the function of every feature and other construct in the representation and asked the user questions in order to build entries in a bottom-up fashion. However, such an approach has several drawbacks.

The complexity of the representation would make a bottom-up approach unwieldy and time-consuming, both for the builder of VEX and for the user, who would have to answer an inordinately long list of questions for every new entry. Furthermore, interaction at the level of individual linguistic features would allow genuinely novel entries to be created, which, given that the user is a nonlinguist, would almost certainly lead to inconsistencies. In addition, endowing VEX directly with knowledge of the representation would mean that as the representation developed, VEX would continually have to be updated.

The copy-and-edit approach, on the other hand, makes VEX independent of most changes to the representation. Furthermore, the fact that its knowledge is specified at the level of word behaviors means that as the CLE's coverage increases, modifications to this knowledge are easy to make. It also makes robust and (relatively) succinct interaction with the user much easier to achieve.

11.3 Assumptions behind the Strategy

The appropriateness of VEX's strategy depends on a number of assumptions, including the following.

11.3.1 Idiosyncrasy and Uniformity

First, it assumes that the syntactic behaviors of arbitrary words are describable in terms of a fixed, manageably small set of paradigms. The alternative view, which has been argued for by Gross (1975), is that in fact *every* word is in some way idiosyncratic. We offer no counterarguments to this position here, but merely observe that as far as copy-and-edit lexical acquisition is concerned, it is a counsel of despair; if every word has its peculiarities, then every lexical entry must be constructed from scratch by a trained linguist (either by hand or using a bottom-up lexical acquisition tool of the kind dismissed above for use by nonlinguists). VEX's approach, on the other hand, can be expected to work if the *approximate* regularities that undoubtedly do exist are strong enough that the exceptions will not cause major problems, and this indeed seems to be the case for open-class words. VEX does not attempt to deal with closed-class words, as these are more idiosyncratic, and in any case are few enough for entries to be written for them by hand as part of the development of the CLE.

11.3.2   Defining Paradigms

Second, however, even once we accept the use of a finite paradigm set, there is the question of what those paradigms are. The definition of paradigms is best understood by following a series of approximations, the drawbacks in each one suggesting the next.

Paradigms as typical words   One might at first consider representing paradigms by "typical" transitive verbs, count nouns, and so on; but in fact, such typical words are very hard to find, because in practice almost every word has a range of behaviors that it shares with various other words. These behaviors must be isolated.

Paradigms as minimal patterns of use   One could therefore define a paradigm in terms of minimal sets of syntactic patterns that always occur together. A word in the language would then be defined using a union of paradigm behaviors.

For example, if the pattern *John <verb>-ed that Mary had left* is grammatical for a given <verb>, then so is *John <verb>-ed Mary had left*, and vice versa. The problem here is that important generalizations can be missed. For example, the patterns *John <verb>-ed the president* and *The president was <verb>-ed/en by John* do not form a minimal set, because although the second only occurs when the first does, the first can occur without the second, for verbs like *become*. If paradigms defined according to this criterion were used to build lexical entries, with each paradigm instance leading to a different predicate name, we would fail to capture the commonality of meaning between active and passive uses of the normal transitive verbs.

There is a related issue of efficiency. One can imagine having two paradigms whose CLE lexicon categories differed only in the value of one binary feature. Then, if a word exhibited both paradigm behaviors, it would be inefficient to define it simply by using both paradigms. Instead, one would want another category, identical to the two paradigm ones except that the value of the offending feature would be unspecified, and therefore cover both options. The definition of the paradigm set therefore needs to be sensitive not only to distributions in the language but to questions of CLE representation as well.

Paradigms as minimal sets of categories   If we imagine an ideal hand-coded lexicon for the whole language, then the entry for a word will consist of a set of categories, each of which allows a number of syntactic patterns of use. The mappings between words and categories, and between categories and patterns, are, as we have seen, both many-to-many.

Our next approximation is therefore to define a paradigm as any minimal nonempty intersection of entries, or, equivalently, as any maximal set of categories with the same distribution among entries. That is, every category in a paradigm will occur in exactly the same set of entries in the ideal lexicon as every other category (if any) in that paradigm; and every entry will be a disjoint union of paradigms. As far as syntax alone is concerned, this "grain size" for paradigms is correct for the following reasons. Any smaller grain size would result in some pairs of paradigms always occurring together in entries, thereby multiplying the number of distinct predicate names and losing generality. A larger grain size, however, would mean that some words either could not be assigned a consistent set of paradigms or would be assigned the same category more than once, leading to spurious multiple analyses.

Adjustments for semantics   When we consider semantics, however, a slightly smaller grain size can be seen to be appropriate:

- It is desirable that each logical form predicate should have one well-defined logical type: for example, a function to propositions from pairs of domain entities, or from a triple of two domain entities and a proposition. Thus, for example, although the uses of *accept* followed by a noun phrase or by a sentential complement are arguably often synonymous (compare *John accepted Mary's claim* and *John accepted that Mary was right*), we need to have a different predicate for each.

- In practice, there is no point in having more than one predicate per paradigm if sorts must be elicited from the user for each one. Separate one-predicate paradigms will do the same job as far as interacting with users is concerned, as well as being required in their own right. The two uses of *accept* just illustrated are an example of this.

Thus our final definition of a paradigm is: a minimal set of categories from our ideal hand-coded lexicon that lead to instances of one single, independent predicate, where each predicate has a single logical type. An example of such a set is the following pair categories for verbs like *want* which, in the use relevant here, takes as complement an infinitival verb phrase that may be preceded by a noun phrase, and where the subject of the embedded clause is that noun phrase if it is present (as in *John wants Mary to leave*) or the matrix subject if it is not (as in *John wants to leave*):

```
[v:[...,subcat=[vp:[vform=to,...]],...],
 v:[...,subcat=[np:[...],vp:[vform=to,...]],...]].
```

The word *independent* in the definition of a paradigm needs some explanation. There are some cases where a CLE paradigm has more than one predicate associated with it; but here, the additional predicates are dependent in that they, and their sortal restrictions, are related to the main one in a predictable way. Examples are the "degree" predicates used for adjectives and the "property" and "proposition" predicates used for some adjectives and verbs (see Section 5.3.3).[1]

11.3.3 Grammaticality Judgments

The third assumption on which VEX's strategy is based is that judgments of grammaticality are to a large extent shared between speakers of the language and tend to be absolute, binary ones. Experience has shown, however, that different users have different intuitions, and even the same user can give different answers on different occasions. To deal with this problem, if VEX receives a set of judgments from which it cannot form a consistent paradigm set, it offers the user a choice of ways in which he can change his mind; this process of negotiation usually arrives at a satisfactory conclusion. Furthermore, some sentence patterns are marked as "neutral" with respect to particular paradigms where gram-

---

[1]One slight drawback of this final definition is that some generality and efficiency can be lost in syntactic analysis, in the case of categories differing in exactly one binary feature value. This drawback is remedied in the CLE by defining a small number of "super-paradigms" each of which subsumes a specified set of normal ones. Super-paradigms play no part in VEX's processing and do not appear in the core lexicon; their only use is that, when the CLE comes to expand and internalize syntactic entries for use in parsing a sentence, then appropriate sets of paradigm instances will, if all present, be replaced by the corresponding super-paradigm instance before expansion.

maticality is unclear; judgments on these patterns will be ignored when deciding whether the paradigms in question are appropriate. The user can also choose to backtrack at any time.

In any case, although grammaticality judgments are sometimes variable and indeterminate, they are much less so than judgments of semantic acceptability, which do not play any part in VEX's main decision-making process. In order to remind the user to judge grammaticality rather than semantic well-formedness, VEX presents example sentences containing "nonsense nouns" such as *thingummy* and *whatsit*. If *use up* is being defined then one of the sentences presented is *The thingummy used the boojum the whatsit up*.

11.4   Eliciting Syntactic Behavior

The algorithm for defining a new word or phrase specified by the user is as as follows. We consider first the case where all paradigms are treated on the same basis, then introduce a modification whereby more common paradigms are presented first.

First, the user is asked for the part(s) of speech of the new item (noun, verb, etc; no further grammatical knowledge is assumed). The rest of the definition process takes place separately for each part of speech. VEX only allows entries for open class (content, lexical) words to be defined. Closed class (function, grammatical) words, of which there are a fixed number, tend to require entries that are more individual but less domain-dependent; they are therefore predefined as part of the core lexicon provided with the CLE. Among open class words, VEX majors on verb and adjective definitions and knows about only very gross syntactic distinctions between noun types (e.g., count vs. mass nouns), because other distinctions, notably those between relational and nonrelational nouns, arguably have as much to do with pragmatics as with syntax and are therefore left for later back-end processing to deal with (see, however, Section 11.5 below). Adverbs are not treated by VEX because those that are not regular inflections (with -*ly*) of adjectives form a closed class.

After determining any irregular inflectional forms, VEX elicits grammaticality judgments from the user. In the delivered version of the system, VEX knows about 60 different paradigms and their grammaticality in the context of 54 different sentential patterns. Its task is to discover the behavior of the new word or phrase by presenting as few example sentences to the user as possible, and then to find the minimal subset of the paradigms that between them account for that behavior. The sets of paradigms and sentences are progressively reduced as follows.

- Paradigms for a different part of speech or number of words from those of the new phrase are eliminated.

- VEX removes sentence patterns which either do not correspond to any surviving paradigms or whose grammaticality can be deduced from that of other patterns in the subset. For example: *if* sentence pattern S1 is grammatical when (and only when) a word or phrase with paradigm P1 is inserted in it; sentence pattern S2 is grammatical only for paradigm P2; and sentence pattern S3 is grammatical only for P1 and P2: *then* there is no point in presenting S3 to the user if S1 and S2 are also to be presented, because S3 will be grammatical when and only when either S1 or S2 (or both) are grammatical. Thus VEX orders the candidate sentence patterns according to the number of paradigms associated with them and eliminates from the resulting list any patterns whose paradigm set is exactly the union of those of one or more later items.

- The remaining sentence patterns, with forms of the item being defined substituted in, are presented to the user, who states which of them are grammatical. Because the number of possible word behaviors is quite large, up to 18 sentences may be presented in this way; instead of immediately making a full choice, therefore, VEX allows the user to make a partial choice and will then provide further guidance by specifying what paradigms might be implied by that choice, and what other sentences would need to be judged grammatical for those paradigms to be acceptable.

- Some of the user's approved sentences may be "false positives" in the sense that they are grammatical only by virtue of resulting from another grammatical sentence by an operation such as the addition of an optional prepositional phrase or the deletion of a noun phrase object. VEX detects any such sentence pairs and eliminates false positives, either automatically or depending on the user's answer to a yes/no question about any implications holding between the sentences.

- VEX then tries to find a minimal set of paradigms that, together, occur in all and only the contexts the user has marked as grammatical. At this point, one of the following occurs:

(a) There is exactly one minimal set. This set is accepted, and VEX moves on to consider semantic aspects of the new entry (see below).

(b) There are no minimal sets, because every set of paradigms that together allows the sentences the user has said are grammatical also allows a sentence that was (by implication) judged ungrammatical. This occurs quite often because users frequently ignore sentences, misread them, or simply have different intuitions on them from those embodied in the CLE's data. VEX responds by asking the user to accept one of several additions to, or deletions from, the grammatical set. The user may either accept a revision or reconsider his assumptions and backtrack to some earlier point in the dialogue. The backtracking mechanism is in fact available throughout a VEX session and allows the user to restart the dialogue from a range of earlier points.

(c) There are several minimal sets of the same size. In this case, VEX prefers less ambiguous sets, that is, those that minimize the number of occasions that two paradigms in the set *both* account for the grammaticality of a sentence (and hence could lead to ambiguity in parsing). If this does not select a unique paradigm set, VEX chooses a set at random and warns the user of the conflict; such conflicts almost always result from VEX being unable to separate two distinct behaviors for a phrase, a situation that can be remedied by the user presenting the behaviors to VEX in two separate dialogues.

A drawback of treating all paradigms on the same basis, as above, is that the number of sentences presented to the user for grammaticality judgment can be quite large: up to 18 for nonphrasal verbs. However, an analysis of the content word part of the core lexicon showed that half of the 52 paradigms used accounted for 94 percent of the entries (i.e., of the individual paradigm occurrences or, equivalently, distinct predicates), and that the most common 10 paradigms accounted for 80 percent of the entries. The behavior of VEX was therefore modified so that, by default, it presents sentences to the user in two passes, considering on the first pass only the subset of paradigms that are defined as "common". For nonphrasal verbs, this means that only four sentences are presented. On the second pass, all paradigms are considered, and all relevant sentences are presented, excluding those whose grammaticality can be inferred from the answers to the first pass (either because they themselves have already been judged, or because they are grammatical only for a set of paradigms whose applicability is already known from the first pass).

The key property of the sentences presented on the second pass is that if the word can be defined using only common paradigms, then none of the second-pass sentences will be grammatical. The user can therefore inspect these sentences with some degree of advance knowledge or expectation, which seems to decrease significantly the overall difficulty of the judgment task. There is, of course, some risk that the user will simply assume that none of the second-pass sentences are grammatical without looking at them carefully. However, the risk of some sentences being ignored is present in the one-pass approach in any case. In the one-pass approach, the consequence will often be the selection of incorrect paradigms, whereas in the two-pass approach, it will typically be that some, but not all, of the correct paradigms are missed, and no incorrect ones are introduced. The latter kind of error is arguably less serious and more easily remedied if it later becomes apparent.

An example As an example of VEX's syntax-based processing, suppose that the user wishes to define the phrasal verb *use up*, and that one-pass sentence presentation is in force. After morphological information has been supplied, VEX presents the following list of sentences:

```
1 The thingummy used up.
2 The thingummy used up the whatsit.
3 The thingummy used the whatsit up.
4 The thingummy used the boojum up very good.
5 The thingummy used the boojum the whatsit up.
6 The boojum was used up the whatsit by the thingummy.
7 The thingummy used up existing.
8 The thingummy used up the whatsit to exist.
9 The thingummy used up the whatsit that the boojum
  existed.
```

and invites the user to specify which ones are grammatical in the domain in question. The user would approve sentences 2, 3, and 8 only. VEX then considers the possibility that, because sentence 3 is grammatical, sentence 8 is grammatical only when *to exist* is an optional modifier. This is in fact the case. It asks the user:

```
Does "the whatsit was used up by the thingummy to exist"
necessarily imply
    "the whatsit was used up by the thingummy IN
    ORDER TO exist"?
```

When the user answers affirmatively, sentence 8 is dropped from consideration. VEX now has enough information to decide that *use up* behaves syntactically as a transitive particle verb.

If, instead, VEX is presenting common paradigms before uncommon ones, then these sentences will be displayed on the first pass:

```
1 The thingummy used up the whatsit.
2 The thingummy used the boojum up the whatsit.
3 The boojum was used up the whatsit by the thingummy.
```

If the user selects only sentence 1 as grammatical, on the second pass the list will be

```
1 The thingummy used up.
2 The thingummy used the whatsit up.
3 The thingummy used up existing.
4 The thingummy used up the whatsit to exist.
5 The thingummy used up the whatsit that the boojum
  existed.
```

Sentences 2 and 4 here are grammatical, because transitive particle verbs are, in the released version of the system, not defined as common. If the user selects these sentences, the same yes/no question as above will be asked, and the same conclusion drawn.[2]

---

[2]Note that sentence 4 of the original nine-sentence list, *the thingummy used the boojum up very good*, is not presented at all in two-pass mode. This is because it can only be grammatical if the sentence *the thingummy used the boojum up the whatsit* is also grammatical, which the user has judged is not the case. (The paradigm that would make both these sentences grammatical is exemplified by a verb like *regard as*: e.g., *The populace regarded the Protector as the King*, and *The populace regarded the Protector as very good*).

11.5   Eliciting Semantic Information

Once a set of paradigms has been established, VEX asks for a name for
the predicate corresponding to each one, and then for sortal restrictions
(see Chapter 9) for the predicate and its arguments. These restrictions
may be given directly as a list (interpreted conjunctively) of atoms occurring in the sort hierarchy currently in force, or indirectly as a pointer
to sortal restrictions on another predicate or one of its arguments. If
an explicit list is provided, its members are checked for existence in the
hierarchy and for mutual consistency (e.g., the list "male female" would
normally be rejected), but no check is made for the existence of other
predicates referred to, since these may not yet have been defined or
incorporated into the system.

VEX allows the user to specify any number of alternative sets of restrictions on a predicate. However, the use of more than one set is dis-
couraged, because if the alternative restrictions are assigned to distinct
predicates then the CLE will be able to provide the back-end system
with more information than would otherwise be possible.

In Chapter 10 we saw that relational nouns are distinguished from
nonrelational ones by the reference resolution component. The distinction takes the form of a lexical entry that links the basic single-argument
predicate for a relational noun sense with a two-argument one to which
reference resolution can resolve it. Therefore when a noun is being defined, VEX not only elicits sortal restrictions on the basic predicate, but
also asks whether a relational sense should also be defined. If the user
answers that it should, sortal restrictions are elicited for the new argument (e.g., for the kinds of things that can *have* mothers or weights),
and a set of possible relational constructions are presented for the user to
decide which ones are grammatical and can mean the same thing. In this
way, dimensional nouns can be distinguished from nondimensional ones;
for example, *John's weight is 60 kilos* can be paraphrased as *John has a
weight of 60 kilos*, but *John's mother is Mary* cannot be paraphrased as
John has a mother of Mary.

11.6   Incorporating New Entries

When sortal restrictions have been acquired, VEX writes out a set of
"implicit" lexical entries, creating a new file whose name reflects the
word or phrase being defined, or, at the user's option, extending an
existing file of user entries. The first type of file can be used as input to
QVEX, a "quick" version of VEX that defines a set of words essentially
as copies of an original. This can be useful when, for example, defining
a list of proper names whose properties as far as the CLE is concerned
are identical.

Implicit lexical entries are instructions interpreted by CLE commands
that make substitutions, for words and predicate names only, in entries
for the paradigms that VEX knows about. The results of these substitutions are explicit, feature-based, entries that the CLE can compile
directly into the internal format used by the parser and semantic interpreter. Both substitution and compilation happen automatically and
are hidden from the user; thus as soon as a word is defined with VEX,
it can be used in an input sentence.

There are three main advantages in introducing this "implicit" level
of representation. First, implicit entries are much smaller than explicit
and compiled ones, which results in considerable saving of space since
the latter are only generated on demand. Second, if the paradigm entries
are later changed, for example because of developments in the feature
system, existing implicit entries will usually not need to be altered; their
explicit and compiled forms will automatically come to reflect those of
the paradigm entries when the system is recompiled. This has occurred
many times during the development of the CLE. Third, implicit entries
are also rather shorter than explicit ones and are therefore easier to edit
by hand where desired. Hand editing is appropriate on those occasions
when VEX has not quite produced the desired results, either because
of peculiarities in the phrase being defined, or more commonly because
the user changes his mind about what detailed responses to VEX are
appropriate (for example, changing a predicate name) and does not wish
to redefine the phrase from scratch. It can also be useful if, for example,
the sort hierarchy is extended after some entries have been defined, and
it is necessary to update the sortal restrictions on those entries to take
full advantage of the extension.

11.7   The Core Lexicon

The CLE core lexicon, which was constructed using VEX, contains definitions for some 1,800 senses of around 1,200 English words and phrases. The words and senses defined were selected according to their frequency of occurrence, as given in sources such as West 1953 and Kucera and Francis 1967 and their usefulness for exploring and demonstrating the features of the CLE.

However, this should not be taken to imply that the CLE can successfully analyze any sentence consisting only of words in the core lexicon and falling, in principle, within the system's grammatical coverage. There are two main reasons for this.

First, while a large number of common words and uses are defined, not every *use* of every word in the lexicon is defined. Some of these gaps are due to the omission of infrequent senses or uses; for example, the word *bill* is defined in the sense of *account* but not in the sense of *beak*.

Second, even where senses are defined, the sortal restrictions defined for them may sometimes result in apparently valid sentences failing to receive an interpretation, and on other occasions in spurious readings being generated. This is partly because it is not possible to anticipate in advance all the contexts in which a particular word sense will be used. Also, even where contexts can be anticipated, a simple binary test using a relatively straightforward sort hierarchy cannot always achieve the desired effect. The more the restrictions are relaxed in order to allow for semantically unusual (but valid) usages, the more they will let through readings that turn out to be spurious. A preference metric, rather than a binary decision, has recently been introduced (see Section 9.6) for use in applications not involving reasoning, but reasoning with a sortally incoherent structure introduces many difficult problems.

Function wordss defined in the core lexicon include modal and auxiliary verbs, personal and relative pronouns, determiners, conjunctions, and prepositions. Various types of closed-class content words are also defined, principally adverbs (other than those derived by adding -*ly* to adjectives) and measure nouns. The open-class content word entries defined fall into three parts of speech: nouns (including proper names), verbs, and adjectives.

The *noun* senses can be normal or relational. Relational nouns are those that presuppose some further information; for example, an *edge* cannot exist on its own but must be the edge of something. Entries for all relational noun senses therefore include pointers to two-place relational predicates that can be accessed by the CLE during reference resolution (see Section 10.5.1). Dimensional nouns such as *weight* are an important subcase of relational nouns. The weight of something is restricted sortally to being a datum (an entity similar to a number). The associated two-place predicate will have the appropriate argument restricted to a physical object (thus *the weight of the machine* will be resolved relationally, but *the weight of the argument* will not).

The *adjectives* include simple pre- and postnominal adjectives such as *red*, adjectives with prepositional complements (*essential for*), and ones with more complex syntactic behaviors (*it is certain that ...*, *John is certain to ...*, *John is certain that ...*).

The *verbs* cover the widest range of syntactic behaviors, including many combinations of nominal, prepositional, and verbal complements. Whereas multiple meanings of nouns tend to be due to homonymy— different, unrelated meanings such as those of *bank*—verbs tend to be polysemous: the different meanings are more or less closely related. For this reason the division of verb meanings into distinct senses is to some extent an arbitrary process. On the one hand, some syntactically similar but semantically varied uses have been conflated into one predicate, as in the different uses of *add to* (sentences like *John added a stone to the pile* and *John added his contribution to the debate* will involve the same predicate); on the other hand, some semantically similar but syntactically different uses will map onto different predicates, as in *John taught Mary French* and *John taught Mary to speak French*. This policy has been adopted because further pragmatic processing is required, on the one hand, to distinguish between the shades of meaning of verbs like *add to* and, on the other, to realize that the two "teaching" sentences are (nearly) synonymous.

While the lack of any explicit link between such nearly-synonymous word senses is a limitation of the current system, to remedy it would require the CLE's logical form representation to be greatly enriched. Pointers to a more powerful treatment of polysemous words are given in Pustejovsky 1989. Such a treatment would greatly reduce the number of distinct predicates for verbs and would also allow sortal restrictions to be applied more powerfully and accurately. This richer formalism would involve predicates (or whatever replaced them) containing more information and interacting in a more active, complex, and contextually determined way, selecting from among each other's knowledge structures to combine in a variety of ways. For example, the predicate for the verb *enjoy* would look for typical actions or uses associated with objects, so that the representation of *John enjoyed the book* would contain (by default) some reference to reading, that of *John enjoyed the beer* to drinking, and *John enjoyed the boulder* would not receive any corresponding interpretation. The sentences *John enjoyed himself dancing* and *John enjoyed himself* would lead to instances of the same *enjoy* predicate, but in the latter case, the argument for the activity enjoyed would be left unspecified (but appropriately constrained) to be resolved during pragmatic processing.

11.8   Summary and Conclusions

The application independence of the CLE leads to a style of lexical acquisition different from that of earlier, dedicated natural language front ends. We have argued for a technique based on a limited number of syntactic paradigms, a subset of which is selected for the construction of new entries according to the user's judgments of sentence grammaticality. This allows the lexical acquisition component to avoid strong dependencies on the CLE's linguistic representation, the application domain, the nature of the back-end system, or the user's knowledge of linguistics.

VEX's concentration on syntactic paradigms allows a wide range of subcategorization types to be recognized and dealt with, and also permits a nontrivial lexicon to be easily maintained while the system is under development. The use of VEX to define the CLE's 1,200-word core lexicon is evidence for the practicality of the approach.

The crucial factor in evaluating VEX, however, is its acceptability to the nonlinguist (but application expert) users for whom it was designed. No formal evaluation of this has been carried out, but informal feedback has been generally positive. It appears that, once they have studied the annotated VEX session transcript distributed with the CLE documentation, those who have so far used the system have had no great difficulty with the idea of using nonsense words or with concepts such as grammaticality and paradigms. In addition, the QVEX subsystem, which creates entries by copying from existing ones or from specified paradigms, greatly speeds up the process of defining classes of similar words.

Perhaps the most difficult task faced by the VEX user is to decide which of the sentences presented are grammatical; however, this task is significantly eased by the possibility of backtracking, by the consistency checker, and by the partial choice facility, all of which were implemented in response to comments by users of earlier versions of the system. The difficulties that remain seem largely due to the fact that the CLE is intended to be usable in as wide a range of hardware and software environments as possible, so that the interface cannot assume any graphical facilities such as cursor-addressable displays. Were such facilities to be available, the system could provide step-by-step feedback on the consequences of individual grammaticality judgments.

The fact that VEX is not specific to any one application domain or type of back-end system, and is relatively loosely coupled to the internal characteristics of the CLE, means that the techniques it embodies should in principle be applicable to (even if not always optimal or sufficient in) a wide range of natural language processing contexts. Indeed, it should be straightforward to produce a version of VEX with clearly defined interfaces at morphological, syntactic, and semantic levels that could simply be "plugged in" to a range of existing systems to provide them with a lexical acquisition capability. The range of systems on which this operation could be carried out would be those that output a logical form, or other representation, that operated on a lexical semantics no richer or deeper than that of the CLE (excluding, therefore, any system based on something like Pustejovsky's treatment discussed in Section 11.7).

12 The CLE in Application Development

Arnold Smith

The Core Language Engine was designed with interactive systems particularly in mind. The CLE was envisaged as a prototype module or package in a complete application, with well-defined interfaces to other system components.

The role that the CLE would play in a larger system was clear in general terms from the beginning of the project. But the precise scope of "the language-processing module" in a general system architecture—the form of its interfaces to other system components, and the precise nature of its requirements for information from those components—was far from self-evident. Had we been designing completely out of context, it would have been easy enough to unwittingly push problems that should really be handled by the CLE across interface boundaries. So from the start an important goal of the project was to build a simple example of a complete system. In this way we hoped to demonstrate, both to ourselves and to others, that the design assumptions of the CLE were at least potentially valid and were workable in practice.

In the end we implemented two such systems, one quite simple and the other somewhat more complex. The first (LF-to-Prolog) is a query system allowing natural language access to facts and simple inferences stored in the standard Prolog database. The second (Opex—the Order Processing Exemplar) implements a small simulation of an order processing system that can be controlled and queried via natural language.[1] Most of this chapter is devoted to describing the salient features of these two systems and to a discussion of some of the lessons to be drawn from our experience with them. In the final section, we will take a quick look at the directions of our current research with respect to language-to-application interfacing.

12.1 Linguistic Applications

One of the obvious categories of language-using systems consists of those applications that deal with language per se. This includes relatively straightforward tools such as context-sensitive spelling checkers and also

---

[1] The design and much of the implementation of Opex were carried out by Barney Pell during the summer and autumn of 1988.

more complex ones such as text summarization and machine translation. With its multiple levels of linguistic representation, the CLE lends itself well to linguistic tool development. Some experiments with interactive translation systems based on the CLE and QLF transfer are currently underway, as described in Chapter 14.

12.2   Model-Based Systems

For another broad class of application systems, the linguistic processing element can be considered as part of the user interface to an underlying system that models a part of the external world. Both LF-to-Prolog and Opex are in this class, and other examples would include straightforward database query systems, computer-aided design systems, command and control systems, and advisory systems. It is this class of system that we will be primarily concerned with in the following discussion.

An important property of this class of system is that natural language queries and statements will appear to refer directly to the world being modeled, even though evaluation really takes place purely with respect to the internal model. Indeed one of the goals of natural language interaction is precisely to encourage the user to adopt this point of view, so that he or she doesn't have to understand the details and structure of the model itself but can instead think directly in terms of the external situation. (A related class of systems deals not with models of the *external* world, but directly with structures internal to the computer. Software engineering tools and database administration facilities are examples of this kind. The crucial difference is that there is in principle no possibility of a discrepancy between model and reality—because the real objects of discussion are directly accessible to the evaluation routines. Actually, even in these cases, the situation is unfortunately not so simple, but this is not the place for a full discussion.)

With other kinds of user interface such as menus and command languages, the available operations will be highly constrained, and "utterances" or actions that don't fit the model will either not be possible at all or fail in some obvious way. A natural language interaction capability relaxes some of the expressive constraints on the user but cannot by itself compensate for the inadequacies of the underlying model. Indeed the poverty of the application domain model in relation to the relevant detail of the world it is supposed to represent may become all too quickly apparent.

12.2.1   CLE–Interface–Model

The CLE in its present form cannot by itself be combined directly with this kind of computational model to create a complete system. Some kind of interface module connecting the CLE to the model is needed to provide a complete interactive environment. The two example applications we have built illustrate somewhat different approaches to doing this, though many other approaches are also possible.

For the LF-to-Prolog system, the model is a standard Prolog internal database of facts about Cambridge colleges. The interface module consists primarily of a translator of CLE logical forms into Prolog, with a few additional routines to do some supporting inferences and to present the results of queries to the user.

For Opex, the model is a discrete-event simulation system implemented in Prolog, providing a very simple model of the activities of several order-processing departments in an imaginary company. The interface module is more like an interpreter of CLE Logical Form, with capabilities for operating the simulation model as well as displaying information to the user.

12.3   The LF-Prolog Query Evaluator

The LF-Prolog query evaluator is a very simple application of the CLE in which the logical forms produced by the CLE are treated as queries to be evaluated against a database of Prolog facts and rules. The evaluator was intended primarily for demonstrating that CLE logical forms, which are in principle capable of supporting complex reasoning, can also be interpreted more or less directly with respect to a simple knowledge base. It also serves to illustrate how to use the CLE interface procedures (Section 10.3), and can be taken as the starting point for Prolog-based applications of the CLE.

If we think of a Prolog database of ground facts as corresponding to a model (in the Tarskian sense) specifying the extensions of relation symbols appearing in logical forms, then we can view the LF-Prolog evaluator as providing a definition of the semantics of the LF language.

Because the evaluator interprets expressions of the LF language in the context of such a model, it can be read as showing the truth-conditional relationship between the language and its models. Given a logical form the evaluator can check if it is true with respect to the model. Used in this way it will return "Yes" or "No" depending on whether or not the logical form holds in the model encoded by the database.

In fact the evaluator is not simply such a logical form truth checker. It can return answers to logical form queries with wh and count quantifiers, and it makes use of the Prolog inference mechanism to apply arbitrary Prolog rules (procedures) for relations.

The LF-Prolog evaluator works in two phases. In the first of these, the logical form is translated into a Prolog term that can be executed directly with the Prolog call procedure. This translation may involve some simplification, since, for instance, existential quantification is implicit in Prolog queries, the restriction and body of absolute quantifiers (Section 2.2.3) can be conjoined, and lambda abstractions in comparative representations can be applied.

As an example, take the query

Who founded more than one college?

which is given the following logical form:

```
[whq,
 quant(wh, A,
       [personal,A],
       quant(N^M^[gt,M,1], D,
             [college_place,D],
             [past,
              quant(exists, E,
                    [event,E],
                    [found_establish,E,A,D])])))].
```

The translation into Prolog simplifies the quantification structure to give the following (commas are used for both conjunction and argument lists in Prolog):

```
wh_ans(A,
       (personal(A),
        abs_qnt(C,M,M>1,
```

```
(college_place(C),
  (event(E),found_establish(E,A,C))))).
```

The predicate abs_qnt implements the semantics of absolute quantifiers by finding the number (M) of instantiations of its variable (C) which satisfy its LF expression, and then checking that this number satisfies the quantifier expression (M>1). (Another predicate ref_qnt implements the semantics of relative generalized quantifiers.) Similarly, wh_ans implements wh-quantification by finding instances of its variable (A) which satisfy its LF expression, and then printing them at an appropriate nesting level (1 in this case since there is only one wh-quantification in the question). The other predicates, personal, college_place, and found_establish, are defined in our particular database about Cambridge colleges. When the above Prolog code is executed with these definitions, the answer "None" is printed. If the quantifier phrase *at least one* appeared in the English question instead of *more than one*, we get the quantifier expression M>=1 in the Prolog translation and a list of all college founders in the database is printed.

The LF for another example,

Is Clare older than Trinity?

includes a conjunct

```
[more,X^Y^[old1_degree,X,Y],clare1,trinity1,D].
```

The translation into Prolog carries out the applications implicit in the predicate more (Section 2.2.12), giving the following Prolog expression for the sentence:

```
((old1_degree(clare1,A),
  old1_degree(trinity1,B)),
  D is A-B,D>0).
```

Evaluation of this expression as a Prolog query against the database about colleges yields the answer "Yes". In this database, the predicate old1_degree is a derived predicate that computes the degree of oldness as the number of years between 1989 and the date when a founding event for the college took place.

12.4   The Order-Processing Exemplar

12.4.1   Language to Behavior

When the CLE is given an English sentence, it produces as output one
or more Logical Form expressions representing possible literal meanings
of the sentence. One of these will be chosen as *the* meaning, by a process
discussed in Section 10.1. For purposes of discussion we will assume that
each utterance results in a single logical form.

In the context of an interactive system, each utterance is a speech
act on the part of the user—a query, a request, a joke, a threat, a
command, an exclamation—and any system will be expected to respond
in an appropriate manner to some subset of these acts. Neither of our
application systems attempts an ambitious classification of speech acts.
LF-to-Prolog interprets all utterances effectively as queries that it tests
against its internal domain model. Opex can handle queries, and some
assertions and commands, and assumes that all utterances fall into one
or other of these categories.

12.4.2   Opex Sentence Handling

In overview, the treatment of sentences by the Opex system is similar to
that in LF-to-Prolog. As indicated in Figure 12.1, during the last two
phases of CLE processing, the application is called on several occasions.
It first collaborates with the CLE to propose reference candidates for
pronouns, descriptive noun phrases, and implicit relations. Then, once
the CLE has produced one or more fully resolved logical forms, the
application is called again to check them in turn for plausibility. The
first reading that succeeds in passing the application's plausibility check
is then passed to the CLE's evaluation phase, which consists primarily of
calling the application once again to interpret and act on the sentence,
and finally calling it one last time to pick up any salient objects that the
application has introduced into the discourse domain (context model).

12.4.3   Opex's Model of Its World

Although Opex's model of the order-processing world is not of great
interest for its own sake, it helps discussion of the application interface
to have a broadbrush understanding of its structure.

As illustrated in Figure 12.2, the model represents a part of a com-

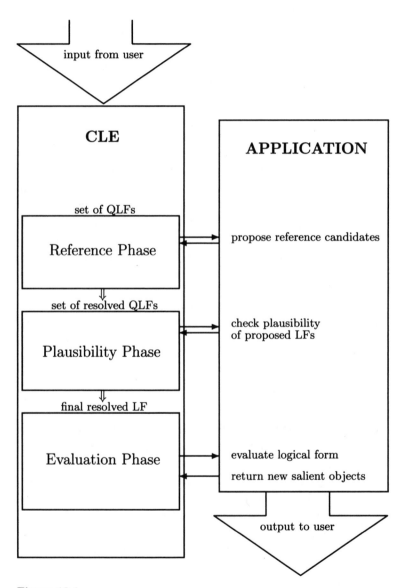

Figure 12.1
CLE-application interface

pany that makes computer components. This company, Compumake has several modeled departments—a sales department that accepts orders from customers, a shipping department that dispatches the items ordered, a billing department, and an accounting department. Several other companies exist as well, each of which has an employee or two who periodically order components from Compumake.

The simulation runs, under the control of natural language commands, in a series of discrete time steps. At random intervals, one of the customer employees creates a new order for a randomly assigned collection of computer components. The new order arrives at Compumake's sales department a short time later, and then spends a variable amount of time in each successive department and a short but variable time in transit between departments. Each department is capable of processing only one order at a time, so each maintains a queue for incoming orders. Orders have variable priorities, and the queues are priority-sensitive.

The point of this simulation is simply to provide an instructive example of an application with just sufficient richness and detail to exercise and illustrate various of the capabilities of the CLE. It includes a fair range of types and individuals, permitting a variety of forms of descriptive reference. It includes time, events, and a history. Commands can be issued and new rules declared that directly affect the way the simulation runs.

12.4.4 Object-Oriented Substrate

The simulation model is implemented partially via a simple object-oriented extension to Prolog, in which entities and their attributes are represented via assertions in the Prolog internal database. It is a temporally oriented object system, in which class and instance relationships are all time-stamped, so that even the shape of the class hierarchy can be dependent on the reference simulation time. The system supports multiple inheritance, object attributes (but without attribute type constraints or defaults), and a simple message-passing semantics that depends in the usual way on the class inheritance structure (except that ancestor precedence is nondeterministic).

The object system is used only for representing objects and some kinds of events (arrivals and departures, for example). Actions and relationships are for the most part implemented directly as Prolog procedures, and a special mechanism was developed for representing states, via state

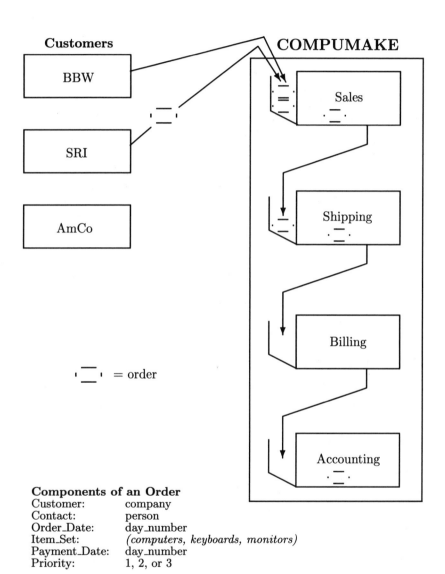

Figure 12.2
The order-processing scenario

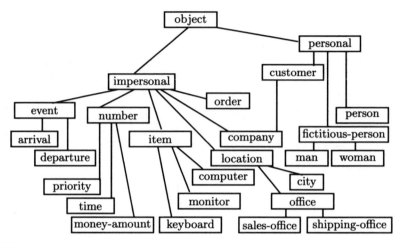

Figure 12.3
Opex object classes

descriptors, which are true over a specified interval in simulation time. Given a real, less inefficient object-oriented programming environment, it would be more elegant and consistent to model everything in the domain as either objects or "messages".

12.4.5   The Two Classification Hierarchies

In general, there is a close correspondence between the sort hierarchy used by the CLE for selectional filtering and the classification hierarchy used by Opex. Near the top (the root) of the trees the correspondence is almost one-to-one. Further down, the application's hierarchy makes more distinctions than the CLE does, but it is also narrower in scope, so that many things that can be classified in a general way by the CLE are not interpretable at all by Opex. A partial view of Opex's class hierarchy is given in Figure 12.3; this can be compared with the CLE sort hierarchy shown in Figure 9.2.

In our situation, the two hierarchies are used to represent rather different types of information. One is used to classify entities in the world on the basis of linguistic well-formedness constraints. The other is used to classify the same entities in terms of their intrinsic attributes and behavior. Nevertheless the relationship is close, and in a unified design it would make sense to represent all the information in a single hierarchy.

12.4.6   Mapping Senses to Domain Concepts

The logical form passed from the CLE to Opex is, obviously enough, a structure containing a lot of symbols. The symbols are of two principal kinds: closed-class symbols that form part of the Logical Form language itself (quant, past, and, ...) and open-class symbols representing word senses from the lexicon. In order to interpret instances of logical form, an application must be able to recognize and "have a definition for" all of these symbols.

For Opex, the lexical word senses will in many cases correspond to object classes in the model, and in other cases to predicates defined for the purpose. Opex maintains a set of translation tables that map word-sense symbols to its own internal names for classes and predicates. The first thing that happens when the CLE hands it a piece of logical form (or quasi logical form) to check or evaluate is that Opex translates it into its own name-space. This serves several purposes. First, it makes the name-space used internal to Opex independent of that used by the CLE. Second, it provides a quick check on whether the application can recognize everything in the LF. If something in the LF fails to translate, Opex immediately rejects whatever the CLE is proposing. The translation step is the first and strongest of the plausibility filters Opex performs on proposed LFs.

An example of the translation of the sentence

What keyboards has AmCo ordered?

will show a little of how the translator works.

The logical form resulting from this sentence is

```
quant(wh,
      A,
      [keyboard_thing,A],
      [pres,[perf,quant(exists,
                        B,
                        [event,B],
                        [order_action,B,amco1,A])]])
```

which when translated, yields the equivalent

```
quant(wh,
     A,
     is_instance_applic(A,keyboard),
     pres(perf(quant(exists,
                     B,
                     is_event(B),
                     order_action(B,amco,A)))))).
```

Note in passing that the list form for predicate notation adopted by the CLE for the Logical Form language (primarily to allow variables in functor position during processing) has been translated to standard Prolog notation for convenience in evaluation. As in Prolog, symbols with uppercase first letters are variables.

In this expression, the symbols quant, wh, exists, and the tense and aspect markers pres and perf are fixed elements of the Logical Form language. Three of the remaining symbols in the Logical Form expression, keyboard_thing, order_action, and amco1, are open-class symbols and are the names of word senses extracted from the lexicon by the CLE.

keyboard_thing is a one-place predicate that is not one of the standard Logical Form language predicates, so it must be either an object-class specification or a one-place relation. In this case the translator finds keyboard_thing in its object-class translation table, so it replaces the original expression with an appropriately instantiated version of Opex's standard two-place predicate

    is_instance_applic(<object>,<class>).

order_action, being a three-place predicate, can only be a relation, and Opex's translator checks to see that it has a corresponding three-place Prolog predicate defined. In this case it does (and its name is the same as the word-sense name), so all is well.

amco1, being atomic (or a zero-place predicate), should be the name of an individual object known to Opex. Sure enough it is, though the corresponding internal name is simply amco.

[event,B] (translated to is_event(B)) is an instance of the event conjunct included in the logical form of many sentences to allow modifiers of the main clause. During evaluation, the is_event predicate binds its argument to a transient structure whose fields can unify with the interpretations of any relevant qualifying phrases in whatever order they may appear. The resulting event objects are used in various ways by other evaluation predicates and are sometimes, but not always, unified with or instantiated as 'real' historical events in the model.

12.4.7 Evaluation of Logical Form

Response strategy Assuming that the translated LF passes the remaining plausibility checks, the application attempts to evaluate (or satisfy) it. There are two primary types of logical forms as far as Opex's evaluator is concerned: truth-functional and answer-producing. Generally speaking, *wh*-questions are answer-producing and everything else is truth-functional. At the top level, the result of evaluating a truth-functional LF is to display "Yes" or "No", and the result of evaluating an answer-producing LF is to display the answer list, or if it is empty, to print "None". This algorithm is extremely simple-minded, and the responses generated, being entirely literal, are sometimes rather unhelpful, but it is surprising how flexible even such a simple tool can be for extracting information.

In addition to the direct responses, evaluation of some kinds of sentences has side effects, an obvious example being the instruction *Print ... or Show me ....* Other commands have internal effects on the model, and some of these (such as the commands to run the simulation) cause effects observable to the user as well.

Evaluation method Like the translation step itself, evaluation is done recursively by a set of Prolog clauses that match each of the variant subforms of the Logical Form language. We will illustrate how this happens by continuing with the same example:

What keyboards has AmCo ordered?

The translated Logical Form expression is, as we saw above,

```
quant(wh,A,is_instance_applic(A,keyboard),
      pres(perf(quant(exists,
                      B,
                      is_event(B),
                      order_action(B,amco,A))))).
```

The top-level expression has the form of a typical quantified expression quant($\langle type \rangle$, $\langle var \rangle$, $\langle restriction \rangle$, $\langle body \rangle$)

where

$\langle type \rangle$ = wh
$\langle var \rangle$ = A
$\langle restriction \rangle$ = is_instance_applic(A,keyboard)
$\langle body \rangle$ = pres(perf(quant(...)))

The effect of evaluating such a form (in the particular case where the quantifier type is wh) is to find all distinct values of $\langle var \rangle$ that can simultaneously satisfy the two LF expressions $\langle restriction \rangle$ and $\langle body \rangle$. Each successful candidate value is paired with the list of answers, if any, resulting from the evaluation of $\langle body \rangle$, and the entire result in the form of a list is returned as the value of the complete quantified expression. If $\langle body \rangle$ is truth-functional then this result is effectively just a flat list, but if $\langle body \rangle$ is itself answer-producing, the result is a structured answer. Note that $\langle restriction \rangle$ is always assumed to be purely truth-functional.

Carrying on with the same example, evaluation of the $\langle restriction \rangle$ expression is as follows:

is_instance_applic($\langle object \rangle$, $\langle class \rangle$)

is defined in Opex as a Prolog procedure that succeeds if $\langle object \rangle$ is an instance of $\langle class \rangle$ in the model. With an uninstantiated first argument, this procedure will enumerate via backtracking all of the instances of $\langle class \rangle$. This is equivalent to the extensional representation of the restriction set in the original quantified expression.

The tense and aspect operators pres and perf are ignored in Opex. However, in a larger system called CLARE that includes the CLE as a subsystem (Section 12.6), such operators are translated as additional conjuncts. These temporal conjuncts typically include first order predicates expressing relations between events and times, or events and other events. The advantage of this translation of LFs with tense operators into first order expressions is that it makes it possible to implement basic reasoning about time and temporal reference with standard inference mechanisms.

The existential quantifier (quant(exists,...)) is handled in a very similar way to the wh-quantifier, except that it stops after finding a single satisfying variable instantiation rather than finding all such instantiations.

Finally, order_action(⟨*event*⟩,⟨*agent*⟩,⟨*order_item*⟩) has a purely ad hoc definition as a Prolog predicate. It succeeds if there is an instance in the model of an order object for which the customer attribute unifies with ⟨*agent*⟩ and a member of the item_set unifies with ⟨*order_item*⟩. The time slot of the event object is also unified with the order_date slot in the order object. With the example sentence, the time-slot unification succeeds vacuously, but if the sentence had been

What keyboards did AmCo order yesterday?

the referent of *yesterday* would have also unified with the time slot of the event object, and the result would have restricted the range of acceptable orders appropriately. In either case, however, the event object is discarded as soon as sentence processing is complete. Although the model does represent some events explicitly, order events happen to be represented only implicitly.

12.5   Extending the Interface

Given the mechanisms already in place in the CLE and Opex, it has proved very easy to extend the range of sentences that the combined system can handle.

The procedures corresponding to word senses for verbs and adjectives are typically five or six lines each, and adding a new definition is a matter of a few minutes. For noun word senses where there is already a corresponding object class in the model, extending coverage is even simpler, since the only change necessary is to add a new entry to the translation table. And VEX makes it easy to add new word senses to the lexicon (Chapter 11).

Of equal concern in a real application will be extending the model itself, in directions that may be pointed out through experience with natural language access. That, however, is a topic beyond the scope of this chapter.

12.6   New Directions

One of the key words in CLE is "Core". It was intended, as we have seen, as a module in larger systems—the module responsible for standard linguistic analysis of syntactic English input. However, to complete the design of a system using the CLE still requires the designer to think about modeling her domain in ways that tie in with the predicates in the lexicon, to worry about presuppositions and plausible inferences from what is said, perhaps to model what the user knows and can be assumed to expect, and so forth.

In research now being carried out at SRI Cambridge as a sequel to the work on the CLE, we are integrating the CLE itself into a more general framework that includes mechanisms for handling some of these issues. The new system, called CLARE (which sometimes stands for Combined Language And Reasoning Engine), will be a more self-contained unit capable of managing a conversation with a human user independently of interaction with other systems, in addition to supporting links to external systems and databases. CLARE contains its own knowledge base, to support reasoning about plausibility of interpretations and appropriate responses and to support models of particular domains. The internal knowledge base includes meta-level information about domain-level knowledge (Alshawi, Rayner and Smith 1991), and to a certain extent it can be extended and maintained via interaction in English. It is intended that some knowledge-based applications may be built entirely within CLARE, while others can take advantage of its self-adaptive capability to make integration with existing systems far easier than at present.

13 Ellipsis, Comparatives, and Generation

Hiyan Alshawi and Stephen G. Pulman

This chapter describes some further developments of the CLE under the topics of ellipsis, comparatives, and generation, which are closely related to the topics covered in earlier chapters. These developments were carried out as part of the CLARE project, which aims to combine language and reasoning capabilities in order to provide a contextual disambiguation and cooperative response environment for the CLE, but we will not be describing the work on reasoning in CLARE which is beyond the scope of this book.[1]

Comparative constructions often involve ellipsis, but there is also a practical link between the topics of ellipsis and generation: our approach to generation allows the results of ellipsis resolution to be paraphrased, giving feedback to users in interactive applications.

13.1 Ellipsis

13.1.1 Analysis of Ellipsis

Elliptical input, in the form of fragmentary input and certain coordination constructions, is common in natural language discourse, especially typed interactive discourse of the kind we expect a user of the CLE to engage in. An elliptical sentence constituent is needed to account for sentence fragments of various kinds:

> *John, Which house?, Inside, On the table, Difficult to do,*
> *John doesn't, He might not want to.*

All of these, as well as more complex sequences of fragments (e.g., *IBM, tomorrow* in response to *Where and when are you going?*) need to be accommodated in a grammar. They do not necessarily need to be treated syntactically as instances of S constituents, although this is the route taken here, as it provides us with a simple characterization of the semantics of ellipsis: an elliptical S consisting of a phrase of type X has as its meaning a function from X→S type meanings to S type

---

[1]This project is funded by the U.K. Department of Trade and Industry, and the CLARE consortium consisting of British Aerospace, British Petroleum, British Telecom, The Royal Signals and Radar Establishment, and SRI.

meanings. An incidental advantage of this decision is that it allows us to use the appropriate ellipsis rules in the analysis of comparatives (and some other constructions) as discussed in Section 13.2, without further ado.

Very many cases of this type of ellipsis can be analyzed by allowing an elliptical S to consist of one or more phrases (NP, PP, AdjP, AdvP) or their corresponding lexical categories. Most other commonly occurring patterns can be catered for by allowing verbs that subcategorize for a nonfinite VP (modals, auxiliary *do*, *to*) to appear without one, and by adding a special lexical entry for a main verb *do* that allows it to constitute a complete VP. In our grammar, the latter two moves allow all of the following to be analyzed:

> *Will John?, John won't, He may do, He may not want to, Is he going to?* etc.

Resolving ellipsis is often a contextually determined aspect of interpretation, so our QLF analysis of elliptical sentences is in terms of suitable a_form constructs (Chapter 10). Ellipsis interpretation can then be treated in a way similar to reference resolution. The semantic analysis of an NP fragment like *John*, parsed as an elliptical S, is represented in QLF as:

```
a_form(<t=ell,p=vp>,P,[P,john]).
```

As with other a_forms, this expression can be interpreted as an existential quantification over a predicate variable P, with the additional assumption that P can be indentified in context. Later in this chapter we discuss different approaches to proposing candidates for P in order to resolve the ellipsis.

13.1.2 Ellipsis and Processing Phases

As well as providing an explicit analysis of ellipsis at the QLF level, the use of a_forms in the CLE analysis is motivated by the aim of providing a uniform framework for contextual resolution of ellipsis, reference, and some cases of vagueness. Our treatment of ellipsis, and particularly verb phrase ellipsis, is therefore more akin to "interpretive" theories of ellipsis in linguistics (for example, Williams 1977) than to those based on deletion (for example, Sag 1980).

Like the resolution of other a_forms in our framework, a_forms arising from ellipsis have their bodies instantiated to a resolved formula in
RQLF, this formula replacing the a_form when an LF is extracted from
the RQLF. Resolution rules for elliptical a_forms have the same format
as those for other unresolved QLF expressions though the control structure for applying resolution rules was generalized to allow appropriate
interaction between ellipsis, reference resolution and quantifier scoping:
further scoping and resolution may take place after ellipsis resolution
that includes QLF constructs.

The nature of ellipsis in English is that its resolution is strongly dependent on the local linguistic context, as provided by the current sentence,
the preceding sentence, or the preceding exchange in a turn-taking dialogue. CLE resolution rules for intersentential ellipsis make use of the
RQLF interpretations of previous sentences which form part of the context model. (In the CLARE system, this information is represented in
the knowledge base together with other, nonlinguistic, contextual knowledge, while the original CLE implementation maintained the context
model as a special set of data structures.) It is not sufficient for ellipsis resolution to proceed simply on the basis of previous QLF analyses
because, in general, the preferred intersentential resolution of an elliptical sentence parallels a previous sentence in aspects such as scoping,
reference, and implicit relations that are not present in a QLF analysis.

An example is resolution of the ellipsis in the second sentence below:

Mary performed an experiment on every sample from the city.
So did Bill.

The required parallelism for the referent of *the city* and the relative scope
of the quantifying determiners *an* and *every* can be achieved by resolving
the a_form in *So did Bill* to an RQLF based on the interpretation of the
sentence providing the context. If instead we had

Mary performed the experiment on every London water sample.
So did Bill.

a parallel resolution of the relation implicit in the compound *London
water sample* can be maintained by resolving on the basis of RQLF.

It might be argued that this parallelism could be achieved by resolving
ellipsis at QLF level and then relying on scoping and reference resolution to produce the same results a second time. However, this would

be ignoring the seemingly reasonable hypothesis that the parallelism in examples like the above is a constraint on coherent discourse: there may be different coherent interpretations of the discourse, but the parallelism should be present in each interpretation. Exceptions to this might also be covered within our representational framework because it is possible to recover the information in a QLF analysis that led to an RQLF interpretation (Section 13.3.4).

13.1.3   Ellipsis Resolution

Our approach to deriving alternative interpretations of elliptical sentences does not depend on parallelism with alternative syntactic or semantic analyses of the "source" clause, that is, the full clause on the basis of which an elliptical (or "target") clause is completed. In this respect our analysis is similar to the one taken independently by Dalrymple, Shieber, and Pereira (1991) using higher-order unification (Huet 1975). They argue against approaches that link ellipsis ambiguities to ambiguities in the analysis of the source (including those of Williams 1977 and Sag 1980).

Our approach is a particularization of the general method proposed by Dalrymple, Shieber, and Pereira (1991) in the sense now explained. Given a correspondence between parallel elements in the source and target clauses, the general method states the ellipsis problem as a pair of equations, solved by higher-order unification. The simplest kind of example is the pair of parallel elements *mary* and *john* in *Has Mary arrived? Has John?* The equations, involving the interpretation of the source clause, let us say $query(arrive(mary))$ for simplicity, is solved for two unknowns, a higher-order relation P and the interpretation of the target clause, T:

$$P(mary) = query(arrive(mary))$$
$$P(john) = T.$$

(As mentioned earlier, in QLF notation, the expression to be resolved to the interpretation T would be a_form(<t=ell,p=vp>,P,[P,john]).) A possible solution proposed for P by higher-order unification of the two sides of the first equation is $\lambda x.query(arrive(x))$. By applying this to *john*, the second equation gives the interpretation of the elliptical clause as $query(arrive(john))$.

However, unrestricted higher-order unification also produces unwanted solutions (e.g., the vacuous $\lambda x.query(arrive(mary))$ in this case), so Dalrymple, Shieber, and Pereira (1991) propose constraints on its application to ellipsis interpretation. They also note that because the source interpretation and the parallel elements are usually fully instantiated, only a special case of second order matching is required to determine the relation P.

These constraints are reflected in our approach in that we apply the parallel elements directly as substitutions. By a substitution we simply mean a pair of expressions e_1 and e_2 where the result of applying the substitution is $I[e_2/e_1]$, that is, the result of replacing all occurrences of e_1 in I by e_2:

$$T = query(arrive(mary))[john/mary] = query(arrive(john)).$$

We will use the notation $[a_1/b_1, \ldots, a_n/b_n]$ for a sequence of substitutions to be applied from left to right.

It seems likely that, on the one hand, higher-order unification is too unconstrained for ellipsis interpretation, while, on the other hand, the use of substitutions alone may turn out to be too constrained, but it is unclear at present which of these extremes gives a better characterization of ellipsis.

13.1.4   Ellipsis Resolution Methods

The common theme among the CLE intersentential resolution methods is that they depend on finding a set of substitutions to apply to an antecedent RQLF interpretation. Rather than giving details of the procedures proposing substitutions for the different resolution methods, we will present the substitutions proposed for a number of cases, particularly follow-on questions that are important for the kind of interactive discourse typical of many applications we are interested in.

The resolution method for an utterance consisting of just a noun phrase finds and applies such a substitution. In a simple case such as resolving the follow-on question:

> *Was Mary nominated by Bill?*
> *Susan?*

identifying and applying the substitution is all that needs to be done. In this example, there are two possible substitutions:

```
[susan/bill]
[susan/mary].
```

The substitution can also replace a `qterm` by a constant, as happens when the preferred method for expanding the answer to a wh-question is applied:

Which candidate did Bill nominate?
Mary.

In this case there is also a substitution to replace the "mood operator" `whq` with the operator `dcl` for declarative utterances:

```
[susan/qterm(<t=quant,l=wh,n=sing>,X,[candidate,X]),
dcl/whq].
```

The RQLF resulting from these substitutions will include a vacuous quantification corresponding to the replaced `qterm`, but this does not affect the truth conditions of the resulting expression. (In fact, the implementation removes such vacuous quantifications to simplify later processing.) The interpretations of the sentences in this example can be passed to the generation component (Section 13.3), producing among others the following paraphrases:

Which candidate was nominated by Bill?
Bill nominated Mary.

In the common case of verb phrase ellipsis where an auxiliary is used to indicate a change of tense or aspect in the elliptical sentence, a substitution for the operator is needed. For example, the substitutions

```
[mary/bill,fut/past]
```

can be used to resolve the ellipsis exhibited by the follow-on question in:

Did Mary nominate Susan?
Will Bill?

However, we still do not have a good model for the required substitutions for tense operators in embedded clauses, and the implementation simply does not apply operator substitutions to such clauses.

An example follow-on question exhibiting the strict/sloppy identity ambiguity is:

Does Bill love his wife?
Does John?

In the RQLF for the first sentence, the resolved pronoun a_term inside the representation for *his wife* will have its variable unified with bill:

```
a_term(Category,bill,
        [and,[male,bill],[personal,bill]]).
```

The "sloppy" reading simply results from applying to the RQLF the substitution [john/bill], both inside and outside the a_term. The generator (arguably exhibiting a certain amount of overgeneration) paraphrases this interpretation as:

Is John's wife loved by John?

For the strict reading, we wish to stop application of the substitution to the resolved pronoun. In general, when substituting a term t2 for a term t1 in an RQLF, if there is an a_term resolved to t1, we wish to allow the possibility of not applying the substitution to the a_term in order to preserve the resolution of the pronoun in the antecedent sentence. In the implementation, we express this by a sequence of substitutions involving an arbitrary new constant c:

```
[c/a_term(Category,t1,Restriction),
 t2/t1,
 a_term(Category,t1,Restriction)/c].
```

The resulting interpretation is paraphrased by the generator as:

Is Bill's wife loved by John?

It is well known that only sloppy readings are available for ellipsis of simple sentences involving control. For example, in

Does John want to leave?
Does Bill?

it is not possible to interpret the second question as asking whether Bill wants John to leave. However, such readings would be predicted by unrestricted use of higher-order unification for resolving the ellipsis (one possibility for the unifier abstracts over the subject of *want* but not that of *leave*). In our approach using substitutions, only the correct reading is proposed by the resolver, this corresponding to the replacement of both instances of `bill` with `john` in the following (shown without event variables):

```
[pres,
   [want,
      bill,[apply,X^[leave,X],bill]]].
```

Another advantage of resolving ellipsis by substitution into RQLF is that it allows constraints on reference resolution to come into effect. For example, in resolving the ellipsis in

Bill likes Mary.
Does she?

unconstrained application of higher-order unification to LFs is problematic because it allows the interpretation *Does Mary like Mary?* This reading is ruled out by the CLE reference constraints that are applied after proposing candidates for all unresolved expressions, including ellipsis. In this case, pronoun configurational constraints disallow the following predication (shown simplified):

```
[like,
   a_term(<t=ref,p=pro,l=she>,mary,[female,mary]),mary].
```

On the other hand, the CLE correctly allows the reflexive resolution of the ellipsis in

Mary likes herself.
Does she?

because in this case the predication is

```
[like,
   a_term(<t=ref,p=refl,l=her>,mary,[female,mary]),mary]
```

which is permitted by the configurational constraints.

In this section, we have concentrated on resolution methods for intersentential ellipsis. Similar resolution methods are also employed in the CLE for handling common cases of intrasentential ellipsis arising from conjunctions and comparatives. Roughly speaking, these resolve the ellipsis `a_form` to a formula resulting from substituting arguments into a subformula of the RQLF interpretation being derived for the sentence.

13.2   Analysis of Comparatives

Many treatments of the English comparative construction have been advanced recently in the computational linguistics literature (e.g., Rayner and Banks 1990, Ballard 1988). This interest reflects the importance of the construction for many natural language applications, especially those concerning access to databases, where it is natural to require information about quantitative differences and limits that are most naturally expressed in terms of comparatives and superlatives.

However, all of these analyses have their defects (as no doubt does this one). The most pervasive of these defects is one of principle: they all place a high reliance on noncompositional methods (tree or formula rewriting) for assembling the logical forms of the expressions being analyzed. As well as needing extra machinery over what the basic syntax and compositional semantics of the language demand, these devices mean that the grammatical descriptions involved lack, to varying extents, the important property of reversibility: they can only be used to analyze, not to generate, expressions of comparison. This is a serious restriction on the practical usefulness of such analyses.

In this section, we present our analysis of the syntax and compositional semantics of the main instances of the English comparative and superlative in a relatively theory-neutral way, abstracting away from details of CLE notation. The main theoretical claim is that by factoring out the compositional properties of the construction from the various types of ellipsis also involved, a cleaner treatment can be arrived at that does not need any machinery specific to this construction.

13.2.1   Syntax of Comparatives

A long tradition in linguistic description sees most instances of comparatives as reduced conjunctions. Intuitively, a sentence like

> *John owns more horses than Bill owns*

seems to consist of two sentences ascribing ownership of horses, together with a comparison of them, where some material has been omitted. Despite appearances, however, this pretheoretical intuition is almost wholly wrong: the sequence *more horses than Bill owns* is in fact an NP, and a constituent of the main clause, as can be seen from the fact that it can appear as a syntactic subject and can be conjoined with other simple NPs:

[More horses than Bill owns] are sold every day
John, Mary, and [more linguists than they could cope with] arrived at the party.

In order to accommodate examples like these we must analyze the whole sequence as an NP, with some internal structure approximately as follows:

```
np:[comparative=-] -->
[np:[comparative=+,postparticle=P,relevantNPfeats=R],
 s':[comparative=+,postparticle=P,relevantNPfeats=R]].
```

An `np:[comparative=+]` is one like:

a nicer horse, a less nice horse, less nice a horse, several horses more several more horses, as many horses, at least 3 more horses, etc.

Some of these NPs can be analyzed by the same rules as are necessary for NPs not containing any expression of comparison, the differences being carried by feature values, but for others, some idiosyncratic statements may be needed.

In the case of the `s':[comparative=+]` constituent, there are several possibilities. Some forms of comparative can be regarded as straightforward examples of unbounded dependency constructions:

... more horses than Bill ever dreamed he would own _
... more horses than Bill wanted _ to run in the race.

These involve wh-movement of NPs. The second type involves a missing determiner dependency:

John owns more horses than Bill owns _ sheep
There were more horses in the field than there were _ sheep.

Rules of the following form will cover [+comparative] sentences of this type, using "gap threading" to capture the unbounded dependency:

```
s':[comparative=+,postparticle=P,relevantfeats=R] -->
  [comp:[form=P],
   s:[comparative=-,
      gapIn=[np:[]/det:[relevantfeats=R]],gapOut=[]]].
```

As well as these "movement" comparatives are those involving ellipsis:

John owns more horses than Bill/Bill does/does Bill/sheep
Name a linguist with more publications than Chomsky
He looks more intelligent with his glasses off than on.

It is noteworthy that sentences like the second of these demonstrate that the appropriate level at which elided constituents are recovered is not syntactic but semantic: there is no syntactic constituent in the first portion of the sentence that could form an appropriate antecedent. We therefore do not attempt to provide a syntactic mechanism for these cases but rather regard them as containing another instantiation of a `comparative=+` sentence introduced by a rule:

```
s':[comparative=+] -->
   [comp:[], s:[ellipsis=+, comparative=-]].
```

The right-hand side of this rule contains an elliptical sentence of the kind discussed in Section 13.1.1.

With this treatment of ellipsis, our syntax will be able to analyze all the examples of comparatives above, and many more. It will also, however, accept examples like

John owns more horses than inside
Bill is happier than John won't

for there is no syntactic connection between the main clause and the elliptical sentence. We assume that some of these examples may actually be interpretable given the right context: at any rate, it is not the business of syntax to stigmatize them as unacceptable.

The requirement that all of these different types of comparative form part of an NP constituent means that when there are other elements in the VP in which that NP occurs, but to the right of it, we must allow for rightward extraposition of the `s':[comparative=+]` out of its containing NP, just as in the case of other types of NP postmodifiers like PPs and relative clauses:

He designed more buildings _ in Cambridge before 1800 [than he de-
signed in Oxford after 1800].

This has the consequence that unextraposed sentences like

He designed more buildings than he designed in Oxford after 1800 in Cambridge before 1800

will also be accepted; rightly, in our view, although they can sound clumsy.

Comparatives with adjectives and adverbial phrases are, *mutatis mutandis*, exactly analogous to those with NPs:

John's horses are [AdjP [AdjP more expensive][S than Bill's horses are _]]
John's horses run [AdvP [AdvP more quickly][S than Bill's horses run _]].

Here an AdjP or AdvP gap is required in the comparative S. The "subdeletion" cases have a "degree" rather than a determiner gap:

This box is [AdjP [AdjP as wide][S as that one is _ tall]]
His organisation runs [AdvP [AdvP as inefficiently][S as yours runs _ efficiently]].

Subdeletion for adverbials is fairly uncommon.

13.2.2   Semantics of Comparatives

In the interest of clarity the semantic analysis will be presented as far as possible in an "intensionless Montague" framework: a typed higher-order logic. In the case of the movement types of comparative we can give the semantics in a wholly compositional way by building up generalized quantifiers that contain the comparison. As explained in Section 2.2.3, we allow generalized quantifiers to be arbitrarily complex expressions. Informally, the gist of the analysis is that in a sentence like *John owns more horses than Bill owns*, there is a generalized quantifier characterizing the set of horses that John owns as being greater than the set of horses that Bill owns. This corresponds to the intuition shared by many linguists that such sentences should be analyzed something like:

John owns [more than Bill owns] horses.

(In this respect, as in the use of generalized quantifiers, this analysis yields logical forms somewhat similar to those of Rayner and Banks (1990) although it was developed independently.)

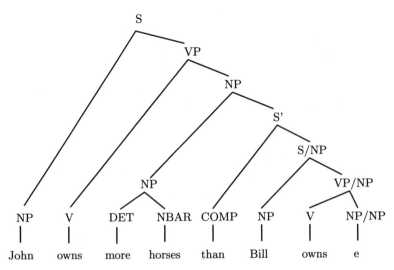

Figure 13.1
Syntax tree for comparative sentence

To build these quantifiers we assume that the various relations signaled by the comparative construction are part of the quantifier. Thus the final analysis of the example sentence is:

quant(λnm.more(m, λx.horse(x) & own(bill,x)),
λy.horse(y), λz.own(john,z)).

More (or *less* or *as*) is the relation used to build the quantifier. To avoid notational clutter we can assume that *more* is "overloaded", and can take as its arguments either a number, or an expression of type e→t, in which case it is interpreted as taking the cardinality of the set denoted by that expression. *More* in fact takes a third argument, which is another quantifier relation. Thus the meaning of a sentence like *John owns at least 3 more horses than Bill owns* would get a logical form like

quant(λnm.more(m, λx.horse(x) & own(bill,x), λab.b≥3),
λy.horse(y), λz.own(john,z)).

The way to read this is "the relation of being more (by a number greater than or equal to 3) than the size of the set of horses owned by Bill holds of the set of horses owned by John". (Where this extra argument is not explicit, we assume it defaults to "greater than 0". However, we shall ignore this refinement in the illustrations that follow.) Note that this quantifier is an absolute quantifier only involving the intersection set: this is always true of comparative quantifiers.

We now give the meanings of each constituent involved in a couple of examples, along with the relevant rules, in skeletal form. We indicate the trail of gap threading using the "slash" notation. For the purposes of this illustration we use the the analysis of the semantics of unbounded dependencies from Gazdar et al. 1985: a constituent C containing a gap of category X is of type X→C. So given a tree of the form [A [B C]], which might normally have as the interpretation of A as B applied to C, the interpretation of a tree [A/X [B C/X]] would be 'λX.B(C(X))'. Since gaps themselves are analyzed as the identity function this will have the right type.

For the sentence *John owns more horses than Bill*, the syntactic analysis is as shown in Figure 13.1. The relevant rules and sense entries in schematic form are:

S → NP VP : NP(VP)

VP → V NP : V(NP)

NP → NP[+comp] S' : NP(S)

S' → Comp S/NP : λx.S(λP.P(x))

S' → Comp S/Det : λx.S(λPQ.P(x) & Q(x))

S/Gap → NP VP/Gap : λG.NP(VP(G))

VP/Gap → V NP/Gap : λG.V(NP(G))

NP/NP → ϵ : λN.N

NP/Det → Nbar : λD.D(Nbar)

NP → bill : λP.P(bill)

NP → Det Nbar : Det(Nbar)

Det → more :λPQR.quant(λnm.more(m,λx.Px&Qx),λy.Py,λz.Rz)

Nbar → horses : λx.horse(x)

V → owns : λNx.N(λy.owns(x,y))

'Gap' abbreviates either NP[-comp] or Det, and G is a variable of the appropriate type for that constituent. N is an NP-type variable; D a

Det-type variable, as are their primed versions. Notice that comparative determiners and their NPs are of higher type than noncomparative NPs, at least for those analyses that analyze relative clauses as modifiers of Nbar rather than NP. Constituent meanings are assembled by the rules above as follows (application of a complex functor to its argument is written [$functor$]($argument$) for ease of readability):

[NP+comp *more horses*]:

$$\lambda QR.quant(\lambda nm.more(m, \lambda x.horse(x) \& \ Q(x)),$$
$$\lambda y.horse(y), \lambda z.R(x))$$

[VP/NP *owns* ϵ]:

$$\lambda G.[\lambda Nx.N(\lambda y.owns(x,y))]([\lambda N'.N'](G))$$
$$= \lambda G.\lambda x.G(\lambda y.owns(x,y))$$

[S/NP *Bill owns* ϵ]:

$$\lambda G'.[\lambda P.P(bill)]([\lambda G.\lambda x.G(\lambda y.owns(x,y))](G'))$$
$$= \lambda G'.G'(\lambda y.owns(bill,y))$$

[S' *than Bill owns* ϵ]:

$$\lambda x.[\lambda G'.G'(\lambda y.owns(bill,y))](\lambda P.P(x))$$
$$= \lambda x.owns(bill,x)$$

[NP [*more horses*][S' *than Bill owns* ϵ]]:

$$\lambda R.quant(\lambda nm.more(m, \lambda x.horse(x) \ \& \ own(bill,x)),$$
$$\lambda y.horse(y), \ \lambda z.R(z)).$$

The remainder of the sentence is straightforward.

The second example for illustration is:

John owns more horses than Bill owns _ sheep.

For the subdeletion cases, a fully compositional treatment demands a separate sense entry for 'more', since the Nbar of the NP in which 'more' appears does not occur inside the comparative quantifier:

$\lambda PQR.quant(\lambda nm.more(m,\lambda x.Qx),\ \lambda y.Py,\ \lambda z.Rz).$

We do not have to multiply syntactic ambiguities: the appropriate sense entry can be selected by passing down into the NP a syntactic feature value indicating whether the following S' contains an NP or a Det gap. Constituents are assembled as follows: remember that D has the type of ordinary determiners: $(e{\rightarrow}t){\rightarrow}((e{\rightarrow}t){\rightarrow}t)$.

[NP/Det ϵ *sheep*]:

$\lambda D.D(\lambda s.sheep(s))$

[VP/Det *owns ϵ sheep*]:

$\lambda D'.[\lambda Nx.N(\lambda y.owns(x,y))]([\lambda D.D(\lambda s.sheep(s))](D'))$
$= \lambda D'.\lambda x.[D'(\lambda s.sheep(s))](\lambda y.owns(x,y))$

[S/Det *Bill owns ϵ sheep*]:

$\lambda D'.[D'(\lambda s.sheep(s))](\lambda y.owns(bill,y))$

[S' *than Bill owns ϵ sheep*]:

$\lambda x.[\lambda D'.[D'(\lambda s.sheep(s))](\lambda y.owns(bill,y))](\lambda PQ.P(x)\ \&\ Q(x))$
$= \lambda x.[[\lambda PQ.P(x)\ \&\ Q(x))](\lambda s.sheep(s))](\lambda y.owns(bill,y))$
$= \lambda x.sheep(x)\ \&\ owns(bill,x)$

[NP+comp *more horses*]:

$\lambda QR.quant(\lambda nm.more(m,\ \lambda x.Qx),\lambda y.horse(y),\lambda z.R(z))$

[NP *more horses than Bill owns ϵ sheep*]:

$\lambda QR.[quant(\lambda nm.more(m,\lambda x.Qx),\ \lambda y.horse(y),\lambda z.R(z))]$
$\qquad\qquad\qquad (\lambda x.sheep(x)\ \&\ owns(bill,x))$
$= \lambda R.quant(\lambda nm.more(m,\lambda x.sheep(x)\ \&\ owns(bill,x)),$
$\qquad\qquad\qquad \lambda y.horse(y),\ \lambda z.R(z)).$

The final logical form for the whole sentence is:

$quant(\lambda nm.more(m,\lambda x.sheep(x)\ \&\ owns(bill,x)),$
$\qquad\qquad\qquad \lambda y.horse(y),\ \lambda z.own(john,z)).$

13.2.3   Comparatives and Ellipsis

Our analysis of intersentential ellipsis generalizes cleanly to some cases
of intrasentential ellipsis, in particular the comparative cases discussed
above. As an example, the NP in a sentence like

Name a linguist with [more publications than John]

will have a structure:

[NP [NP more publications] [S' than [S+elliptical [NP John]]]].

The meaning of the elliptical S will be as above, and the appropriate
version of the semantics for the S' rule will (as was the case with the
analysis of the movement comparatives given earlier) arrange things so
that the type of the whole elliptical expression is e→t. The meaning of
the entire NP will then be:

$$\lambda R.quant(\lambda nm.more(m, \lambda x.publication(x) \,\&$$
$$[\lambda x'.a\_form(c,P,P(\lambda Q.Q(john)))](x)),$$
$$\lambda y.publication(y), \lambda z.R(z))$$

where the meaning of the elliptical sentence figures in the second term
of the comparison after beta-reduction. An appropriate candidate for
P in ellipsis resolution here, given that the constituent resulting from
the application of P to the meaning of *John* must be of type e→t is the
following (we assume *with* to be synonymous in this context with the
transitive verb *have*):

$$\lambda N.N(\lambda y.have(y,x'))$$

where N is a variable of the type of an (ordinary) NP. After beta-
reduction the second argument of *more* will be:

$$\lambda x.publications(x) \,\& \, have(john,x)$$

and the final meaning of the whole NP will be equivalent to *more publications than John has.*

Now we have succeeded in analyzing all the types of comparative so
far discussed using either purely compositional means or a device for
contextual interpretation of ellipsis whose properties are motivated on
grounds other than its use for comparatives. Furthermore, with the
ellipsis mechanism in place, it is a simple matter to extend it to account
for comparatives in which the whole comparison is missing:

John has more horses.
There are at least as many sheep.

As Rayner and Banks (1990) somewhat ruefully note, these are in many
texts the most commonly encountered form of comparative, although
their analysis, in common with others, fails to handle them.

Syntactically, what we do is to give the various comparative morphemes an analysis in which they are marked as [comparative=-].
Thus a phrase like *at least as many sheep* will be analyzed as either a +
or - comparative NP. In the first case, the syntax will only permit it to
occur with an explicit complement, as detailed above, and in the second
case the syntax will prevent an explicit complement from occurring. Semantically, however, the second contains an elliptical comparison. Thus
the meaning of *more* in this type of comparative will be:

$$\lambda PQ.quant(\lambda nm.more(m,\lambda x.\ P(x)\ \&\ a\_form(c,R,R(x))),$$
$$\lambda y.P(y),\ \lambda z.(Q(z)).$$

In a context where *John has more horses* follows a sentence like *Bill has
some horses*, R should be resolved to '$\lambda a.have(bill,a)$'. Notice that it
may be necessary to provide interpretations for *more* in these contexts
corresponding to both the NP-gap and the Det-gap cases. The elliptical
portion is different depending on whether the preceding sentence was *Bill
has some horses* or *Bill has many sheep*: the latter is like the Det-gap
type of explicit comparison.

13.3   Generation

Since the CLE grammar formalism is declarative, it can be used for generation (synthesis) as well as analysis. In particular, given that QLF
analyses are built up by unification rules for syntax, semantics, and
morphology, it is also possible to devise algorithms for building a tree
of constituents by unification by applying these rules in the "reverse"
direction. If the semantic rules had been more in the style of traditional Montague semantics, generation from structures that had under-
gone lambda reductions would have presented search difficulties because
the reductions would have to be applied in reverse during the generation process. This turns out to be an important practical advantage of
unification-based semantics over the traditional approach.

In the context of a system like CLARE for interaction with a knowledge base, generation is potentially useful to the aim of natural cooperative dialogues in a number of ways. These include the generation of responses: answers, asking the user to confirm consequences of their requests (e.g., changes to the knowledge base), explanations of analysis failure, and so on. Generation is also useful for interactive disambiguation as it often allows user inputs to be paraphrased in a way that makes explicit their interpretation by the system.

The CLE component for generation from QLF employs an algorithm that is based on the "semantic head driven" (SHD) generation algorithm (Shieber et al. 1990). We will briefly describe the original algorithm and then discuss some steps we have taken in the CLE implementation to make generation efficient in the context of a large grammar.

13.3.1   The SHD Generation Algorithm

The SHD algorithm is usually applied to a pair consisting of the semantic structure being generated from (in our case a QLF), together with a category for the phrase type we are attempting to generate. We will refer to such a pair as a *node*, so semantic rules in the CLE grammar formalism are lists of such nodes. At the start of the process, the category may be more or less instantiated, it may simply be the start category for the grammar, or it may be a suitably instantiated sentence or noun phrase category. In the CLE implementation, the output (which is nondeterministic) is a phrase structure tree for some sentence having the input QLF as its semantic analysis.

The SHD algorithm proceeds as follows. The QLF for the node currently being generated is matched against the QLF of the mother of a *nonchain rule*, that is, a rule in which the QLF for the mother is different from that of any of its daughters. The choice of rule is constrained further to rules for which there is a sequence (or chain) of categories, $C_1, \ldots, C_n$, where C_1 is the category of the node being generated, C_n is the mother node category of the chosen rule, and each pair (C_i, C_{i+1}) corresponds to the mother and daughter categories of a *chain rule*. A chain rule is one in which some daughter (the semantic head) has the same QLF as the mother node of that rule. To complete the construction of the phrase structure tree, all that is needed is to apply the algorithm recursively to the daughters of the chosen nonchain rule and to the non-head daughters of each chain rule in the sequence.

The effectiveness of the algorithm comes from the way it quickly leads to a backbone of the target phrase structure tree being proposed according to the input QLF and the semantic head relation for the grammar. For a more detailed presentation of the algorithm and a discussion of its merits, the reader is referred to Shieber et al. 1990.

Applying Rules for Generation

In the CLE implementation, the rules used in generation are those built by unifying the categories in semantic rules with the categories in their syntactic counterparts (syntactic rules with matching rule identifiers) and the categories in word sense derivation rules with those in corresponding morphology rules. It is also possible to run the generator simply with semantic rules and sense derivation rules, and apply the constraints from the syntactic rules in a second stage, but this leads to much increased nondeterminism and a consequent increase in processing time. Syntactic constraints for lexical entries are also unified into sense entries when these are being applied, as daughterless nonchain rules, during generation.

The more compositional the semantic rules of the grammar, the more efficient generation becomes with this algorithm. In the context of the CLE semantic rules, this corresponds to having the mother QLF in a rule built from daughter QLFs rather than in from the values of semantic features. As a result, applying the CLE grammar in the generation direction, rather than the analysis direction for which it was originally designed, was more effective after some re-organization of the rules that increased the compositionality of the grammar—this also made the grammar easier to understand.

Different uses to which a generator is employed require different trade-offs between efficiency and the number of paraphrases that the generator needs to produce for a given QLF. To control the set of rules that the generator applies, the rule compilation process is sensitive to declarations specifying which rules are to be included, and the order of their application, in the generation process.

13.3.2   Rule and Lexicon Precompilation

The CLE implementation of the SHD algorithm includes a number of control structure and precompilation optimizations. The first of these is precompilation of the transitive closure of the semantic head relation for the categories of the grammar to allow more efficient application of the chaining step. This precompilation proceeds in a similar fashion to the computation of the left-corner linking relation used by the CLE parser in that pairs in the relation are kept in their most general form with subsumed pairs being deleted.

Further preprocessing takes place by unifying the daughter element of pairs in the semantic-head relation with the mother categories of nonchain rules producing composed rules of the form

```
gen_rule(Index,ChainCategory,MotherNode,DauNodes).
```

These rules are applied at run time by matching the mother QLF and the chain category against the target QLF and category being generated. It is further assumed that these two terms (the QLF and category) will be instantiated when the rule is applied, so a combined index is derived from them to improve the efficiency of rule look-up. This assumption can be enforced by reordering the generation of daughter nodes dynamically, as explained in the next section.

As mentioned above, sense entries are treated by the algorithm as daughterless nonchain rules, so it is possible to include them in the precompilation process. However, this results in a very large set of gen_rule entries (several times the number of entries in the lexicon) with corresponding increased storage and access overheads. Our strategy is to only include lexicon entries in the compilation process if they cannot be indexed effectively by a unique (or almost unique) symbol, such as the word sense predicate symbols in the QLFs for most noun, verb, and adjective entries. In effect, the precompilation process decides which words are to be treated as "function" words whose entries are compiled together with grammar rules, and which are treated as "content" words. Applying the former will be constrained during generation by the semantic-head relation, while the latter will only be considered when generating from a QLF (sub)expression if the symbol under which it is indexed is present in that QLF. Since there is a constant number of function words, and a constant number of content words indexed from the symbols in a QLF, the time taken for generation is effectively independent of the size of the lexicon.

Literals appearing in grammar rules (i.e., daughters that are specified as words rather than categories) are compiled directly into the run-time rules, so no access to the lexicon is necessary for them; they are treated as daughters whose generation has been completed at compile time.

13.3.3 Control and Search

The CLE implementation of the SHD algorithm includes an improvement to the basic control structure: when the recursive generation of a list of daughters of a rule is taking place, these are not necessarily generated from left to right, although that is the default order. Instead, if the next daughter to be generated has an as-yet uninstantiated QLF, the generation of this daughter is delayed until the other daughters have been generated. Generating from daughters with instantiated QLFs reduces unguided search and allows the improved indexing mentioned above. There are cases where delaying generation of one daughter until others have become instantiated is essential. An example of this is generation of subject-auxiliary inversion questions like *Will John sleep?* if these are treated by a rule of the form:

```
sem(s_aux_np_vp,inverted,
    (AuxQLF,s:[type=ynq,...]) -->
    [(AuxQLF,aux:[arglist=[(VpQLF,VpCat)],subjval=Np],
    (Np,np:[...]),
    (VpQLF,VpCat)]).
```

When this rule is used for analysis, the subject noun phrase meaning Np is passed to the verb phrase meaning VpQLF via the sense entry for the auxiliary. During generation, however, the noun phrase meaning variable Np will only become instantiated after the verb phrase node (VpQLF,VpCat) has been generated. It is therefore necessary to delay generation of the noun phrase node until this has happened, as otherwise all possible noun phrases compatible with the noun phrase category will be generated before their meanings are matched against the noun phrase meaning in the input QLF.

The search strategy for generation in the CLE implementation is an iterative deepening strategy whereby a series of depth-limited searches are performed to successively higher limits (Korf 1985). The depth of a solution corresponds here roughly to the number of applications of rules or lexical entries during the search, so a shallower solution usually corresponds to a simpler sentence. The strategy is thus often able to find simple solutions closer to the top of the search space than the depth-first strategy. This is particularly suitable for generation because in many applications we are only interested in a single, simple rendering of the semantic representation in natural language. This is in contrast to parsing where we are often interested in all possible analyses, the reason for the asymmetry being that the semantic representation language is less ambiguous a representation than natural language. The iterative deepening strategy also means that finite solutions will be found eventually, even if the grammar allows infinite phrase structure derivations for the input semantic representation.

In order to reuse intermediate results from one search path (or from a previous depth iteration), whenever a possible phrase structure for a constituent is generated, this is stored together with the QLF-category node associated with it, provided that it is not subsumed by an existing intermediate result. When a daughter node is being generated it is first matched against previously generated nodes, so that the stored phrase structure can be reused. Again, the fact that we do not want to exhaustively search for all possible solutions means that such a simple caching technique can be effective in reducing the time spent finding initial solutions.

13.3.4   Generation from RQLF

Although the SHD algorithm is limited to generation from the semantic representations that are built by unification (QLF in the case of the CLE), the CLE also allows generation from the RQLF, or sentence interpretation, level. This proceeds by first mapping the RQLF to a suitable QLF which is then passed to the generation component described above. The capability for generation from fully interpreted (RQLF) representations is relatively easy in the CLE because an RQLF preserves the information in a QLF from which it is derived (Chapter 10). In fact, this was one of the motivations for preserving qterms in full in later versions of the scoping module.

What counts as a suitable QLF for generation to extract from an RQLF depends on the purpose of the generation. If this purpose is to provide a paraphrase of a user's utterance giving feedback on how the utterance is being interpreted, then the QLF should show how unresolved expressions (referential or elliptical) have been resolved. This is achieved in the implementation by replacing a_term, referential qterm, and a_form expressions by their referents. Quantified formulae aris-

ing from scoping nonreferential qterms can be replaced by their body
(scope) formulae because in the RQLF representation such a body formula still contains the qterm for the quantified variable. It would also
be possible to replace any vague determiners that have been resolved to
a quantifier by a less ambiguous determiner (e.g., 'any' being replaced
by 'some' or 'all' depending on whether it was resolved to an existential
or a universal).

For example, the QLF analysis chosen for *She saw one* might be the
following:

```
[past
  [see1,
    qterm(<t=quant,n=sing,l=ex>,E,[event,E]),
    a_term(<t=ref,p=pro,l=she,n=sing>,Y,[female,Y])
    qterm(<t=quant,n=sing>,X,
          a_form(<t=pred,p=one>,P,[P,X]))]],
```

while the QLF extracted from an RQLF interpretation of the analysis
might be

```
[past
  [see1,
    qterm(<t=quant,n=sing,l=ex>,E,[event,E]),
    mary1
    qterm(<t=quant,n=sing>,X,[zebra1,X])]],
```

from which the sentence *Mary saw a zebra* can be generated. Examples of generation from resolved ellipsis have already been given in Section 13.1.4.

In the present version of CLARE, the most important use of the generator is to allow users to confirm interpretations by generation from
RQLF. We had expected that its use for paraphrasing QLF analyses
for structural disambiguation would be more important. In practice, it
turns out to be difficult to generate paraphrases exhibiting a choice of
structure without introducing further ambiguity. On the other hand,
generation from RQLF to exhibit the choices made during reference and
ellipsis resolution turns out to be informative and useful to users.

Using the generator for producing English statements corresponding
to knowledge base assertions will require another phase in generation

that builds QLF expressions like the qterms corresponding to descriptions of objects. To some extent, the process of building QLF descriptions corresponds to the inverse of reference resolution, so it is possible that the reference resolution rules could be used in reverse for this process. If it is possible to do this, we will have extended the reversibility of the language description from analysis into interpretation.

For an application like translation, in which the form of some linguistic expressions such referential definite descriptions needs to be preserved, it is not always appropriate to include all resolutions from an RQLF in the QLF to be generated from. It may be desirable, for instance, to only include a resolution if not including it would introduce an ambiguity or vagueness in the target language that was not present in the source language, but clearly this would require additional contrastive knowledge about the two languages.

14 Swedish-English QLF Translation

Hiyan Alshawi, David Carter, Björn Gambäck, and Manny Rayner

14.1 Introduction

In this chapter, we describe a translation project with the aim of building an experimental Bilingual Conversation Interpreter (BCI) allowing communication through typed text between two monolingual humans using different languages (cf. Miike et al. 1988).

The two main components of the prototype system are the English and Swedish versions of the Core Language Engine (the Swedish version is described below in Section 14.2). Input sentences are analyzed by the source language version of the CLE as far as the level of quasi logical form (QLF, Chapters 2 and 10), and then, instead of further interpretation, undergo transfer into another QLF having constants and predicates corresponding to word senses in the other language. The transfer rules used in this process can be viewed as a kind of meaning postulate. The target language CLE then generates an output sentence from the transferred QLF, using the same linguistic data as is used for analysis of that language. The components of the BCI system are shown in Figure 14.1.

QLFs were selected as the appropriate level for transfer because they are far enough removed from surface linguistic form to provide the flexibility required by cross-linguistic differences. On the other hand, the linguistic, unification-based processing involved in creating them can be carried out efficiently and without the need to reason about the domain or context; the QLF language has constructs for explicit representation of contextually sensitive aspects of interpretation.

When it is necessary for correct translation to resolve an ambiguity present at QLF level, the BCI system interacts with the source language user to make the necessary decision, asking for a choice between word sense paraphrases or between alternative partial bracketings of the sentence. There is thus a strong connection between our choice of a representation sensitive to context and the use of interaction to resolve context-dependent ambiguities.

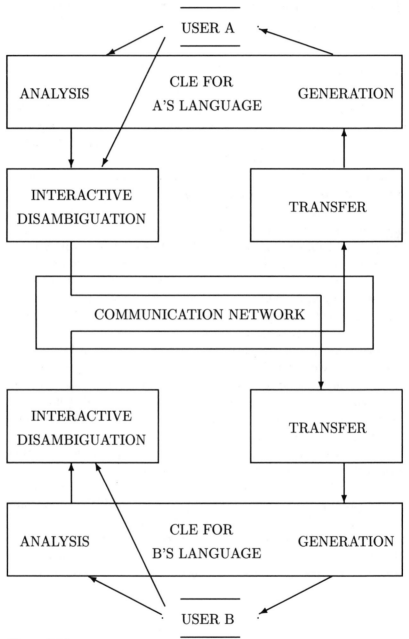

Figure 14.1
The bilingual conversation interpreter

14.1.1   Which Level for Transfer?

Before proceeding to the main body of the chapter, we will explain in more detail the reasoning that led us to select QLF as the appropriate level on which to carry out transfer. We begin by noting that the representational structures on which transfer operates must contain information corresponding to several linguistic levels, including syntactic and semantic information. For transfer to be general, it must operate recursively on input representations. We call the level of representation on which this recursion operates the "organizing" level; semantic structure is the natural choice, since the basic requirement of translation is that it preserves meaning.

Experience has shown that syntactic phrase structure transfer, or deep-syntax transfer, results in complex transfer rules (e.g. Thurmair 1990, Nagao and Tsujii 1986). McCord's (1988) organizing level appears to be that of surface syntax, with additional deep syntactic and semantic content attached to nodes. As we have argued, this level is not optimal, which may be related to the fact that McCord's system is explicitly not symmetrical: different grammars are used for the analysis and synthesis of the same language, which are viewed as quite different tasks. Isabelle and Macklovitch (1986) argue against such asymmetry between analysis and synthesis on the grounds that, although it is tempting as a shortcut to building a structure sufficiently well specified for synthesis to take place, asymmetry means that the transfer component must contain a lot of knowledge about the target language, with dire consequences for the modularity of the system and the reusability of different parts of it. In the BCI, however, the transfer rules contain only cross-linguistic (contrastive) knowledge, allowing analysis and generation to make use of exactly the same data.

Kaplan et al. (1989) allow multiple levels of representation to take part in the transfer relation. However, Sadler et al. (1990) point out that the particular approach to realizing this taken by Kaplan et al. has problems of its own and does not cleanly separate monolingual from contrastive knowledge.

In contrast to systems such as Rosetta (Landsbergen 1986), which depends on stating rule by rule correspondences between source and target grammars, we wish to make the monolingual descriptions as independent as possible from the task of translating between two languages. Apart from its attractions from a theoretical point of view, this has practical advantages in allowing grammars to be reused for different language pairs and for applications other than translation.

Both form (e.g., the form of referring noun phrases) and content need to be considered in designing a representation for transfer, but syntactic phrase structure trees are inappropriate because they are too closely related to the surface form of a source language: the transformations required for mapping between differing syntax trees result in complex transfer rules and a general loss of compositionality. In contrast, QLFs appear to have excellent properties from this point of view. In Section 14.3.2 below, we consider this argument in more detail. The predicate-argument structure required for the application of sortal restrictions is also absent from syntactic analyses. Sortal restrictions can be very significant to translation because of the importance of word sense disambiguation to performing this task.

At the LF (Logical Form) level, sortal restrictions can be applied but at this level the form of noun phrase descriptions used and also information on topicalization is no longer present. Vagueness present in specifier phrases will also have been removed by an explicit commitment to a particular quantifier. It is also well-known that producing completely resolved interpretations can require arbitrary knowledge of the domain of discourse, knowledge that is usually not available to an automatic translation system.

This leaves us with the QLF and RQLF (see resolved QLF, Chapter 10) levels. Both these levels are deep enough to allow the application of sortal restrictions for word sense disambiguation. Both representations also contain noun phrase descriptions and syntactic information in the categories of QLF constructs. However, not all the information appearing in the RQLF about how QLF constructs have been resolved is necessary for translation. For example, while pronoun resolution is sometimes required for translation between language pairs with differing pronoun systems (especially with regard to gender), definite descriptions are often best translated into target definite descriptions rather than referents, since otherwise the view of the referent in the source is lost during translation. Similarly, translation from resolved ellipsis (Section 13.1.4) can result in unwieldy target sentences. Scoping and collective/distributive distinctions do not normally manifest themselves in paraphrases of RQLF interpretations (Section 13.3.4), so ambiguities corresponding to these distinctions are often preserved during translation.

It would thus appear that, for many constructions, there is little advantage to be gained for the purpose of translation from the process of interpreting unresolved QLF constructs. For practical systems, aspiring to unrestricted domain translation, there might even be something to be lost by doing so: the lack of contextual knowledge and appropriate means for applying it mean that the interpretation process would be error prone. Contextual knowledge is available to humans in the machine-aided translation setting, so we are concentrating at present on systems in which humans can provide contextual resolution for the cases where this is required. The BCI application is well suited to this approach.

In arguing for QLF-level transfer, we are asserting that predicate-argument relations of the type used in QLF are the appropriate organizing level for compositional transfer, while not denying the need for syntactic information to ensure that, for example, topichood or the given/new distinction is preserved.

The organization of the rest of the chapter is as follows. The next section describes the Swedish version of the CLE; following this, Section 14.3 describes the process of QLF transfer. In the final section, we discuss the BCI's interactive aspects, in particular with reference to clarification of semantically ambiguous input.

14.2 The Swedish CLE

This section will describe the Swedish version of the CLE (hereafter S-CLE); in practice, the S-CLE grammar was not so much written from scratch as adapted from the English version, exploiting the large overlap between the structures of the two languages. We will begin in Section 14.2.1 by giving a brief overview of Swedish, concentrating on those aspects that turn out to have important consequences for Swedish-English transfer; in the following section, we describe in fair detail how the actual adaptation process was carried out. The only parts of the system we will examine in depth are morphology, syntax and semantics, and the lexicon. Processing beyond the level of generation of QLFs was not included in the project, but we have observed that the scoping

and reference resolution modules continue to function for Swedish with
at most very minor changes. The general level of functionality of the
Swedish version is comparable to that of the English one, except that
the lexicon is currently somewhat smaller (approximately 1000 entries,
or half as many as in the English system). The total development effort
was about 16 man-months over a period of a year.

14.2.1   An Overview of Swedish

Swedish is a Germanic language, spoken by about eight million people in Sweden and a half million in Finland, where it is the official
second language. It is related very closely to Danish and Norwegian,
and somewhat less so to Dutch, English, and German; the similarity
to Norwegian is sufficiently great that the two languages are mutually
intercomprehensible. Except phonetically, it is generally regarded as a
fairly easy language for people whose native tongue is English. Here, we
will describe some of the more significant divergences between Swedish
and English, not necessarily because they all are relevant to the task of
translation as it is done in the BCI (our translation model allows the
grammars to be developed independently), but partly to give a rough
indication of the relative level of difficulty of this particular language
pair.

Morphology   An immediate and obvious difference is inflectional morphology, which in Swedish is much more complex[1]. Swedish allows inflection of verbs, nouns and adjectives: verbs have nearly the same inflections as their English equivalents, with two main exceptions. Firstly,
there is an extra form (the *supine*), which is used to form the per-
fect tense, and which is generally distinct from the past participle; secondly, most inflectional forms have a "passive" counterpart, formed by
adding the suffix -*s*. This is explained in more detail below. There
are three conjugations of weak verbs (the second being divided into two
subclasses), and one conjugation of strong verbs, divided into three subclasses. Nouns are marked for both number and definiteness; thus *bil*
is "car", *bilar* is "cars", *bilen* is "the car", and *bilarna* is "the cars".
They also have grammatical gender (*common* or *neuter*). There are five

---

[1]There is also a rich system of derivational morphology, especially for forming
compound nouns. Since the S-CLE has as yet no capacity to deal with this, we will
not discuss it here.

different declensions of nouns, corresponding to the plural endings *-or*, *-ar*, *-er*, *-en*, and "null" (i.e., the singular and plural are the same). Adjectives are marked for number, gender, and definiteness, but these are conflated so that there are actually only three distinct forms.

Syntax   Moving on to syntax, the most important differences in word-order stem from the strongly verb-second nature of Swedish: formation of both yes/no and wh-questions is by simple inversion of the subject and verb, without the introduction of an auxiliary. This is illustrated in the following examples:

Han såg Maria.	*He saw Mary.*
Såg han Maria?	*Did he see Mary?*
Vem såg han?	*Who did he see?*

The same process is used to form topicalized clauses, which are extremely common, especially in spoken or colloquial language:

Maria såg han.	*Mary, he saw.*
Idag såg han Maria.	*Today, he saw Mary.*

Another significant difference at clause-level concerns negation, which is expressed with the particle *inte* ("not"); *inte* is placed after the main verb in a main clause, but before it in a subordinate clause, thus:

Han såg inte Maria.	*He did not see Mary.*
Han sade att han inte såg Maria.	*He said that he did not see Mary.*
Kvinnan som han inte såg.	*The woman that he did not see.*

Similar considerations also apply to a number of other common adverbials (so-called mobile adverbs), including *ofta* ("often"), *alltid* ("always"), and *troligen* ("probably").

The third important divergence at this level is formation of passives, which as already mentioned can be expressed by addition of the suffix *-s* to the corresponding active form:[2]

Den skrevs av Maria.	*It was written by Mary.*
	(lit. It wrote-PASSIVE by Mary.)
Den ska skrivas av Maria.	*It will be written by Mary.*
	(lit. It will write-PASSIVE by Mary.)

[2]The only exception is the present passive, which is formed from the imperative.

With regard to the NP structure, most of the differences derive from
the previously mentioned fact that Swedish marks for definiteness. This
means that the definite article can often be omitted, although it is obligatory before an adjective: thus "the car" is *bilen*, but "the red car" is
den röda bilen. Prenominal adjectives agree in number, gender, and
definiteness with their nouns. There are a number of other divergences
concerned with prenominal modification, but these are of a somewhat
esoteric nature.

As with any language, there are a number of syntactic phenomena that
are hard to fit into a systematic classification. Of these, we single out
for special attention the very common *vad ... för* construction (which is
analogous to the German *was für*):

> *Vad såg du för bil?*   *What kind of car did you see?*
>   *(lit. What saw you for car?)*

A thorough treatment of Swedish morphology and syntax can be found
in Thorell 1973 for example.

14.2.2   Adapting the CLE to Swedish

We begin by indicating roughly how the work performed in the adaptation was divided between the various parts of the system: for each module, Table 14.1 shows in the first column an estimation of the number
of person-months (PM) devoted, and in the second and third, the overlap between the Swedish and English sets of rules and rule interpreters,
respectively, expressed as percentages.[3]

In some cases, the basic formalism was generalized to some degree,
necessitating corresponding extensions to the rule interpreters; these are
noted in the fourth column, together with other comments. In general,
it is clear that the amount of work needed to adapt the various CLE
modules to Swedish declined steadily as a function of their "distance"
to surface structure. It seems likely that this would be the case with
adaptation to other European languages.

In the remainder of the section, we will discuss some specific technical
problems and their solution within the S-CLE.

---

[3]For the purposes of the present discussion, we will use the term "interpreter"
indiscriminately to refer both to interpreters and compilers.

Table 14.1
Breakdown of work performed in Swedish adaptation of the CLE

Module	Effort (PM)	Overlap (%) Rules	Interpreter	Comments
Segmentation	2	10	90	rewritten; generalized
Morphology	2	25	90	basic ideas retained; generalized
Lexicon	3	70	100	adaptation
VEX	4	60	80	adaptation; generalized
Syntax	3	80	100	adaptation
Semantics	1	90	100	adaptation
Generation	1	90	90	minor extensions

These figures do not include effort expended on repairing software problems judged to be unrelated to Swedish.

Morphology   In the English morphology rules, affixes are always literals whereas in Swedish a compact grammatical description requires giving affixes categories with feature specifications.

There are basically two tricks that, suitably applied, can be used to capture all the morphological structure fairly compactly; we illustrate them first with one of the simpler examples, namely, the rules that describe pluralization of nouns. Recall that Swedish nouns can be pluralized in several different ways, depending on their declension, but that singular and plural forms coincide for 5th declension nouns. The main rule takes care of the 1st, 2nd, 3rd and 4th declension nouns; simplified slightly, it is as follows:

```
morph(nbar_nbar_plural,
  nbar:[agr=plur, synmorphc=M, def=n, subcat=S, ...],
  -->
  [nbar:[agr=sing, synmorphc=M, def=n, subcat=S, ...],
  'PLURAL':[synmorphc=M]]).
```

The rule is supplemented by four lexical entries for the plural suffixes, one for each relevant declension; the number of the declension is encoded in the **synmorphc** ("syntactic morphological category") feature. The first two entries are thus

```
lex('-or','PLURAL':[synmorphc=1]).
lex('-ar','PLURAL':[synmorphc=2]).
```

An additional rule, however, is needed for the 5th declension nouns. Here we need an extra Nbar feature `nullmorphn`, which when set indicates that the plural affix is null. The null plural rule is consequently

```
morph(nbar_nbar_nullplural,
   nbar:[agr=plur, synmorphc=M, def=n, subcat=S,
         nullmorphn=n, ...]
   -->
   [nbar:[agr=plur, synmorphc=M, def=n, subcat=S,
         nullmorphn=y, ...]]).
```

The same basic mechanism is used to deal with verb and adjective morphology, although the details are considerably more complicated; since these are unlikely to interest readers not well-acquainted with Swedish, we omit them here. A full account can be found in Gambäck, Lövgren, and Rayner 1991.

The lexicon We had anticipated a large overlap in the English and Swedish grammars. Perhaps somewhat surprisingly, it turned out that the amount of structure shared between the English and Swedish lexicons was also very significant. This is most obviously apparent when considering function words, where the great majority of function words in one language have a clear counterpart in the other; in general, differences are often confined to variance in surface form and changes to the values of a small number of features. We illustrate this with examples of entries for a determiner (*någon*, the common-gender singular equivalent of *some*), a modal verb (*måste*, equivalent to *must*), and an interrogative pronoun (*vem*, equivalent to *who*).

```
lex(some,
   det:[type=norm, gaps=g(G,G,F,F), simple=y,
        lexical=y, of=_])

lex(någon,
   det:[type=norm, gaps=g(G,G,F,F), simple=y,
        lexical=y, of=_,
        def=n, agr=(sing/\common/\3)]).
```

(*Någon* is indefinite and common-gender.)

```
lex(must,
    v:[mainv=n, subjform=SForm, mhdfl=n, gaps=Gaps,
       vform=fin,
       subcat=[vp:[vform=inf, modifiable=_,
                   mainv=_, gaps=Gaps,
                   subjform=SForm, headfinal=_]]])

lex(måste,
    v:[mainv=n, subjform=SForm, mhdfl=n, gaps=Gaps,
       vform=(fin/\present), agr=Agr, subordinate=_,
       subcat=[vp:[vform=inf, modifiable=_,
                   mainv=_, gaps=Gaps,
                   subjform=SForm, headfinal=_,
                   agr=Agr, subordinate=y,
                   lexpassivized=_]]]).
```

(Swedish modals need to pass the **agr** feature to their arguments.)

```
lex(who,
    np:[simple=y, mass=n, determined=n, name=n,
        pron=y, wh=y, hascase=n, gaps=g(G, G, F, F),
        type=(q\/r), agr=3])

lex(vem,
    np:[simple=y, mass=n, determined=n, name=n,
        pron=y, wh=y, hascase=n, gaps=g(G, G, F, F),
        type=q, def=y, agr=(sing/\common/\3)]).
```

(*Vem* is definite and common-gender. Unlike *who*, it must be singular and cannot be used as a relative pronoun.)

A count of the Swedish function word lexicon revealed that only 33 of the 401 entries had not been derived from a close English equivalent. Among these, the following deserve mention: the negation particle *inte*; the reflexive pronoun *sig*; the preposition *hos* (like French *chez*); the adjective *sådan* (like German *solch*); and the verbs *finnas* (existential *to be*), *komma att* (a future construction), *låta bli* ("refrain from"), *heta* (like German *heissen*), *det går att* ("it is possible to"), *det gäller att* ("it is important to") and *ligga* and *stå* (existential verbs meaning roughly "to be somewhere").

With regard to content words, the main problem is that Swedish verbs, like French and German ones, can subcategorize for reflexive pronouns; for example, *marry* is *gifta sig med* (literally, "marry oneself with"), and *decide* is *bestämma sig för* ("decide oneself for"). This means that the number of verbal paradigms is approximately doubled, since most paradigms have a counterpart with an extra reflexive. The prototype entries for the reflexive variants are straightforward extensions of those for the normal verbs.

Syntax and semantics   We will now examine the syntactic phenomena described in Section 14.2.1 in more detail, in particular with reference to the structure of their representations at QLF level. Most of the differences that arise are in essence fairly trivial and involve only minor extensions to the English grammar rules.

To take a comparatively hard example: although the *vad ... för* construction mentioned at the end of Section 14.2.1 lacks any near-English equivalent, it can be dealt with by a straightforward application of the constituent movement mechanism, letting an NP gap matching a fronted occurrence of *vad* be absorbed by a constituent consisting of the preposition *för*, followed by an Nbar. The syntactic rule and one of the semantic rules (there is a second one for plural Nbars) are as follows:

```
syn(np_för_nbar,
    np:[agr=Agr, def=n, type=q, ...,
        gaps=g([npgap:[lexform=vad,gaptype=wh]|Gn],
               Go,Fn,[g|Fo])]
    -->
    [p:[lexform=för],
     nbar:[agr=Agr, def=n, ..., gaps=g(Gn,Go,Fn,Fo)]]).


sem(np_för_nbar, singular,
    (qterm(<t=quant,n=sing,l=wh_type>, V, Nbar),
     np:[quantform=quant, handle=V, ...,
         semGaps=([(qterm(_,_,_),_)|Sn],So)])
    -->
    [(för,p:[pptype=subcategorized]),
     (Nbar,nbar:[agr=sing, arg=V, ...,
                 semGaps=(Sn,So)])]).
```

The QLF for *Vad såg han för bil?* ("What kind of car did he see?")
is thus

```
[whq,
  [past,
    [se_3p,
      qterm(<t=quant,n=sing,l=ex>, A,
        [entity,A]),
      a_term(<t=ref,n=sing,l=han>, B,
        [and, [male,B], [personal,B]]),
      qterm(<t=quant,n=sing,l=wh_type>, D,
        [bil1,D])]]].
```

It would be tedious to list explicitly all the small adjustments that have
been made in the grammar. In particular, the more complex agreement
structure of Swedish means that the **agr** feature must be propagated
to many more constituents. We refer once again to Gambäck, Lövgren,
and Rayner 1991 for a full account. We now proceed directly to the
two problematic cases where the English and Swedish analyses exhibit
nontrivial structural differences at QLF level.

Verb-second We begin with the word-order problems deriving from
the verb-second rule: essentially, the modifications to the English rules
are the following:

- Any verb (not just auxiliaries) can be inverted.

- Any NP, PP, ADJP, or ADVP (not just those whose **wh** feature is
  set) can be fronted by wh-movement.

- The rules for topicalized clauses are removed, since they are now
  subsumed by the movement rules used in English for wh-question
  and relative clause formation.

- Consequently, the top-level "sigma" rule for topicalized clauses
  expands to an S with the features for inversion and wh-movement
  set, thus:

```
syn(sigma_topic, core,
    sigma
    -->
    [s:[type=norm, inv=y, whmoved=y,
        subjcase=subj, vform=fin]]).
```

Although this analysis adequately describes the syntactic facts and produces plausible QLFs, a closer examination unfortunately reveals that things are not quite as good as one might hope; the QLFs produced by the Swedish and English grammars still contain some information originating in their divergent syntactic realizations. The problem can be exhibited in its simplest form in a yes/no question with a VP modifier, for example, *Did he sleep today?* In English, the past tense operator applies to the auxiliary *did*, and the tensed auxiliary applies to the VP *sleep today*. The QLF is thus schematically

```
[ynq,
  [past,
    [and,[sleep1,<event>,<he>],
          <today>]]].
```

In the corresponding Swedish sentence, *Sov han idag?*, the past tense is applied directly to the main verb, *sova*, to which the VP operator *idag* subsequently applies. This gives the QLF

```
[ynq,
  [and,
    [past,[sova1,<event>,<han>]],
    <idag>]].
```

In other words, the tense operator has wide scope over the VP operator in English, but narrow scope in Swedish.

Negation Similar, but more complex, considerations apply to the treatment of Swedish negation. In view of the data presented in Section 14.2.1 above, and for other reasons, it seems fairly clear that the negation particle *inte* should be regarded as forming a constituent with its verb; to ensure that the word-order constraints are enforced, there is a feature subordinate, which has the value n for main clauses and y for others. This feature is percolated down to the V, where it is available to rules like the following one:

```
syn(v_not_v, core,
    v:[subordinate=y, fronted=n,
       agr=Agr, vform=VForm,
       mainv=MainV, modifiable=Mod,
       gaps=Gaps, subcat=S, ...]
```

```
-->
[neg:[],
v:[subordinate=y, fronted=n,
   agr=Agr, vform=VForm,
   mainv=MainV, modifiable=Mod,
   gaps=Gaps, subcat=S, ...]]).
```

Since negation in English is viewed as applying to a VP rather than a
V, the relative scopes of operators representing negation, tense, and VP
modification are correspondingly affected. For example, in the English
sentence *He did not sleep*, the negation *not* is considered to modify the
VP *sleep*, producing a VP that subsequently appears as an argument to
the tensed auxiliary *did*. The QLF is accordingly

```
[past,
  [not,[sleep1,<event>,<he>]]].
```

The Swedish counterpart, *Han sov inte* has the tensed main verb *sov*
modified by the negation *inte*, giving a QLF with the scopes of the tense
and negation operators reversed:

```
[not,
  [past,[sova_2p,<event>,<han>]]].
```

In the following sections, we will describe more exactly how the problems
just discussed affect the process of QLF transfer.

14.3   QLF-Based Translation

14.3.1   Transfer Rules

QLF transfer involves taking a QLF analysis of a source sentence, say
QLF_S, and deriving from it another expression, QLF_T, from which it
is possible to generate a sentence in the target language. Leaving aside
unresolved referential expressions, the main difference between QLF_S
and QLF_T is that they will contain constants, particularly predicate
constants, that originate in word sense entries from the lexicons of the
respective languages. If more than one candidate source language QLF
exists, the appropriate one is selected by presenting the user with choices
of word sense paraphrases and of bracketings relating to differences in the

syntactic analyses from which the QLFs were derived. This interaction is described in Section 14.4.

Performing transfer at a level as deep as QLF highlights the fact that many, perhaps most, difficulties in translation do not arise from differences between the constructions used in two languages under consideration but from differences between the mapping of concepts to such constructions; it is perfectly possible for nontrivial problems to occur when translating between two dialects with exactly the same set of syntax rules, or indeed when paraphrasing within the same language. For example, translating *I want him to go* as *Jag vill att han ska åka* (literally, "I want that he will go") is at QLF-level essentially isomorphic to paraphrasing *I expect him to go* as *I expect that he will go*.

We now descend to concrete implementation details. A transfer rule specifies a pair of QLF patterns. The left-hand side matches QLF expressions for one language and the right-hand side matches those for the other:

```
trans(<QLF pattern 1>
      <Operator>
      <QLF pattern 2>).
```

The QLF patterns in these rules can be QLF (sub)expressions, or such expressions with "transfer variables" showing the correspondence between the two sides, as explained later on. If the operator is <=> this states that the rule is bidirectional, otherwise a single direction of applicability is indicated by use of one of the operators => or <=.

As will be described below (in Section 14.3.2), most transfer rules are simple bidirectional relations between two atoms, like the following English-Swedish examples:

```
trans(car1 <=> bil1).
trans(pay1 <=> betala1).
```

Transfer rules often correspond directly to interlingual meaning postulates: when the expressions in a transfer rule are formulae, the symbols <=>, =>, and <= can be read as the logical operators $\leftrightarrow$, $\rightarrow$, and $\leftarrow$, respectively. A more complicated rule like

```
trans([and,[bad1,X],[luck1,X]] <=> [otur1,X])
```

translating between the English *bad luck* and the Swedish *otur*, can thus, as well as the examples above, be expressed as postulates in a logical language for which the set of predicate constants is the union of the set of such constants in QLF expressions for both languages:

$\forall$X(car1(X) $\leftrightarrow$ bil1(X))
$\forall$E$\forall$S$\forall$O(pay1(E,S,O) $\leftrightarrow$ betala1(E,S,O))
$\forall$X(bad1(X)$\wedge$luck1(X) $\leftrightarrow$ otur1(X)).

Transfer rules are applied recursively, this process following the recursive structure of the expression tree for the source QLF. In order to allow transfer between structurally different QLFs, rules with transfer variables need to be used. These variables, which take the form tr(*atom*), show how subexpressions in the source QLF correspond to subexpressions translating them in the target QLF. Transfer variables may appear more than once on either side of a transfer rule. For example, the following rule expresses an equivalence between the English *to be called* (*I am called John*), and the Swedish *heta* (*Jag heter John*):

```
trans([call_name,
       tr(ev),
       qterm(<t=quant,n=sing,l=ex>,A,[entity,A]),
       tr(ag),
       tr(name)]
<=>
[heta1,tr(ev),tr(ag),tr(name)]).
```

Transfer rules are not restricted to the logical elements of QLF, but are also used to indicate the correspondence between unresolved QLF expressions containing QLF categories. For example, the a_term for a pronoun may be transferred into an a_term with a category having linguistic features that are specific to the target language. Transfer between qterms for descriptive noun phrases also requires translation of the categories and the restrictions:

```
trans(qterm(tr(cat),X,tr(rest))
      <=>
      qterm(tr(cat),X,tr(rest))).
```

Other transfer rules for categories would then indicate the correspondence between definiteness, number, and gender in the two languages.

Formally, we can regard a `qterm` for a referential definite description as a function from (linguistic and non-linguistic) contexts to referents. The linguistic featural information in these terms is an important part of the specification of such a function. A bidirectional transfer rule between two referential terms can thus be regarded as a meaning postulate stating equality of two functions, `f1` and `f2`:

$$\forall C \forall X (\texttt{f1(C)=X} \leftrightarrow \texttt{f2(C)=X})$$

where `C` ranges over contexts and `X` over referents. Similarly, a unidirectional transfer rule, corresponds to an implication in one direction

$$\forall C \forall X (\texttt{f1(C)=X} \rightarrow \texttt{f2(C)=X})$$

so that, in this case, it is not possible to infer from the fact that the unresolved expression corresponding to `f2` refers to `X` in a given context that the one corresponding to `f1` will also refer to `X` in that context.

14.3.2   Effectiveness of QLF Transfer

We will now assess the method's strengths and weaknesses, as they have manifested themselves in practice. We will pay particular attention to the following criteria:

- *Expressiveness*: Intuitively valid generalizations about transfer should be expressible in the transfer formalism.

- *Compositionality*: The fewer special cases arising from idiosyncratic interactions between rules, the better.

- *Simplicity*: The simpler the rules are, the better. Of course, simplicity is to some extent subjective; however, we think it fairly clear that the ideal rule is simply an equivalence between two terminal symbols, and that as many rules as possible should be of this form.

- *Reversibility*: Reversible rules are better than unidirectional ones.

- *Monotonicity*: Adding new rules should not invalidate old ones.

Most of these are not easy to measure objectively, if they are not absolute properties of the formalism. (In particular, a formalism like ours, which is purely unification-based with all rules applied nondeterministically, is guaranteed to be monotonic). The big exception seems to be compositionality; in Section 14.3.2, we will describe a method for measuring compositionality and present fairly detailed test results. First, however, we present what facts we can on the remaining criteria.

Expressiveness   Since we are intentionally limiting ourselves by disallowing access to full syntactic information (but only that placed in QLF categories) in the transfer phase, it is legitimate to wonder whether the formalism can really be sufficiently expressive. Here, we will attempt to answer this criticism; we begin by noting that shortcomings in this area can be of several distinct kinds. Sometimes, a formalism can appear to make it necessary to write many rules, where one feels intuitively that one should be enough; we treat this kind of problem under the heading of compositionality. In other cases, the difficulty is rather that there does not appear to be any way of expressing the rule at all in terms of the given formalism. In our case, a fair proportion of problems that at first seem to fall into this category can be eliminated by having adequate monolingual grammars and using the target grammar as a filter; the idea is to allow the transfer component to produce unacceptable QLFs that are filtered out, during generation, by fully constrained target grammars.

A good example of the use of this technique is the English definite article, which in Swedish can be translated as an article (*den* or *det*, depending on gender) but preferably is omitted; however, an article is obligatory before an adjective. Solving this problem at transfer level is not possible, since the transfer component has no way of knowing that a piece of logical form will be realized as an adjective; there are many cases where an adjective-noun combination in English is best translated as a compound noun in Swedish. Exploiting the fact that the relevant constraint is present in the Swedish grammar, however, the "transfer-and-filter" method reduces the problem to two rules defining equivalences of qterm categories, namely,

```
trans(<t=def,n=sing,l=the> <=> <t=def,n=sing,l=bare>)
trans(<t=def,n=sing,l=the> <=> <t=def,n=sing,l=den>).
```

The intrinsic limitation of the "transfer-and-filter" method is that there are still a certain number of cases where the requisite information is present in neither the source QLF nor the target grammar: this can be caused by the presence of unresolved relations in the source QLF, or simply by deficiencies in the formalism that make it impossible to express certain distinctions. We present an example of each type of problem.

To illustrate the problem with unresolved relations, we consider the rule that defines an equivalence between the English verb *have* and its Swedish counterpart *ha*. This is generally correct; however, in some exceptional cases like *to have an accident*, a different Swedish verb must be used. Although it is possible to ensure that the correct translation is always produced first, by suitably ordering the rules, there is no way to block the default rule altogether; since *ha* (like *have*) is associated at QLF level with an unresolved relation (cf. Section 10.5.1), sortal information cannot be used to filter out constructions where it takes an inappropriate object. Similar problems can occur with other unresolved relations, like those arising from noun-noun and genitive constructions, although they seem in the case of the present language-pair to be less frequent.

An example of the second case, where the problem arises due to limitations in the QLF formalism's representational adequacy, is the Swedish present tense: as in many other languages, this can have either a specific or a generic/habitual reading, the first corresponding to the English present progressive, and the second to the plain present. Thus, for example, *Det regnar i Stockholm* can be used to mean either *It is raining in Stockholm* (the specific reading) or *It rains in Stockholm* (the generic). Since both of these get the same QLF, it is not possible to do more than produce both translations and query the target language user as to which one is more appropriate (see Section 14.4).

Simplicity and reversibility   The most obvious way to evaluate simplicity is to give a count of the various categories of rule and provide evidence that there is a substantial proportion of rules that are simple in our framework but would not necessarily be so in others.

The transfer component currently contains 718 rules. Of these, 576 (80.2%) have the property that both the right- and left-hand sides are atomic and 502 members of this first group (69.9%) translate senses of single words to senses of single words as, for example,

```
trans(car1 <=> bil1)
trans(buy1 <=> köp1)
trans(for_benef <=> åt_benef)
```

giving the correspondence between predicates for a noun, a verb, and a preposition sense respectively. The remaining 74 (10.3%) translate atomic constants representing the senses of complex syntactic constructions, most commonly verbs taking particles, reflexives, or complementizers. An example is the following rule, which defines an equivalence between English *decide to* (*John decided to go*) and Swedish *bestämma sig för* (*John bestämde sig för att åka*, literally "John decided himself for to go"):

```
trans(decide_to_do <=> bestämma_sig_för_att_göra).
```

Since vocabulary has primarily been selected with regard to utility,[4] we think it reasonable to claim that QLF-based transfer is simplifying the construction of transfer rules in a substantial proportion of the commonly encountered cases.

On the score of reversibility, we will once again count cases; here we find that 659 (91.8%) of the rules are reversible, 17 (2.4%) work only in the English-Swedish direction, and 42 (5.8%) only in the Swedish-English direction. These also seem to be fairly good figures.

Compositionality Perhaps the most important factor in keeping transfer simple is the degree to which the transfer relation is a homomorphism, that is, the degree to which transfer rules are compositional. For compositionality to be a meaningful notion in the first place, it must be possible for transfer rules to apply to partial structures. These structures can occur consequently in different contexts; other transfer rules will apply to the contexts as such. The question is the extent to which particular combinations of rules and contexts give rise to special problems. In a perfectly compositional system, this will never happen, although it seems a safe bet that no such system exists today. What we want is a method that objectively measures how closely we approach the compositional ideal.

As far as we know, there is no accepted benchmark for testing compositionality of transfer. Our first step in this direction has been the construction of *compositionality tables*, in which a set of rules and a set of contexts are systematically combined in all possible meaningful combinations. The question is the extent to which the complex transfer

---

[4]We have, for example, made considerable use of frequency dictionaries (Allén 1970).

Table 14.2
Examples of complex transfer types

Complex transfer type	English→Swedish example
Different particles	John **likes** Mary John **tycker om** Mary
Passive to active	Insurance **is included** Försäkring **ingår**
Verb to adjective	John **owes** Mary $20 John **är skyldig** Mary $20
Support verb to normal verb	John **had** an accident John **råkade ut för** en olycka
Single verb to phrase	John **wants** a car John **vill ha** en bil (lit.: "wants to have")
Idiomatic use of PP	John **is in a hurry** John **har bråttom** (lit.: "has hurry")

rules continue to function in the different contexts. In the following three diagrams, we give an example of such a table for the current version of the BCI. Table 14.2 gives a set of rules, which exemplify six common types of complex transfer. Table 14.3 gives a set of twelve common contexts in which the constructions referred to by the rules can occur. Finally, Table 14.4 summarizes the results of testing the various possible combinations.

Of the ten sentences in Table 14.4 that the transfer component was unable to handle, six were due to the rule for object raising, which currently only functions in the English to Swedish direction (the other direction requires the transfer component to produce an abstraction for the infinitive). The other four were caused by the combinations "passive to active + VP modifier" and "idiomatic use of PP + negation", which failed to transfer in either direction. The problem for the first pair is another variant of the one we have already seen several times: the tense operator in the passive English sentence derives from the auxiliary *is* and thus has scope over the VP modifier. However, the Swedish sentence has active mood, and the tense operator gets narrow scope. The problem for the second pair is caused by the treatment of negated *be* in the English

Table 14.3
Examples of transfer contexts

Transfer context	English→Swedish example
Present tense	John likes Mary John tycker om Mary
Perfect tense	John has liked Mary John har tyckt om Mary
Negated	John doesn't like Mary John tycker inte om Mary
yes/no question	Does John like Mary? Tycker John om Mary?
wh-question	Who does John like? Vem tycker John om?
Passive	Mary was liked by John Mary blev omtyckt av John
Relative clause	The woman that John likes Kvinnan som John tycker om
Sentential complement	I think John likes Mary Jag tror John tycker om Mary
Embedded question	I know who John likes Jag vet vem John tycker om
VP modifier	John likes Mary today John tycker om Mary idag
Object raising	I want John to like Mary Jag vill att John ska tycka om Mary ("I want that John shall like Mary")
Change of aspect	John stopped liking Mary John slutade tycka om Mary ("John stopped like-INF Mary")

Table 14.4
Compositionality table (Swedish→English shown above English→Swedish)

Transfer context	Different particles	Active→ Passive	V→ Adj	Supp.→ Normal	V→ Phrase	PP Idiom
Present	OK	OK	OK	OK	OK	OK
tense	OK	OK	OK	OK	OK	OK
Perfect	OK	gen	OK	OK	OK	OK
tense	OK	OK	OK	OK	OK	OK
Negated	presNot	presNot	presNot	pastNot	presNot	trans
	presNot	presNot	presNot	pastNot	presNot	trans
yes/no	OK	OK	OK	OK	OK	OK
question	OK	OK	OK	OK	OK	OK
wh-	OK	OK	OK	OK	OK	OK
question	OK	OK	OK	OK	OK	OK
Passive	OK	–	–	–	–	–
	OK	–	OK	–	OK	–
Relative	OK	OK	OK	OK	OK	OK
clause	OK	OK	OK	OK	OK	OK
Sentential	OK	OK	OK	OK	OK	OK
complement	OK	OK	OK	OK	OK	OK
Embedded	OK	OK	OK	OK	OK	OK
question	OK	OK	OK	OK	OK	OK
VP	OK	trans	OK	OK	OK	OK
modifier	OK	trans	OK	OK	OK	OK
Change of	OK	OK	OK	OK	OK	OK
aspect	OK	OK	OK	OK	OK	OK
Object	trans	trans	trans	trans	trans	trans
raising	OK	OK	OK	OK	OK	OK

Each square in Table 14.4 consists of two entries, the first for the Swedish to English direction, and the second for English to Swedish. The entries are:

- – The construction referred to by the rule cannot occur in this context.

- OK Analysis, transfer, and generation all functioned correctly, without extra rules being necessary to deal with the particular context.

- gen The generation component failed to produce the correct target sentence.

- trans The transfer component was unable to produce a correct representation.

  Other entries are names of rules needed to deal with special combinations of rule and context. For this table, only two extra rules were needed: **presNot** and **pastNot**, reversing the relative scope of the operators for negation and a tense (present and past, resp.) as described in Section 14.2.2).

grammar, where negation receives narrow scope.

One may note that all failures of compositionality occurring in the table, with the exception of the *be*-negation case, were caused by the same phenomenon, namely scope mismatches involving tense operators. It is thus of considerable significance that this problem can be eliminated in the alternate QLF representation mentioned in Section 10.5.4, where tense and aspect are represented not as operators but rather as a_forms; we expect to use this representation in later versions of the BCI.

It should also be pointed out that the compositionality table presented here is still too small to detect more than a fraction of the bad rule-interactions that may occur in the current system. Most important is to extend systematically the set of contexts, taking proper note of the fact that many of the features they are intended to represent are in fact orthogonal to each other.

A full set of contexts would include, at a minimum, all legal combinations of independent choices along the following dimensions:

- *Tense*: Present, past, or future.

- *Mood*: Active or passive.

- *Negation*: Positive or negative.

- *Modification*: Unmodified; modified by PP, by ADVP, by fronted constituent.

- *Clause-type*: Declarative, yes/no question, wh-question, relative clause, sentential complement, embedded question, progressive VP complement, control.

Multiplying out all the choices gives a total of 384 distinct contexts; this must then be multiplied by the number of transfer rule types to be tested and doubled to get both directions of transfer. A set of noun phrase contexts would also be needed in addition to the clausal contexts listed above. Developing the software support needed to be able to run tests of this size regularly is clearly not a trivial task, but our opinion is that being able to do so would greatly contribute to maintaining the system's reliability and integrity.

14.4   Disambiguation and Interaction

The linguistic information available to the BCI defines a mapping of source language sentences onto source language QLFs, another of source language QLFs onto target language ones, and a third of target language QLFs onto target language sentences. In general, a given input will map onto several values, and it will be necessary for the system to choose which value is appropriate at each stage.

$$sentence_S\text{--analysis} \rightarrow QLF(s)_S\text{--translation} \rightarrow$$
$$\rightarrow QLF(s)_T\text{--generation} \rightarrow sentence(s)_T$$

There are two observations to be made here. First, there will be sentences for which the composition of the three mappings yields no values, that is, which are untranslatable; so some means of recovery is desirable. This is discussed in Section 14.4.4. Secondly, a particular choice between values may be spurious in that each choice leads to the same, or a very similar, meaning being conveyed to the target language user. This occurs in different ways in all of analysis, transfer, and generation.

Thus when faced with a choice at any stage, the system can take any of the following actions, which are discussed in turn.

- Choose one option arbitrarily, on the grounds that the choice makes little or no difference to the meaning of the end result.

- Decide that one of the options is intrinsically better, for example, because it conforms more closely to sortal restrictions, or because (if a QLF) it contains more salient or more frequent word senses. Reasoning, if performed, also comes into this class of actions.

- Present one of the users with (paraphrases of) the choices, and perhaps ask for a decision.

14.4.1   Recognizing Spurious Choices

It turns out to be easier to recognize a choice as spurious or unnecessary the closer we are to generating the output.

The simplest case is **generation**. In generating from target language QLFs, spurious choices are the rule rather than the exception, because sentences corresponding to the same QLF will normally just be syntactic variants of one another. The BCI therefore presents the first sentence it generates from a QLF, only considering alternatives if the user asks for them.

In **transfer**, spurious choices can arise because QLFs are not canonical: different QLFs can have identical, or very similar, meanings. If the Swedish sentence *Jag äter gärna godis* is transferred to English QLFs for, say, *I like to eat sweets* and *I enjoy eating sweets*, the difference would not be important. Such choices can be much reduced by taking advantage of the directionality of transfer rules; when one term in language A corresponds to two alternatives in language B, but one of those alternatives will always in fact be acceptable, the transfer rule involving the other can be made unidirectional. Thus, for example, we have the following rules, where the Swedish *angående* and *beträffande* can both map onto the English *concerning*, but in the other direction *concerning* is always translated as *angående*:

```
trans(concerning1 <=> angående1).
trans(concerning1 <=  beträffande1).
```

The same technique could be applied to structural alternatives as well.

In **analysis**, a choice (this time between distinct meanings) can be spurious when source and target languages share an ambiguity; for example, the English *John drove the car without any insurance* and its Swedish translation *John körde bilen utan försäkring* are both ambiguous with respect to whether the car itself, or John's driving of it, is uninsured.

There are two ways in which one might recognize a spurious choice between analyses. One is by "look ahead": for example, if two source language QLFs differ only in the sense selected for a given word, the difference is unimportant if the two senses transfer to senses of the same target language word. In the English CLE lexicon, the word *bank* is defined with senses corresponding to (among other things) banks as buildings and banks as organizations. This distinction can be important in other language processing applications, but the same Swedish word is used for both.

In general, one might attempt to establish whether any given choice of analyses is spurious by following each option through all the way to generating multiple target language sentences, and seeing whether any generated sentence occurred in both sets. However, this is likely to be too time consuming to be practically useful. It may also have

other practical difficulties in an architecture where the BCI components
for the two languages run on two machines connected over a wide-area
network.

14.4.2   Selecting One Option

Nonspurious choices occur principally in analysis but also to some extent
in transfer, when the competing QLFs represent different meanings that
cannot be expressed by the same sentence in the target language. In
analysis, this is the familiar problem of linguistic ambiguity. In transfer,
it will normally involve a lexical distinction made in the target language
but not in the source language; the source language word cannot truly
be called ambiguous, but nevertheless, in any given context, only one of
the target words is correct. An example would be translating the English *grandfather* to the Swedish *farfar* (paternal grandfather) or *mor-
far* (maternal grandfather), there being no single Swedish translation of
grandfather.

The fundamental choice of strategies here is between making the
choice automatically and querying one of the users, although in practice
a mixed approach has been adopted, the system doing what it can and
consulting a user when it cannot decide on its own.

Automatic decision-making can be carried out

- on context-independent, sentence-internal grounds, such as sortal
  restrictions on predicates;

- using general linguistic or domain-specific tendencies, such as fre-
  quencies of word senses or grammatical constructions;

- using reasoning about the relation between the analyses under consideration and the specific or general context, as in the CLE processing levels that (in other applications) follow QLF construction.

In the BCI, the first type of decision is currently made by the system during the analysis phase and may optionally be applied to target
language QLFs too. The second could in principle be made, while the
third, in general, is dependent upon advances in the state of the art, or
at least on the availability of domain-specific back-end systems.

The CLE's procedure for checking sortal restrictions has been adapted
in the BCI to work on a preferential basis: a QLF that disobeys sortal constraints is only rejected if there is another QLF that disobeys

fewer. This is because, especially in a relatively unconstrained domain, unpredictable uses such as metaphor may be quite common. A literal translation is better than nothing, but should be received with caution. Thus if a translation is produced from a sortally imperfect QLF, the fact can be indicated by attaching a query to the output, for example:

User 1:
    `The engine of this car has died.`

System to user 2:
    `... possible translation violated sorts`
    `Ignore sort violation? (y/n): y`

    `"Den här bilens motor har dött."`

It would be quite feasible to attach weights, possibly domain-specific, to particular word senses and grammar rules, so that in the absence of convincing sortal differences, the reading that resulted from the most frequent senses and rules would be preferred. The potential already exists to do this in the CLE, to some extent, by ordering rules and lexical entries. The CLE's representational levels also allow the results of reasoning to be incorporated if suitable intelligent systems become available.

14.4.3 Querying Users

When the BCI is unable to decide by itself on a QLF in analysis or transfer, it needs either to query one of the users or to proceed with all the options, producing alternative outputs. The strategy that has been adopted in the BCI project is as follows:

- The system interacts with the source user to decide on a single QLF to be transferred, that is, to resolve any source language ambiguities. This is done by using bracketing to indicate possible structures of a sentence or presenting the user with paraphrases of the senses of an ambiguous word.

- One or more target language QLFs may be produced from the single approved source QLF. Where possible, senses are conflated as shown in the example below. A sentence is generated from the first QLF, and presented to the target user. If the user disapproves of the translation, other target QLFs may be tried.

- Sentences generated from the same QLF will be fairly close paraphrases of each other. For clarification, the target user may request a second paraphrase of any of the sentences presented to him.

- The target user may query the source user (via the BCI, of course) about any remaining ambiguities.

An exchange involving most of these stages might be as follows:

User 1:
```
His poor grandfather is ill.
```

System to user 1:
```
What does "poor" mean?
    1 penniless
    2 unfortunate
    3 unimpressive
Enter a number: 2
```

System to user 2:
```
"Hans stackars farfar/morfar är sjuk."
```
His unfortunate (father's father / mother's father) is ill.
```
Accepteras översättningen? j
```
Accept translation? **y**

User 2:
```
Är det hans farfar?
```

System to user 1:
```
"Is it his paternal grandfather?"
```

A choice between target language QLFs that is a matter of a single lexical item is finessed by defining what might be called "pseudowords" involving slashes. In this example, `farfar/morfar` is defined as a Swedish (pseudo)lexical item whose predicate is associated with the predicate for the English *grandfather*. It is not necessary for the system to be told which of the options the target user prefers.

The reasons for the division of labor shown here between source user, target user, and system are as follows.

It is more appropriate for the source user to choose between source language QLFs, first because only the source user can reliably be expected to know which meaning he intended, and second because users may feel happier if they know that the system will not generate anything for the other user that might derive from an unintended meaning.

Correspondingly, the target user is better placed to choose between target language QLFs (implicitly, by inspection of the resulting generated sentences) for the practical reason that to ask the source user to do this would mean having to transfer structures back into *different* source language QLFs, which would not always be possible, and in any case would be beset by almost all the linguistic problems facing the whole translation process.

The strategy of presenting sentences generated from multiple QLFs should not swamp the target user with information because the transfer rules will have been written so as not to produce large numbers of results (as in the case of *concerning* on page 301 above).

This overall interaction strategy allows a variant of the BCI's interactive use in which it can be used to encode speech or e-mail messages in QLF format, eliminating source language ambiguities, and to decode them on reaching the other user.

If there are multiple source language ambiguities in a sentence, they are factored out, with the user's attention being focused on one distinction at a time. Structural ambiguity, corresponding to different syntactic bracketings of the sentence giving rise to different QLFs, is tackled first. For example, if the user inputs the sentence *I telephoned the man from France*, he will be asked to make the following choice:[5]

```
Consider the following bracketings...
    1: I {telephoned the man} from France
    2: I telephoned {the man from France}
Enter the number of one that you like, or minus the
number of one that you don't like:
```

If more than one such ambiguity is present, as in *He drove the car to the garage without any insurance*, several menu options, each still with

---

[5]For the case of English-Swedish, it is rare for a choice between source language bracketings to make a difference to the target language structure because the word order in the two languages is quite similar. However, decisions of this type are very important for other, less closely related language pairs.

only *one* pair of brackets, are presented. The user makes a decision, positively or negatively, about any one option, and the process repeats, with the numbers both of alternative QLFs and of menu options being reduced until only one possible full bracketing remains.[6]

The set of syntactic categories that give rise to bracketings that may be presented to users is configurable by the grammar writer. Currently, the categories **s**, **np**, and **vp** are used on both the English and Swedish sides.

The full bracketing eventually selected may correspond to several QLFs, partly because of straightforward lexical ambiguity as with *poor* above, and partly because of structural differences at the QLF level that happen to give rise to the same bracketings of the syntactic categories deemed to be significant. The latter case is currently handled simply by making an arbitrary choice, but this could be improved on by defining rules that allowed competing QLFs to be paraphrased (using the system's generator) in ways that bring out the contrast between them.

14.4.4 Recovery

In the sections above, the problem was that there were a number of possible interpretations to choose from. But sometimes, the problem is the opposite: there are sentences for which the composition of the three mappings (analysis, translation, and generation) yields no values. For these untranslatable sentences, some means of recovery is desirable.

In analysis the same means of recovery as in the CLE proper are available, that is, spelling correction, proper name inference, and so on. In transfer a pragmatic approach has been adopted; if no applicable rule can be found for a given construction, it will be translated as it stands. For nonlexical items, this is normally the correct choice, due to the similarities between English and Swedish—many constructions are simply the same in both languages. For lexical items, however, this approach is the correct one for proper names only; in general it leads to a lot of undesirable target QLFs, for which generation is doomed to fail.

Due to the adopted "transfer-and-filter" approach, the target language generator normally should fail to generate from some of the QLFs it is presented with. If it, however, fails to generate from *all* the QLFs

---

[6]We have also experimented with a facility which allows the experienced user to specify the desired bracketing explicitly in the input sentence.

given by the translation component, some graceful recovery should be available. At present, the BCI system only allows for recovery from sortal restriction violations, as described in Section 14.4.2.

14.5   Summary and Further Directions

We have described the development of a version of the CLE for Swedish, a transfer mechanism based on QLF representations, and the use of these components in a translation system for interactive communication between monolingual users. The current version of the BCI has vocabularies of about 2000 English words, and 1000 Swedish: most Swedish word-senses have associated transfer rules, which allow them to be translated into English. The system has been tested on a corpus of about 400 sentences, the majority of which were constructed within a hypothetical car-hire domain.

As we have argued in Section 14.3.2, QLF transfer appears to score particularly well from the point of view of compositionality. Moreover, nearly all compositionality failures are caused by the "operator" representation of tense and aspect, a problem that can apparently be solved by the QLF representation of tense and aspect described in Section 10.5.4. An experimental version of the English system using the revised format is already operational, and there is every reason to believe that it is possible to implement the same solution for Swedish, modifying the transfer component accordingly; with these changes, the system should hopefully be almost perfectly compositional, which would greatly simplify its further expansion and refinement. We hope to report on the results of these experiments, and further work resulting from them, at a later date.

References

Aho, A. V., and J. D. Ullman. 1972. *The Theory of Parsing, Translation and Compiling: Volume I—Parsing.* Englewood Cliffs, N.J.: Prentice-Hall.

Allen, S., ed. 1970. *Frequency Dictionary of Present-Day Swedish.* Stockholm: Almqvist & Wiksell.

Alshawi, H. 1987. *Memory and Context for Language Interpretation.* Cambridge, England: Cambridge University Press.

Alshawi, H. 1990. "Resolving Quasi Logical Forms". *Computational Linguistics* 16:133–144.

Alshawi, H., and J. van Eijck. 1989. "Logical Forms in the Core Language Engine". Proceedings of the 27th Annual Meeting of the Association for Computational Linguistics, Vancouver, British Columbia, 25–32.

Alshawi, H., and D. B. Moran. 1988. "The Delphi Model and Some Preliminary Experiments". In *Logic Programming*, edited by R. A. Kowalski and K. A. Bowen. Cambridge, Massachusetts: The MIT Press.

Alshawi, H., and R. S. Crouch. 1991. "Monotonic Semantic Interpretation". CCSRC Technical Report, Cambridge Computer Science Research Centre, SRI International, Cambridge, England.

Alshawi, H., M. Rayner, and A. G. Smith. 1991. "Declarative Derivation of Database Queries from Meaning Representations". *Proceedings of the 1991 BANKAI Workshop on Intelligent Information Access*, edited by the Society for Worldwide Interbank Financial Telecommunications. Amsterdam: Elsevier.

Ballard, B. 1988. "A General Computational Treatment of Comparatives for Natural Language Question Answering". Proceedings of the 26th Annual Meeting of the Association for Computational Linguistics, State University of New York at Buffalo, Buffalo, New York, 41–47.

Barwise, J., and R. Cooper. 1981. "Generalized Quantifiers and Natural Language". *Linguistics and Philosophy* 4:159–219.

van Benthem, J. 1986. *Essays in Logical Semantics.* Dordrecht, Holland: D. Reidel.

Boguraev, B., and E. Briscoe. 1989. "Utilising the LDOCE Grammar Codes". In *Computational Lexicography for Natural Language Processing*, edited by B. Boguraev and E. Briscoe. Harlow, Essex: Longman.

Bresnan, J. 1982. "The Passive in Lexical Theory". In *The Mental Representation of Grammatical Relations*, edited by J. Bresnan. Cambridge, Massachusetts: The MIT Press.

Carlson, G. N. 1977. *Reference to Kinds in English*. Ph.D. dissertation, Indiana University Linguistics Club.

Carter, D. M. 1987. *Interpreting Anaphors in Natural Language Texts*. Chichester, England: Ellis Horwood.

Carter, D. M. 1989. "Lexical Acquisition in the Core Language Engine". Fourth Conference of the European Chapter of the Association for Computational Linguistics, Manchester, England, 137–144.

Coltheart, M. 1981. "The MRC Psycholinguistic Database". *Quarterly Journal of Experimental Psychology* 33:497–505.

Cooper, R. 1975. "Montague's Semantic Theory and Transformational Syntax". Ph.D. dissertation, University of Massachusetts, Amherst, Massachusetts.

Cooper, R. 1983. *Quantification and Syntactic Theory*. Dordrecht, Holland: D. Reidel.

Dalrymple, M., S. M. Shieber, and F. C. N. Pereira. 1991. "Ellipsis and Higher-Order Unification". *Linguistics and Philosophy* 14:399–452.

Davidson, D. 1967. "The Logical Form of Action Sentences". In *The Logic of Decision and Action*, edited by N. Rescher. Pittsburgh, Pennsylvania: University of Pittsburgh Press.

Dowty, D. R., R. Wall, and S. Peters. 1981. *Introduction to Montague Semantics*. Dordrecht, Holland: D. Reidel.

van Eijck, J. 1988. "Quantification". Technical Report CCSRC-7, SRI International, Cambridge Computer Science Research Centre, Cambridge, England. To appear in *Handbook of Semantics*, edited by D. Wunderlich and A. von Stechow. Berlin: de Gruyter.

Fauconnier, G. 1975. "Do Quantifiers Branch?" *Linguistic Inquiry* 6:555–567.

Gambäck, B., A. Lövgren, and M. Rayner. 1991. "The Swedish Core Language Engine", *SICS Research Report*, Swedish Institute of Computer Science, Stockholm.

Gazdar, G., E. Klein, G. Pullum, and I. Sag. 1985. *Generalized Phrase Structure Grammar*. Oxford: Blackwell.

Geach, P. 1962. *Reference and Generality*. Ithaca, New York: Cornell University Press.

Groenendijk, J., and M. Stokhof. 1987. "Dynamic Predicate Logic". Faculteit der Wijsbegeerte, University of Amsterdam.

Gross, M. 1975. *Méthodes en Syntaxe*. Paris: Hermann.

Grosz, B. J. 1977. "The Representation and Use of Focus in Dialogue Understanding". Ph.D. dissertation and Technical Note No. 151, Artificial Intelligence Centre, SRI International, Menlo Park, California.

Grosz, B. J., D. E. Appelt, P. Martin, and F. Pereira. 1987. "TEAM: An Experiment in the Design of Transportable Natural-Language Interfaces". *Artificial Intelligence* 32:173–243.

Hobbs, J. R. 1976. "Pronoun Resolution". Technical Report 76-1, Department of Computer Science, City College, City University of New York.

Hobbs, J. R. and J. Bear. 1990. "Two Principles of Parse Preference". Vol. 3, Proceedings of the 13th International Conference on Computational Linguistics, Helsinki, 162–167.

Hobbs, J. R., and S. M. Shieber. 1987. "An Algorithm for Generating Quantifier Scopings". *Computational Linguistics* 13:47–63.

Huet, G. 1975. "A Unification Algorithm for Typed Lambda Calculus". *Theoretical Computer Science* 1:27–57.

Isabelle, P., and E. Macklovitch. 1986. "Transfer and MT Modularity". Proceedings of the 11th International Conference on Computational Linguistics, Bonn, West Germany, 115–117.

Kamp, H. 1981. "A Theory of Truth and Semantic Representation". In *Formal Methods in the Study of Language*, edited by J. A. G. Groenendijk, T. M. V. Janssen, and M. B. J. Stokhof. Mathematisch Centrum, Amsterdam.

Kaplan, R., and J. Bresnan. 1982. "Lexical-Functional Grammar: A Formal System for Grammatical Representation". In *The Mental Representation of Grammatical Relations*, edited by J. Bresnan. Cambridge, Massachusetts: The MIT Press.

Kaplan, R. M., K. Netter, J. Wedekind, and A. Zaenen. 1989. "Translation by Structural Correspondences". Proceedings of the Fourth Conference of the European Chapter of the Association for Computational Linguistics, Manchester, England, 272–281.

Karttunen, L. 1984. "Features and Values". Proceedings of the 10th International Conference on Computational Linguistics, Stanford, California, 28–33.

Karttunen, L. 1986. "D-PATR: A Development Environment for Unification-Based Grammars". Proceedings of the 11th International Conference on Computational Linguistics, Bonn, West Germany, 74–80.

Korf, R. E. 1985. "Depth-first Iterative-deepening: An Optimal Admissible Tree Search". *Artificial Intelligence* 27:97–109.

Koskenniemi, K. 1984. "A General Computational Model for Word-Form Recognition and Production". Proceedings of the 10th International Conference on Computational Linguistics, Stanford, California, 178–181.

Kucera, H., and W. N. Francis. 1967. *A Computational Analysis of Present-Day American English*. Providence, Rhode Island: Brown University Press.

Kuno, M. 1987. Functional Syntax. Chicago, Illinois: The University of Chicago Press.

Ladusaw, W. 1980. "Polarity Sensitivity as Inherent Scope Relations". Ph.D. dissertation, Department of Linguistics, University of Texas, Austin, Texas.

Landsbergen, J. 1986. "Isomorphic Grammars and Their Use in the Rosetta Translation System". In *Machine Translation Today: the State of the Art*, edited by M. King. Edinburgh: Edinburgh University Press.

Lasnik, H. 1976. "Remarks on Coreference". *Linguistic Analysis* 2:1–22.

McCord, M. 1988. "A Multi-Target Machine Translation System". Proceedings of the International Conference on Fifth Generation Computer Systems, Tokyo, Japan, 1141–1149.

McDonald, D. B. 1982. "Understanding Noun Compounds". Ph.D. dissertation, Carnegie–Mellon University, Pennsylvania.

Matsumoto, Y., H. Tanaka, H. Hirakawa, H. Miyoshi, and H. Yasukawa. 1983. "BUP: A Bottom-up Parser Embedded in Prolog". *New Generation Computing* 1:145–158.

May, R. 1985. *Logical Form: Its Structure and Derivation.* Linguistic Inquiry Monographs 12. Cambridge, Massachusetts: The MIT Press.

Mellish, C. S. 1988. "Implementing Systemic Classification by Unification". *Computational Linguistics* 14:40–51.

Miike, S., K. Hasebe, H. Somers, and S. Amano. 1988. "Experiences with an On-line Translating Dialogue system". Proceedings of the 26th Annual Meeting of the Association for Computational Linguistics, State University of New York at Buffalo, Buffalo, New York, 155–162.

Montague, R. 1974. "The Proper Treatment of Quantification in Ordinary English". In *Formal Philosophy*, edited by R. Thomason. New Haven: Yale University Press.

Moore, R. C. 1981. "Problems in Logical Form". Proceedings of the 19th Annual Meeting of the Association for Computational Linguistics. Stanford University, Stanford, California, 117–124.

Moore, R. C. 1989. "Unification-Based Semantic Interpretation". Proceedings of the 27th Annual Meeting of the Association for Computational Linguistics, Vancouver, British Columbia, 33–41.

Moran, D. B. 1988. "Quantifier Scoping in the SRI Core Language Engine". Proceedings of the 26th Annual Meeting of the Association for Computational Linguistics, State University of New York at Buffalo, Buffalo, New York, 33–40.

Nagao, M. and J. Tsujii. 1986. "The Transfer Phase of the Mu Machine Translation System". Proceedings of the 11th International Conference on Computational Linguistics, Bonn, West Germany, 97–103.

Partee, B. 1978. "Bound Variables and Other Anaphors". Proceedings of TINLAP-2, edited by D. Waltz, University of Illinois, Urbana, 79–83.

Pelletier, F. J., ed. 1979. *Mass Terms: Some Philosophical Problems.* Dordrecht, Holland: D. Reidel.

Pereira, F. C. N. 1981. "Extraposition Grammars". *Computational Linguistics* 7:243–256.

Pereira, F .C. N. 1990. "Categorial Semantics and Scoping". *Computational Linguistics* 16:1–10.

Pereira, F. C. N., and D. H. D. Warren. 1980. "Definite Clause Grammars for Natural Language Analysis—A Survey of the Formalism and a Comparison with Augmented Transition Networks". *Artificial Intelligence* 13:231–278.

Pollack, M. E., and F. C. N. Pereira. 1988. "An Integrated Framework for Semantic and Pragmatic Interpretation", Proceedings of the 26th Annual Meeting of the Association for Computational Linguistics, State University of New York at Buffalo, Buffalo, New York, 75–86.

Pulman, S. G. 1987. "Passives". Proceedings of the 3rd Meeting of the European Chapter of the Association for Computational Linguistics, Copenhagen, Denmark, 306–313.

Pustejovsky, J. 1989. "Current Issues in Computational Lexical Semantics", Proceedings of the Fourth Conference of the European Chapter of the Association for Computational Linguistics, Manchester, England, xvii–xxv.

Rayner, M., and A. Banks. 1990. "An Implementable Semantics for Comparative Constructions". *Computational Linguistics* 16:86–112.

Reinhart, T. 1983. *Anaphora and Semantic Interpretation.* London: Croom Helm.

Rosenkrantz, D. J., and P. M. Lewis. 1970. "Deterministic Left Corner Parsing". Conference Record of the 11th Annual Symposium on Switching and Automata Theory, IEEE, 139–152.